Kitchen Planning Guide
for Builders, Designers, and Architects

Kitchen Planning Guide for Builders, Designers, and Architects

Second Edition

by Patrick J. Galvin

STRUCTURES PUBLISHING COMPANY   1978
Farmington, Michigan 48024

Manufactured in the United States of America.

Edited by Shirley M. Horowitz

Designed by Richard Kinney.

Current Printing (last digit)

10 9 8 7 6 5 4 3 2 1

Structures Publishing Company
Box 423, Farmington, Michigan 48024

Jacket photo courtesy of Allmilmo, German cabinet mfr.

Library of Congress Cataloging in Publication Data

Galvin, Patrick J.
    Kitchen planning guide for builders, designers, and
architects.

    First ed. published in 1972 under title: Kitchen
planning guide for builders and architects.
    Includes index.
    1. Kitchens. I. Title.
NA8330.G35   1978   728   77-25423
ISBN 0-912336-57-9

Contents

Foreword

The kitchen is now the most important and expensive room in the house.

In the homes in which we over-fifty folk were brought up, the kitchen was a necessary evil, closed off from the rest of the house. The only requirement for its location was proximity to the dining room. The room had to be close to a rear or side door so that the "icebox" could be replenished by the messy "iceman who cometh" nearly every day. The kitchen was equipped by the builder with a sink and little else. Cabinets were often supplied by the occupant. The gas range was obviously an item to be moved when the family moved and you could have any color you wanted, so long as it was stove black. The garbage disposer was a smelly pail under the sink which we had to carry out to the garbage can in the alley.

Today the kitchen is a thing of beauty, a joy to work in, and a proud possession. It is efficient, easy to clean, safe, well lit, sound conditioned, and well ventilated. Equipment includes one or more built-in ovens, ranges, refrigerators, a garbage disposer and lots of factory-built cabinetry styled to suit a variety of tastes. No longer is this room masked from the rest of the house, but other rooms are allied to it by open planning, folding doors and pass-throughs. The kitchen frequently accommodates table-type eating space or a snack bar. A wet bar, a cooled wine cellar, a trash compactor, menu planning desk, built-in mixing center, and a communication center are increasingly incorporated.

In addition to all of this, it should be economical to build, but per square foot or per room it is by far the most expensive room in the home.

The need has long been recognized for an authoritative kitchen guide that will bring order out of conflicting rules, suggestions, and customs. As with our other books in the structures field, this has been our objective in bringing you the *Kitchen Planning Guide*. Pat Galvin, a most experienced and competent author, has ably demonstrated his command of the subject.

How To Use the Guide

First, scan the book from cover to cover so that you are generally aware of its contents. At the same time, get rid of any misconceptions you may have had about kitchen design criteria.

Then, when you need answers to a kitchen problem, from a complete design to selection of a ceiling material or appliance, consult the index and then the book for your answers.

For better kitchens . . . .

> *R. J. Lytle*, Publisher
> Structures Publishing Company

6

A kitchen with a country air, where the mellow fruitwood cabinets are styled with ageless Provincial detailing. The dishwasher, sinks and cooktop are along one wall and a preparation counter surfaced with a hardwood cutting board is convenient to both wall ovens and the refrigerator-freezer. Floor and backsplash are of mosaic tile. (American Olean Tile Co., photo)

1

Introduction: The Room that Makes/ Sells/Rents the House

To anyone selling a house, the kitchen can be worth a dozen salesmen.

Or, conversely, it can just sit there, occupying its space and contributing more than its share to the cost.

Think about it. Except for the bathroom, it is the only room in the house that comes fully furnished, and with "furniture" that costs a lot and cannot be moved. Its sink location is slave to the plumbing lines, its range to the location of the separate 220 circuit. Its cabinets have been screwed to the walls and fitted into the corners.

A new buyer who wants to make a house a home can control the design and decor of all other rooms, trying them one way and then another to express a distinctive lifestyle. But the kitchen, an important socializing center and one of the most lived-in areas in daytime and evening, was designed by someone else and must be taken the way it is. This is why the architect, the builder, the designer — whoever has the final say — must consider it the most important room in any home or apartment.

Buyers and renters may not be aware of the importance of the kitchen, even though they have owned homes themselves. But let us consider two typical situations that every builder will understand.

Mr. and Mrs. X visit Model Home A. They wander through, probing for features they like, whispering to each other, avoiding salesmen, and considering its price as they depart for the next model. But when Mr. and Mrs. Y visit model Home B, the first thing they notice is the interesting peninsula separating — and yet connecting — the dining area and the kitchen. They open a kitchen drawer that glides smoothly and noiselessly. They open the refrigerator door, where the builder has placed a sign that reads: "You will *Never* have to defrost this beautiful refrigerator." Next they open the cabinets and see the certification seal of the American National Standards Institute. Above the range hood is the Home Ventilating Institute seal certifying air delivery and sound rating. The dishwasher, disposer, and built-in appliances are there, as well as lighting over all the work areas. They note the extras — a chopping board, inserts in the counters for hot pans, etc. Everywhere the builder has put little signs calling attention to the advantages of this "living kitchen."

Here is no furtive whispering. Mrs. Y's eyes light up as she discovers all the special features, and Mr. Y is already thinking, "It's $3,000 more, but maybe we can swing it if . . ." — *and they haven't even looked at the rest of the house!*

This is how a great kitchen makes a great difference, whether the unit is for sale or rent. Mr. and Mrs. X may have seen a very nice home, and it may have been a good buy, but there was nothing striking about it. Mr. and Mrs. Y did see something striking — and the deal was already started.

A good kitchen can bring a family closer during the hours they are home together, but if poorly designed it can be a source of annoyance. It can separate them psychologically as well as physically, by a series of minor frustrations.

The builder invariably pays for poor kitchen design. When he cuts corners and fails to engineer a kitchen for human needs, he is losing his customer

Small kitchen is dressed up with decor and lighting to look like more than it really is. Wall is textured with an artificial stone, with down lights in panel across room, sculptured fish for nautical motif. Cabinets and design by Coppes, with Coppes Ranch Oak cabinets in Waikiki White.

U.S. approximation of European look — contemporary, but with face frames showing — is by Yorktowne. Note effective under-cabinet lighting at left, "space age" feeling imparted by wall covering. Cabinet line is "Spacemaker II."

Spectacular greenhouse window treatment makes a showcase of this kitchen, with theme extended using green lattic wall coverings. Cabinets are Riviera's Country Squire.

Small island gives added work space and storage in kitchen with Boise Cascade's Olde Dominion cabinets. It's a traditional styling enhanced by wicker in soffit area, and green wall covering.

Combination of St. Charles steel cabinets, tile walls and tile and wood countertops add textural interest to this small kitchen, which has 2-burner cooktop supplementing 4-burner range.

Weldwood paneling is used as wall covering, then as decorative panel on dishwasher and cabinets in this "idea corner" from Champion. Closed-circuit TV monitors kids at play.

The futuristic look of this kitchen is available to anyone right now.

Designed by General Electric, it has today's appliances and materials but, obviously, is customized. The black, red and white surfaces are of GE Textolite, a high-pressure plastic laminate, which comes in 4 x 8- or 5 x 9-foot sheets, but the seams are all up high where they don't show.

Country Maple kitchen was designed by Coppes with cabinets in Cinnamon Frost finish. Wall of artificial brick and wood beams help give antique look. Note dishwasher has decorative panel to match cabinetry.

Complete entertainment center can be a stunning adjunct to the kitchen. This includes bar sink, under-counter refrigerator, and the small metal plate to right of sink is built-in mixing center. Fluorescent tubes under wall cabinets cast light down to work space, up through bottom of cabinets to illuminate glassware. Plastic laminate on counter simulates maple butcher block. (Mutschler photo)

Contemporary kitchen uses Weldwood paneling from Champion Building Products for beams and walls, Decolam for cabinets. Luminous ceiling gives a lot of illumination.

Experimental new solar house by Architect Harry Wenning was built near Poughkeepsie, NY. Kitchen cabinets are built from Champion Building Products decorative overlay panels, Decolam/hpt, and countertops of DuPont Corian. Note integral sink in counter, NuTone mixing center recessed in near corner.

Multi-colored ceramic tile countertop creates a kitchen in open area of this home. Ceramic tile also is used on floors, counters, and island cooking/cleaning center.

Newest Cooking Method, by Fasar, uses magnetic induction for cooking. Cooking elements can be placed under ceramic tiles, at random, for new design freedom. Elements never become hot to the touch.

Contrast of the American look is exemplified in these Country Classic cabinets by Riviera. Note kitchen wall covering duplicated in draperies in living room, decorative rail treatment of soffit area.

Artistry of Charles Cressent, 18th century French cabinet maker and sculptor, inspired this Country French cabinetry by Mutschler, and Cressent's combinations of wood and metal were emulated in kitchen design. Protruding countertop angles at sink add a design element, but also add work space.

Luminous ceiling adds most modern touch to kitchen in which Wood-Mode's Lexington cabinets and old-style wall covering suggest earlier era. Corner sink in far corner is for cleanup, near dishwasher. Island sink with built-in mixer (near corner) makes this a food preparation center.

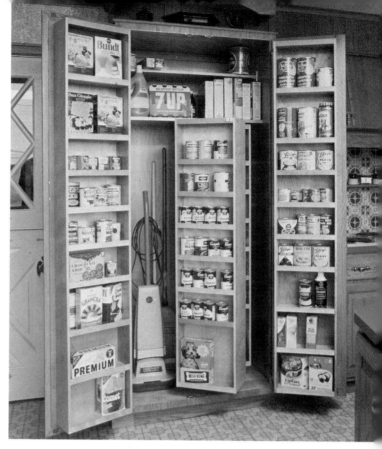

Storage options available with custom cabinetry include these from Quaker Maid: Lazy susan corners for wall and base cabinets, with small appliance compartment on counter; fold-out pantry compartments in tall cabinets; similar fold-outs under the counter.

This Patriot Pine kitchen by Quaker Maid was exhibited by Lone Star Gas in State Fair of Texas. Under-cabinet lights above sink shine on work area, island with vegetable sink has lowered brunch counter, and Quaker Maid's decorative panels blend on the refrigerator, compactor and dishwasher.

Modernistic European look is by Allmilmo, German cabinet manufacturer now marketing in U.S. While all cabinets are built to German metric measure, here all U.S.-made appliances are used, all built-ins, to show compatibility.

Colors, materials and textures have a heyday in this eclectic "hodge-podge." Floor, counters and walls are ceramic tile in varying patterns, sizes and colors. Glass case holds fruits, nuts, candies and flowers. Pots and pans and other decor items hand from polished brass rails above. Portable butcher block table rolls around for use or out of the way, and it all goes to prove that a kitchen is one place where one can express individuality and lifestyle.

Fully-luminous ceiling lights this traditional country kitchen by Coppes, with brick wall adding atmosphere, and decorative fronts on dishwasher and compactor to match cabinets. Custom cabinet companies such as Coppes also make matching furniture items, such as peninsular table.

Design idea of integrating rooms with cabinetry is shown in this Coppes oak kitchen-dining room combination.

Versatility of custom cabinetry is shown here in combination of drawers and doors to right of desk area. Cabinets are oak traditional, by Coppes.

Floor covering is extended up wall of peninsula in this Coppes kitchen by Dick Martin, of Gallery of Kitchens, Elgin IL. Light-colored ceiling panels couple with high window (right background) to make the room light and cheerful.

Use of kitchen cabinets to furnish other rooms of the house is shown here, with Overton standard cabinets supplemented by furniture pieces made for furniture groupings.

Country Oak is the name of these cabinets by Yorktowne. Stone
wall adds texture, island has bar sink which also can be used for
cleaning vegetables and mixing center.

New contemporary cabinets by Rutt hit a balance between U.S.
and European look. Unlike most U.S. cabinets, these are minus face
frames, with fully adjustable hinges and extra built-in rigidity.

Variations of brown integrate all elements of this kitchen, brightened by the pattern of backsplash and soffit. Counter lighting is recessed under wall cabinets, and a hydronic heating unit is almost hidden in kick space under sink. (Formica photo)

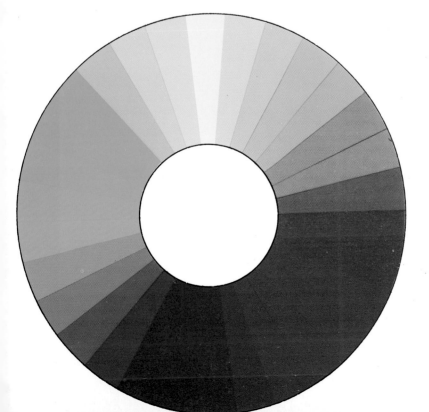

Color wheel from The Oxford Companion to Art, edited by Harold Osborne, 1970, by permission of the Clarendon Press, Oxford.

Textures and contrasts are the story in this
kitchen, small but complete. Cabinets are wood,
painted white to contrast with black decorative
hinges and pulls.

Kemper's Manor Oak cabinets form a cooking
island in this kitchen, giving a work triangle not
interrupted by passing traffic.

Modernistic kitchen at Horizon House, Lake Lindera, Cal., has eye appeal and total cleanability. Note the modern hanging lighting fixtures, supplemented by valance light at top of ventilating hood housing.

Even a one-wall kitchen can be distinctive. This one by Connor has pass-through at sink area to adjacent room and decorative opening over wall cabinets. And floor covering is duplicated on backsplash.

for a second home in years to come. He is also losing word-of-mouth referrals that could presell his homes before he gets them on the drawing board.

When there is little in a kitchen design to excite the buyer, the couple will settle for something adequate. Price will be the determining factor. But when the kitchen excites the buyer, all the powers of rationalization will be brought in to justify the price the builder sets.

The purpose of this book is to make builders, architects, designers or other professionals more aware of what it takes to make a kitchen exciting.

Of course, many professionals already have kitchen departments that make it their business to find out what kitchen features appeal to the buyer. But in this rapidly changing field an architect, builder, or designer must know about new products and materials on the market.

With all of the new things builders, designers, and architects must learn, it is difficult for them to be aware of the more than 10,000 items available from even one single kitchen range manufacturer. Furthermore, there are more than 500 items available from a single cabinet builder. Keeping track of the names and locations of the more than 1,500 basic suppliers to the kitchen industry is a monumental task itself. The interior furnishing and design of modern kitchens is thus a complicated endeavor. Vast resources of kitchen expertise are available to builders and architects. Most major cabinet and appliance manufacturers, for example, supply design services for builders.

But probably the best source for the large builder is a good, local independent distributor. Many kitchen distributors not only bid jobs as specified, but also are prepared to suggest alternate kitchen plans to contractors.

The warmth of redwood brings both elegance and a country flavor to this highly individual kitchen, augmented by good artificial lighting and a skylight that admits daylight. (Architect, Don Batchelder; Photo, Karl Riek; Courtesy California Redwood Association)

Custom-home builders often prefer to deal with local retail kitchen specialists. Many such specialists are available, but the more reliable ones will probably be members of the American Institute of Kitchen Dealers, an association with extremely high standards for membership and with about 1,000 members in the United States. Builders will also find individuals who use the initials CKD after their names. These individuals are not necessarily members of the American Institute of Kitchen Dealers. CKD, for Certified Kitchen Designer, indicates certification of the individual by a certifying branch of the American Institute of Kitchen Designers.

The expertise of the specialists mentioned above may not be readily available to you as an architect or builder in your locality, but the services of these individuals can indeed be valuable. This book will help you in working with the professional kitchen designer.

An attempt has been made to include all the information required to design modern kitchens for single and multiple family dwellings. This book is meant to aid you in designing, specifying, and installing the kinds of kitchens desired by modern home buyers.

This book will be of value to architects in designing and specifying components. It will be of value to certified kitchen designers as a valuable reference to supplement their professional knowledge. It should be of special value to busy contractors and builders faced either with designing their own kitchens or in working with kitchen designers.

2

Basic Kitchen Measurements

The kitchen has no basic measurement standards that cannot be varied for cause. But unless there is cause, everything will work out better if the standardized measurements are followed. For example, the 84-inch total height of a kitchen installation from floor to top of wall cabinets squares off approximately with the top of the door trim, and it squares off precisely with the height of tall cabinets such as those used for broom storage, appliance enclosures, and pantries.

Basic Kitchen Dimensions. Here are the basic dimensions:

1) *Base cabinet* — height is 34-1/2 inches.
2) *Countertop* — 1-1/2 inches thick.
3) *Blacksplash attached to countertop* — 4 inches high, minimum, can be 5 or 6 inches, or can extend upward all the way to the wall cabinets.
4) *Blacksplash area from countertop to bottom of wall cabinets* — 15 or 18 inches, depending on height of wall cabinets.
5) *Wall cabinets* are 30 or 33 inches high. The preferred height is 33 inches, but the most common is 30 inches.

All of these measurements combined will total 84 inches, from floor to the top of the wall cabinets.

Some multiple-housing builders, particularly in New York City, Chicago, scattered other cities, and on the West Coast, have begun using 42-inch wall cabinets extending all the way to the ceiling. They claim they do this for esthetic reasons — for a cleaner look — and to gain added storage space in small kitchens.

It should be noted, however, that the minimum property standards do not accept storage space in the kitchen above the 74-inch line, and from a practical point of view such space is simply too hard to reach. Other standard kitchen dimensions are listed below:

1) *Wall cabinets* — 12 inches deep, varying to 13 inches. Standard heights progress in 3-inch increments from 12 to 42 inches. Standard widths progress in 3-inch increments from 12 to 60 inches.
2) *Wall cabinets for general storage* — 30 or 33 inches high.
3) *Wall cabinets over a range* — 18 to 21 inches high.
4) *Wall cabinets over a refrigerator* — 12 to 18 inches high, with 15 inches preferable.
5) *Wall cabinets over the sink* — if present these should be 21 to 27 inches high.
6) *Base cabinets* will be 24 to 24-1/2 inches deep, and will have a 4-inch kick-space. Height will be 34-1/2 inches, and widths will vary in 3-inch increments from 9 to 60 inches.
7) *Base cabinets used for kitchen desks or for buffets* — 28-1/2 inches high. Units used for bathroom vanities are 30 inches high.
8) *Tall utility cabinets (84 inches)* — usually 24 or 24-1/2 inches deep, although some are half-sized at 12 inches or more. Width ranges from 12 to 42 inches in 3-inch increments. These come in variable configurations. Some have space for upright broom storage in addition to open shelving and/or drawers. Those used for pantries might have a series of

Table 2.1.

Kitchen Cabinet Requirements

	Minimum Frontage		
Work Centers	Two Bedrooms	Three Bedrooms	Four or More Bedrooms
Sink	24"	32"	32"
counter and base cab. at each side	20"	24"	30"
Range	24"	30"	30"
counter and base cab. at one side	20"	24"	30"
Refrigerator (space)	36"	36"	36"
counter at latch side	15"	15"	18"
Mixing (base and wall cabinet)	36"	36"	42"

PROFILE DIMENSIONS

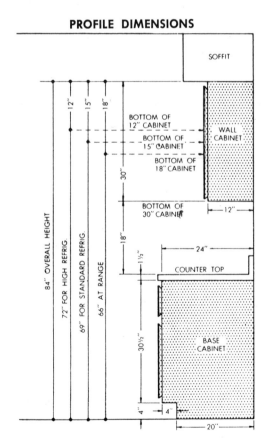

Basic measurements for kitchen cabinets.

revolving shelves or vertical shelving systems that fold out into the room.

HUD Minimum Property Standards. The Minimum Property Standards of the U.S. Department of Housing and Urban Development furnish a starting point in kitchen space planning, because these standards must be met or exceeded in any housing units where federally insured mortgages are involved.

Through 1971 and 1972 these standards were totally rewritten (for the first time since 1956), and builders and architects will probably find the new standards much easier to work with. As a whole, they recognize more fully the environmental factors in the home and in the urban area, are oriented more toward performance, and tend to encourage design innovations and improved building technologies.

The new MPS are in four volumes: for *One and Two Family Dwellings*, for *Multifamily Housing*, for *Care-Type Housing* (nursing homes and the like), and a fourth publication called *Manual of Acceptable Practices*, which contains back-up material for the three volumes of mandatory standards.

The paragraph numbering system is the same for all three volumes and is similar to the system used in the old MPS, so a builder or architect can easily check differences between requirements for one-family houses and multifamily by checking the same sections and paragraph numbers in the two appropriate volumes.

Following are all requirements pertinent to kitchens in one- and two-family houses with, where appropriate, the differences in multifamily housing.

Chapter 4, Building Design. Paragraph 401-1.2 applies to the dining area, regardless of whether it is a separate room or combined with living room or kitchen. It specifies:

Space for accommodating the following size table and chairs with proper circulation space in the dining area shall be provided, according to the intended occupancy, as shown:

(2 bedrooms) 4 persons -2'6"x3'2"
(3 bedrooms) 6 persons -3'4"x4'0" or 4'0" round
(4 bedrooms) 8 persons -3'4"x6'0" or 4'0"x4'0"
(5 bedrooms) 10 persons -3'4"x8'0" or 4'0"x6'0"
(6 bedrooms) 12 persons -4'0"x8'0"

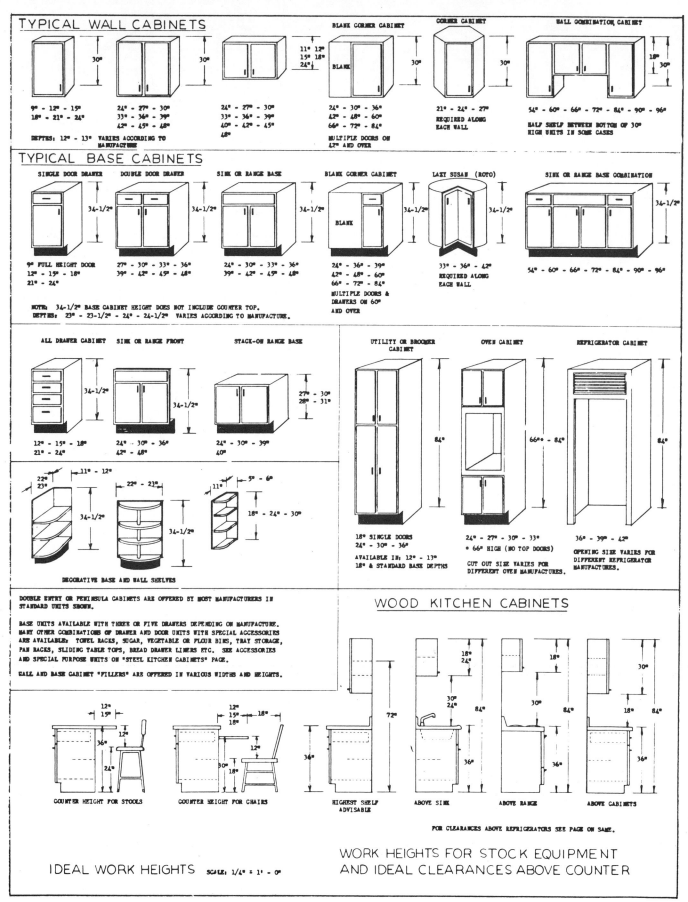

Specifications page by the National Kitchen Cabinet Association shows typical wall, base, and tall cabinets with their customary sizes as made by most stock cabinet manufacturers.

Dining chairs   -1'6"x1'6"

In multifamily, this paragraph is the same except for the addition of this specification: "(Efficiency or 1 bedroom) 2 persons -2'6"x2'6"."

Paragraph 401-2.1 applies to the kitchen specifically, with the following provisions:

The kitchen design shall provide for efficient food and utensil storage, and serving, as well as cleaning up after meals.

The kitchen shall be directly accessible to the dining area and shall be conveniently located near the living area.

Circulation space in food preparation areas shall not be less than 40" in width.

Kitchen cabinets shall be provided according to Table 4.1. (Reproduced here as Table 2.1.)

Specific provisions. The following specific provisions are included:

1) Work centers may be combined; the kitchen multiple-use space shall at least equal the largest frontage of any one of the work centers being combined, plus 6 inches.
2) Provide a drawer at each base cabinet, or equivalent group of drawers.
3) Frontage may continue around a corner, except a space less than 12" may not be counted.
4) Frontage of wall cabinets shall equal the required frontage for base cabinets.
5) The frontages are based on typical cabinets. Base cabinet approximately 24 inches deep by 36 inches in height with one shelf and drawer. Wall cabinet approximately 12 inches deep by 30 inches in height with two shelves.

6) Provide at least 9 inches from the edge of the sink or range to any adjacent corner cabinet, and 16 inches from the latch side of the refrigerator to any adjacent corner cabinet.
7) Refrigerator space may be 33 inches when a refrigerator is provided and the door opens within its own width.
8) Where dishwashers are provided, 24-inch sinks are acceptable.

Differences for multifamily housing. A number of differences exist. These are shown in Table 2.2.

Work centers are basically the same except that when requirements for work centers are combined for efficiency and one-bedroom units the combined work centers must at least equal the largest work center being combined, i.e., dropping the extra 6 inches. A 72-inch compact kitchen with adequate wall cabinets may be substituted in efficiency apartments.

Light and ventilation. Paragraph 402-3.1 is a table with minimum requirements for natural light and ventilation in the various house areas. There is no requirement for natural light in the kitchen, but the ventilation requirement is for natural ventilation as 4 percent of the floor area or, if mechanical ventilation is substituted, 15 air changes per hour.

In multifamily housing, the natural ventilation requirement is the same. But for mechanical ventilation the table specifies 15 air changes per hour with a room-controlled exhaust fan or, with other mechanical means such as central system, 10 changes per hour.

Chapter 5, Materials. Paragraph 509-4.3 specifies that walls in kitchens, bathrooms and laundries shall be resistant to grease, water, detergents, and normal household chemicals.

Hardboard. When hardboard is used for interior walls in the kitchen or bath, it must be Class I Decorative grade.

Flooring. When resilient flooring is used, minimum thickness of various materials are as specified in Table 2.3.

Wall coverings. Wall covering requirements are as follows:

Table 2.2.

Work Centers		Minimum Frontage			
	Efficiency	One Bedroom	Two Bedrooms	Three Bedrooms	Four or More Bedrooms
Sink	18"	24"	24"	32"	32"
counter and base cab. at each side	15"	18"	20"	24"	30"
Range	21"	21"	24"	30"	30"
counter and base cab. at one side	15"	18"	20"	24"	30"
Refrigerator (space)	30"	30"	36"	36"	36"
counter at latch side	15"	15"	15"	15"	18"
Mixing (base and wall cabinet)	21"	30"	36"	36"	42"

509-8.1 Wall coverings shall be of such kind and quality for a given material to assure (a) intended life, (b) renewability, and (c) walls in kitchens, bathrooms and laundries resistant to grease, water, detergents and normal household chemicals.

509-8.2 Vinyl covering shall be cotton cloth coated with plasticized polyvinyl chloride resin or copolymer thereof conforming to applicable requirements of Federal Specification CCC-A-700. Minimum weights and thickness shall be:

Total weight per square yard . . . . . . 7 ounces
Coating thickness . . . . 5 mils

When *wallpaper* is used, of course it must be sunfast, waterfast and of waterproof type.

Mechanical Ventilation. Mechanical ventilation is covered in 515-2.1 and 2. It states:

Ventilating equipment shall comply and be tested and rated in accordance with the "Air Flow and Sound Test Procedures of the Home Ventilating Institute" dated October, 1968. Evidence of compliance shall be a Home Ventilating Institute or manufacturer's label showing capacity and sound characteristics. Sound levels on kitchen exhaust and range hood fans rated 500 cfm or less shall not exceed 9.0 sones. Bathroom fans not to exceed 6.5 sones. Electrical equipment shall comply with the National Electric Code.

Kitchen range hoods must be labeled and listed by Underwriters Laboratories.

Construction (Chapter 6). The 611-1 paragraphs cover kitchen cabinets and countertops. The requirement is that all manufactured factory-finished cabinets must comply with ANSI A161-1, "Recommended Minimum Construction and Performance Standards for Kitchen and Vanity Cabinets," or an equivalent standard. Further, they must bear a label of an independent inspection agency acceptable to HUD, and the label must indicate compliance with the standards.

Cabinets. Custom or job-built cabinets must be equivalent in quality and construction.

Table 2.3.

Material	Minimum Thickness	Material	Minimum Thickness
Asphalt tile	0.09 in.	Unfilled vinyl sheet	0.065 in. or 0.055 in.
Homogenous vinyl tile	0.050 in. (3/64 in.)	Vinyl-asbestos tile	0.0625 in. (1/16 in.)
Linoleum tile or sheet	0.090 in. (std. gage)	Vinyl sheet (backed) Grade B Grade C	0.070 in. 0.065 in.
Rubber tile	0.80 in. (5/64 in.)		

Countertops. Countertops must be securely bonded "to reinforced steel core or to 3/4-inch plywood or other equivalent material. Top material shall be phenolic laminate, vinyl plastic covering, ceramic tile, stainless steel or other material suitable for the intended use. Also required is at least a 3-inch back and end splash against all abutting vertical surfaces. All edges, including sink and built-in surface units, must have non-corrodible metal molding or other suitable edging installed.

The MPS reference to linoleum is no longer of interest; the material has not been produced in the U.S. since 1974.

A new countertop performance standard has been developed by the National Association of Plastic Fabricators, and it probably will become an ANSI standard and eventually work its way into the MPS. To get it, write NAPF, 4720 Montgomery Lane, Washington, DC 20014.

Kitchen and bathroom ventilation. The 615-2 paragraphs outline requirements for kitchen and bathroom ventilation. Following are the kitchen requirements:

1) *Fan capacity* in cfm, based on air changes per hour, shall be calculated by this equation:

$$cfm = \frac{\text{cu. ft. room vol. x no. air changes per hr.}}{60}$$

2) *Discharge openings* to exterior must be protected against rain entry, and have automatic backdraft dampers or louvers.

3) *Kitchen air* must be exhausted directly to outdoors, either by vented range hood or a ceiling or wall fan, if natural ventilation is not provided.

Table 2.4.

Electrical Equipment Demand

	Diversified demand (KW)
Basic demand	4.0
Clothes washer	.8
Dishwasher	1.2
Range	12.
Oven, built-in	4.5
Top, built-in (4 units)	6.0
Clothes dryer:	5.0
Water heater: (high recovery)	5.5
Food freezer	.6
Food waste disposer	.4
Water pump	.4
Attic fan	.4
Electric bathroom heater (each)	1.3
Central heating system (1)	.5
Room air conditioner (each)	1.2
Central air conditioner (1)	(2)

(1) Only the larger of the heating or cooling load need be considered.
(2) Rated wattage.

Table 2.5.

Measurements: Minimum Vs. Recommended

	Counter (Lineal)	Base Cabinets (Lineal)	Wall Cabinets (Lineal)
1 or 2 bedrooms			
(HUD minimums)	52"	68"	68"
(Generous)	84"	96"	96"
3 bedrooms			
(HUD minimums)	60"	72"	72"
(Generous)	96"	120"	144"
4 bedrooms			
(HUD minimums)	72"	84"	84"
(Generous)	108"	120"	168"

4) A *range hood* must be at least as long as the range, at least 17 inches wide, and the bottom of the hood rim must not be more than 30 inches above range top.

5) *Range hood fan* must have a minimum capacity of 40 cfm of hood length, increased to 50 cfm when in island or peninsula location.

In the multifamily book, the specifications change drastically because of the nature of the central vent systems normally used. But for low multifamily walkups, such as townhouse complexes, the multifamily book refers to the one-family requirements.

Electrical requirements. These are spelled out in the 616 paragraphs. Demand for the various needs in the home, including all kitchen appliances, is listed in the Table 2.4.

As for lighting, the MPS requirement first is that there must be permanent lighting fixtures, controlled by wall switches, in dining areas, kitchens and all other habitable areas.

No point along a floorline can be more than 6 feet from a convenience outlet, and there must be at least two duplex receptacle outlets over counter work spaces in kitchens.

Recommended Kitchen Measurements. The HUD Minimum Property Standards are workable, and they represent a tremendous improvement over those used for the previous 15 years. But they are minimums, and even for dwellings intended for small families the prudent builder would do well to expand the countertop and cabinet capacities. And since they leave more open to interpretation than the old standards, it is possible to make them even more minimal. For example, by combining work areas it would be possible to get off with as little as 52 inches of lineal counter space in a two-bedroom house. But in this instance a little added cost can add a great deal of appeal and usefulness.

The countertop is for the purpose of serving the sink and appliances, and thus basic countertop needs do not change greatly as the size of the family increases.

Basic cabinet requirements do change as the size of the family increases because of the need for increased food storage and the necessity of storing additional dishes. Other requirements, such as storage for utensils and small appliances, remain largely the same.

In Table 2.5 the HUD minimums (by the wildest possible interpretation) are compared with other figures more in line with what a kitchen expert might recommend.

In augmenting the minimums for larger kitchens for larger houses and larger families, there are the following recommendations:

1) *Dry vegetable storage* is best accommodated by a 3-drawer base cabinet (no shelves).

2) *Bread and cake storage* is best accommodated by a 3-drawer base cabinet.

3) *Sink area* (within easy reach of sink) is best accommodated by a 2-drawer base cabinet (which will have one shelf). This augments the storage provided by the floor of the sink cabinet.

4) *General storage* is adequately accommodated by 1-drawer 2-shelf base cabinets. This includes pots and pans.

5) *Small appliance storage* is best accommodated by pull-out shelves.

For basic needs and measurements in the distribution of countertop space and for kitchen brunch and dining areas, see Chapter 7.

3

What to Do about Energy Efficiency

In past years, the basic measurements in the kitchen were in inches and feet.

But this is a new era, the energy-conscious era, and we must now also be concerned with *btus* gained and lost, with kilowatts and kilowatt hours, with conservation of energy and, as the costs of our kitchen fuels go up, with conservation of dollars.

Builders, architects and other kitchen designers are caught in a squeeze in this new era. They are pressured by governmental, quasi-governmental and consumer agencies and groups to design-in and build-in energy economies that the American buying public is often not willing to accept. The representative American buying a home or re-modeling an older home has worked hard for whatever affluence he has, and his point of purchase is no time to tell him that it is he who must bear the brunt of any austerity program and forego things he has worked and planned to own.

So we must think of energy-efficient houses and energy-efficient kitchens, true, but generally it is not the appliance that wastes the energy, it is the person operating it.

First, let's check some of the facts.

Windows and Doors

It is often said that after the heating plant, the biggest user of energy in the home is the hot water heater.

This is not true. The biggest wasters of energy in the home — hence the biggest users — are the windows and doors. We should consider them first, as the kitchen usually has at least one window and

often an outside door.

According to HUD studies, the windows and doors of a house account for 70 percent of the heating load and 46 percent of the cooling load.

Heat, of course, moves right through a single-pane window. A house loses three times as much heat by conduction through glass as it does through infiltration, or leakage, around the sash and frames, assuming a 1/16-inch gap all around. So if there are 12 windows it's like having a hole in the house about 150 inches square!

Windows also waste energy through radiation. A hole in the wall has a thermal conductivity, or "U" value, of 1.00. When you put a single pane of glass into that opening the "U" value rises to 1.13, or 13 percent greater in transmitting solar heat to the inside or inside heat to the outside. A University of Illinois study indicates that 10 single-pane windows will leak enough heat in cold weather to consume about 100 extra gallons of fuel-oil in a season, compared with storm windows with tightly-installed storm sash. And an NAHB Research Council study reports that a poor-fitting un-weatherstripped window can lead to 5-1/2 times more air infiltration than a window properly weatherstripped.

The answers are careful fitting of frames and sashes, and double-glazing. Beyond that, outside shade is the best protection against solar heat, and this can be provided either with trees or awnings. Heat-absorbing and reflecting glasses also can reduce solar heat, from 40 percent to 70 percent according to the U.S. Office of Consumer Affairs.

Beyond that the builder or designer can take the extra effort to educate the home buyer. The buyer

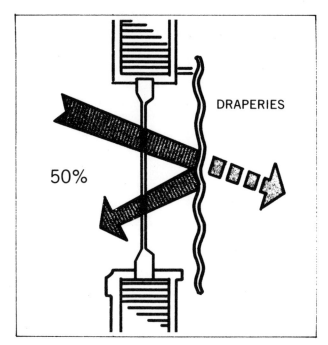

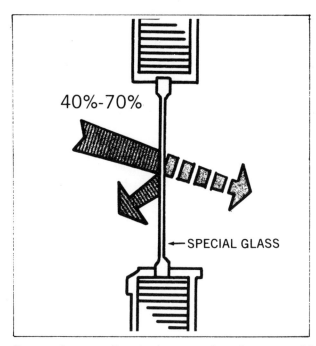

Draperies aren't as good as a shade tree outside, but they can reflect 50 percent of solar heat to conserve on indoor cooling. Special glass that absorbs and/or reflects heat can reduce solar heat by 40 to 70 percent according to the Office of Consumer Affairs in Washington.

Even a drawn roller shade can reduce heat or cold transmission through windows. Tests at the Illinois Inst. of Technology showed that a drawn shade can prevent more than 25 percent of heat loss through the window in winter. In summer, a drawn shade admits only half as much heat as an unshaded window. This means a saving of 8¢ on every dollar spent on heating, of 21¢ on cooling.

should be aware of the periodic need to recaulk, and of factors such as use of light-colored, opaque inside draperies to reflect solar heat. Draperies are only 50 percent effective because they reflect heat that already is in the house, but that is still 50 percent saved.

Appliances

In the kitchen perhaps more than in any other room, appliances use energy, but there are misconceptions here too.

A pyrolytic self-cleaning oven is one of the most-appreciated modern conveniences. However, because cleaning comes in a separate cycle in which the oven heats up to about 900°F, there have been charges that it is a big energy-waster. Disputing that, appliance people claim it has greatly improved insulation and actually saves energy because cooking heats are retained with much less fuel expenditure. And this is correct. It also is true that the self-clean feature is not used every day and often not even once per week.

But even at worst, estimated annual kwh for a conventional range is about 1,175 and for a self-cleaner it is 1,205, a difference of only about 2 percent.

Moving on to other appliances, the difference between a frost-free refrigerator and a manual defrost model is considerable. A 14-cu.-ft. frost-free model will use an estimated 1,829 kwh annually, compared with 1,137 for a manual. That's an increase of more than 50 percent. But manual defrosting of a refrigerator is one of the most-hated tasks in the home, second only to cleaning an oven. The housekeeper who has tried both, if given a choice, usually will opt happily for the extra expense of frost-free.

In addition, that higher energy cost is open to challenge: Manual defrosting uses a lot of energy, too, in bringing a warm box and warm foods back to cold. Frequent manual defrosting will not wipe out the cost differential, but it certainly will minimize the difference.

Here again, the builder can do some constructive educating. Homeowners should be informed that putting hot foods into a refrigerator or freezer increases the load and wastes energy. Foods should be allowed to cool before they go into the box.

Doors should not be opened with unnecessary frequency, and should be kept open for the shortest possible time. And door gaskets should be checked occasionally for tight fit, using the time-honored test of slipping a dollar bill in between the gasket and the box, closing the door and pulling out the bill. If it comes easily with no drag, the gasket is loose. This should be tried at different points around the door.

	average wattage	est. kwh consumed annually
Food Preparation		
Blender	386	15
Broiler	1,436	100
Carving Knife	92	8
Coffee Maker	894	106
Deep Fryer	1,448	83
Dishwasher	1,201	363
Egg Cooker	516	14
Frying Pan	1,196	186
Hot plate	1,257	90
Mixer	127	13
Oven, microwave (only)	1,450	190
Range		
with oven	12,200	1,175
with self-cleaning oven	12,200	1,205
Roaster	1,333	205
Sandwich Grill	1,161	33
Toaster	1,146	39
Trash Compactor	400	50
Waffle Iron	1,116	22
Waste Disposer	445	30
Food Preservation		
Freezer (15 cu ft)	341	1,195
Freezer (Frostless 15 cu ft)	440	1,761
Refrigerator (12 cu ft)	241	728
Refrigerator (Frostless 12 cu ft)	321	1,217
Refrigerator/Freezer (14 cu ft)	326	1,137
(Frostless 14 cu ft)	615	1,829

More appliance-makers have been developing products with energy-saving in mind. An electric dishwasher uses only about 363 kwh annually, again a cheap energy price for the time and human energy it saves. A homeowner can cut that figure down considerably by buying the more expensive model with a choice of several cycles. For example, the KitchenAid Superba or the Waste King 911, to pick two at random, offer a push button that simply rinses dishes so they can then wait until there is a full load, saving water and electricity. Or they can be shut off to eliminate the heated drying cycle, allowing the dishes to air-dry, or to dry with a flow of fanned air with no heat. These features help pay back the added cost of the upgraded model.

Instructions to consumers should be to read the literature to find the ways to conserve energy (and water) and, where possible, to save up the dishes for one full load per day rather than multiple washings of light loads.

The electric garbage disposer and the compactor, the other two clean-up appliances in the kitchen, have to be used when they are needed. But it would be difficult in any case to cut down on the 1.01 kwh per month of the compactor, or the 0.68 kwh per month of the disposer, a combined cost of only about 4¢ per month or less.

To return to cooking equipment, there are other instances where the highest-priced products save the most. A Jenn-Air range will cost at least 300 percent more than the cheapest similar configuration available. But with built-in down-draft ventilation, it obviates the need for a ventilating hood. And, the most important energy-saving feature is the opportunity it offers of cooking with convected heat, which surrounds both bake and broil elements with a power-driven stream of air. This means a cook can use temperatures 50°F lower and reduce cooking time as much as 30 percent, which represents real fuel savings.

Or, for $2,000, you can have a double-combination wall oven by Thermador that combines conventional cooking, microwave cooking and self-cleaning. The energy savings of microwave, supplemented by conventional heat only for the browning-appearance factor, is unbeatable for energy savings.

It would be impossible to cover properly the subject of energy savings in the kitchen without talking about microwave.

They are nearly always called microwave "ovens." More properly they are microwave "cookers," not ovens. An oven surrounds food with heat and the food cooks slowly as the heat seeps inward, cooking from the outside in.

With microwaves there is no heat. Radio frequency waves driven by a magnetron tube penetrate the food in the cooker. The waves cause the food molecules to rotate 180 degrees with such rapidity that they generate heat within the food, causing cooking. Microwave frequencies are allocated by the Federal Communications Commission to prevent interference with radio broadcasts. The two ranges permitted in the U.S. are 890 to 940 megacycles, and 2400 to 2500 megacycles.

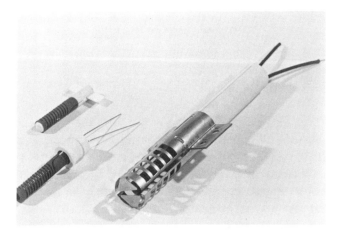

Newest thing in gas cooking is pilotless ignition. Such ranges have no pilot light, and gas is lit by this silicon carbide igniter.

Insulating Skylight by Solartron can cut use of electric light but minimize problem of heat gain. It is a sandwich panel, with dead air space between and a U value of 0.425 btu/hr/sq ft.

NATIONWIDE ENERGY COST COMPARISONS
OF MAJOR COOKING APPLIANCES

Per Cent of U.S. Households Using Microwave Ovens

	1970	1975	1980	1985
Microwave ovens and ranges	–	3	20	50
Conventional ranges	100	97	80	50

Cost of Electricity (In Millions)

	1970	1975	1980	1985
Microwave ovens	–	$ 48.4	$ 296.1	$ 739.1
Conventional ranges	$2,952.6	$2,688.0	$ 1,991.9	$ 1,082.7
TOTAL:	$2,952.6	$2,736.4	$ 2,288.0	$ 1,821.8

Cost Savings (From 1970 Level)

	1975	1980	1985
Dollar (In Millions)	$ 216.2	$ 664.6	$ 1,130.8
Kilowatt Hours (In Millions)	6,177.1	18,988.6	32,308.6

Assumptions: — U.S. households held constant at 70 million.
— Cost per kilowatt hour held constant at 3.5¢.
— Operating costs of gas and electric ranges are about the same.
— Life expectancy of all major cooking appliances at 15 to 16 years.

Source: Litton Microwave Cooking Products, May, 1976.

At 890 megacycles, food molecules oscillate at a rate of 890 million times per second, causing the rapid cooking. Greatest oscillation occurs about 1 inch below the surface of the food, and from that point on the energy is used up slightly so a roast can be rare in the center. A microwave cooker uses only about 190 kwh annually.

Their virtues are the tremendous speed with which they cook, the low power demand, and the fact that they do not (or anyone else) become hot and so do not heat up the kitchen. Nor can a child burn a hand accidentally. Microwave shortens cooking time generally by about 75 percent and at lower wattage rates. It saves as much in human energy. A hot dog can be cooked wrapped in a paper napkin, since there is no heat, or chicken parts can be cooked or reheated in a paper plate. So cleanup is reduced, dishwasher use is reduced, oven-cleaning becomes prehistoric. And the new generation of microwave cookers have variable power, microprocessor touch control, and they make up their own minds on when to shut themselves off or cut power to deliver a meal cooked the way the cook wants it.

Are they dangerous? It is unfortunate that this question even has to be raised, but there have been scares based on loose talk and on uninformed opinions from consumerists, doctors and elected officials. The fact is that in millions of cooking hours in the U.S. since 1955 there has never been a case of injury attributed to microwave cooking. Microwave researchers work bathed in microwaves and scoff at danger charges.

The key fact is that microwave radiation is non-ionizing radiation. X-Rays are ionizing; radiation from color TV sets is ionizing. Ionizing radiation can build up within the body. Microwave radiation is like radio waves, not harmful. Conversely, the microwave cooker is possibly the safest appliance in the home. By contrast, how many times have you or your spouse showed up at dinner time with an arm burn or hand burn from a conventional range? How many fires start in the kitchen from a conventional range?

So the equipment the builder puts into the kitchen can be a significant factor in energy-saving, with or without the homeowner's subsequent cooperation. And his structural practices can also have an effect. The merits of insulation go without saying and the kitchen is only a small part of the whole. But double-glazing, or even triple-glazing is something to consider.

Also of great help are fluorescent fixtures. Every incandescent bulb is a little heater that increases the cooling load (and, conversely, lessens the heating load in winter also). But fluorescents are more energy-efficient, about 250 percent more. A 20-watt fluorescent tube gives more light than a 60-watt incandescent bulb. And the tube will last about seven times longer.

Use of a skylight is worth considering to provide natural light and save on electricity. If there is an attic space above the kitchen, the light from the skylight can be "piped" down through the intervening space by building a "tube" of ordinary 1/4-inch plywood from roof to ceiling below. This could be flared to increase the light below. The trouble with a skylight is that it is another window, and we've already talked about window problems. But at least one brand, Solartron, uses a 1-1/2-inch-thick sandwich panel forming a 1-3/8-inch dead-air insulating space between, giving it a good insulation rating. The company claims this cuts out about 65 percent of the solar

Price pfister offers a 3 gallon per minute shower-head in both the regular and Jet Setter lines; this is about half the normal flow.

Eljer Plumbingware claims 40 percent average savings in water flow through use of its water-saving faucets. This Ultima line for the lavatory was recently converted to 2.25 gallons per minute, compared with the conventional 4.5 gallons per minute.

Swivel-spray aerator for sink or lavatory is part of Water Gate line by JKW 5000. It can cut water consumption by 33 percent, and swivels 360 degrees.

"Flow-Rator" by Moen is a restrictor now standard on all Moen sink and lavatory faucets, auto-matically cuts flow by 25 percent less than conventional single-handle faucet with conventional aerator.

Kohler flow-control showerheads can cut water use in half, the company claims, limiting water use to 3 gallons per minute at 40 psi. Assuming 5-minute daily showers for a family of four, this could mean savings of 20,000 gallons per year.

Water-Plus makes a faucet accessory it calls Aqua-Touch, which can be fitted to any faucet and permits instant shutoff. The lever has a spring which, when released, shuts the flow. It can save a lot of water in families where children or others are very slow to shut off the water.

Water-saving kitchen sink aerator by Baron Industries is said to conserve 66 to 75 percent of water use, maintaining constant flow regardless of line pressure. It is threaded to fit either male or female connection.

Keystone Brass and Rubber offers an assortment of water-restricting devices designed to cut flow by 50 percent or more.

radiation, but it still brings in the light.

In the "Energy-Efficient Residence" developed by NAHB for HUD, there were these features in water-heating and appliances:

1) A heavily-insulated water heater with isolated jacket, set back to 120°F;
2) Hot and cold water pipes insulated to reduce heat loss and control condensation;
3) Low-water-use devices on kitchen and bathroom faucets and shower head;
4) High-efficiency refrigerator with improved insulation and energy-saving feature (most good refrigerators are being improved to this point now);
5) Electric range with heavily insulated standard oven plus microwave cooker;
6) Energy-saving dishwasher, used for minimum water and air circulation drying;
7) Fluorescent lighting.

These are only the kitchen features; there were many other structural pointers given for other rooms. But estimated savings were $630 in a year, for a savings of 61,400,000 btu/year.

NAHB estimates that, with an annual increase in the price of energy running about 10 to 12 percent, the extra costs of this home would be recouped in 5 to 7 years.

A new feature in gas ranges that a builder should always look for, incidentally, is pilotless ignition. The gas industry estimates it can reduce gas used by a gas range over a year's time by 30 percent. The system uses a silicon carbide igniter by Carborundum, electrically heated to ignite the gas.

With it all, a builder can possibly do his customers, himself, and his country the biggest favor by providing some energy-related literature with the house. Such literature is available from local utilities, from the Federal Energy Administration, from NAHB, from HUD and other sources.

4

The Coming Metric Kitchen

The kitchen industry is not pushing it, but the U.S. has made a lukewarm commitment to metrication and over the next 10 years, more or less, metrication will creep into the kitchen.

Necessarily, the cabinet industry must wait until the lumber industry sets its metric standards. Cabinet metrics will have to conform to the sizes of sheet plywood and particleboard to cut down on the waste factor.

And, necessarily, cabinets must wait for or work closely with appliances. It can be easy to adapt a cabinet size to fit appliances. But it cannot be easy to adapt or modify the expensive tooling required by the appliance industry to conform with cabinets.

While decisions must wait, the cabinet industry has done extensive preliminary work. Louis Himelreich, technical director of the National Kitchen Cabinet Association, has made thorough studies and whatever develops probably will be based largely on his work. A. F. Kimmel, chairman of the metric committee of the American Institute of Kitchen Dealers, also has made studies and is chairman of a Cabinet & Casework subcommittee in the American National Metric Council, representing both associations.

Two objectives the industry will be guided by are to make the transition period easy on stocking distributors by not multiplying their inventory with old and new sizes, and to maintain compatibility with old and new appliance sizes. The inventory-mixing problem is an obvious one and probably will call for a mixing of hard and soft conversion in the transition period. The compatibility problem calls for a solution that will

permit the fitting of new metric replacement appliances into old kitchens.

Another objective will be to maintain the basic simplicity of the metric system itself. For example, the industry in the U.S. commonly uses two thicknesses of 3/4-inch particleboard to get the 1-1/2-inch thick countertop. But 3/4-inch converts to 18.75 mm, a fractional millimeter that adds to complication. It would maintain simplicity to change particleboard thickness to 20 mm and eliminate fractional measurements.

The lumber industry is not hanging back. It is working on metrication. However, if the appliance industry is hanging back, its hesitation can be understood. Retooling for new appliance sizes is something that must last for up to 12 years for profitable amortization. But a contributing factor in appliance retooling is that the great majority of appliance companies in Canada are subsidiaries of U.S. appliance companies. They must provide for the Canadian market, which should pave the way for action in the U.S.

The cabinet industry in the U.S. originally thought it could simply copy procedures from some other country that had gone metric. This has turned out to be not as easy as it looked. European countries have metric systems designed to protect their own national industries, and there are significant differences between German, Dutch and other European systems, as well as Canadian. So it cannot be a copycat process.

A simple and obvious solution would be to go with our present 3-inch modules, which are used almost universally in cabinet manufacture, but changing them to a rounded-off metric which

The difference is metric — The same kitchen, drawn in both U.S. inches and metric system, by Robert A. Cuccaro, CKD, of Worcester, MA, shows difference in working with German and U.S. cabinets. The drawings are different sizes although of the same room, because U.S. scale is 1/2 inch = 1 foot, whereas metric scales the drawing 1 = 20. Metric drawing uses German Allmilmo cabinets, while U.S. drawing uses U.S. Wood-Mode. They have slightly different dimensions, but add up to the same kitchen.

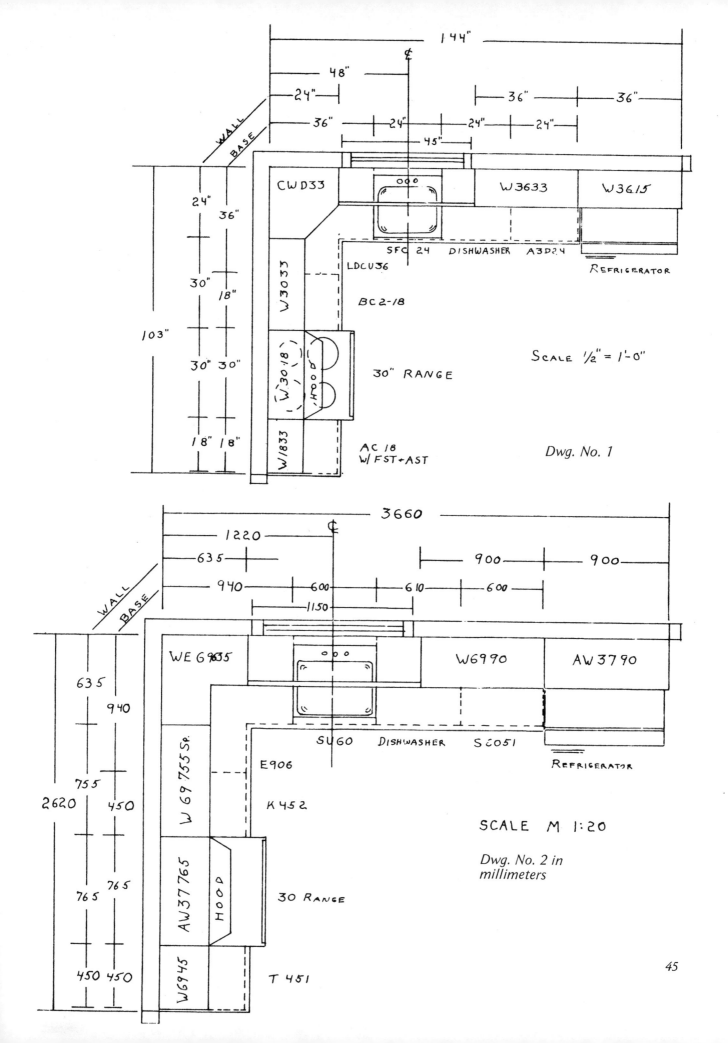

Dwg. No. 1

144"

48"

24"

36" 24" 24" 24" 36" 36"

45"

CWD33

W3633 W3615

SFC 24 DISHWASHER A3D24

REFRIGERATOR

24"

36"

W3033

LDCU36

BC 2-18

30"

18"

SCALE ½" = 1'-0"

103"

30" 30"

W3018 HOOD

30" RANGE

18" 18"

W1833

AC 18
W/ FST+AST

Dwg. No. 1

3660

1220

635

900 900

940 600 610 600

1150

WE G935

W6990 AW3790

SU60 DISHWASHER SC051

REFRIGERATOR

635

940

W 69 755 Sp.

E906

755

450

K 452

2620

SCALE M 1:20

765 765

AW37765 HOOD

30 Range

*Dwg. No. 2 in
millimeters*

450 450

W6945

T 451

would be slightly smaller than current sizes. This would permit cabinet-appliance compatibility through the use of fillers and/or extended stiles to bring cabinets up to assumed larger dimensions of any new appliances and actual larger dimensions of existing appliances.

The present 3-inch module converts, on this basis, to a 75 mm (2.95 inches) module easily.

Base cabinet and wall cabinet widths, then, as normally sized by stock cabinet manufacturers, would convert as follows:

Present dimension	Converted dimension
9 in.	225 mm (8.86 in.)
12 in.	300 mm (11.81 in.)
15 in.	375 mm (14.76 in.)
18 in.	450 mm (17.72 in.)
21 in.	525 mm (20.67 in.)
24 in.	600 mm (23.62 in.)
27 in.	675 mm (26.57 in.)
30 in.	750 mm (29.53 in.)
33 in.	825 mm (32.48 in.)
36 in.	900 mm (35.43 in.)
39 in.	975 mm (38.39 in.)
42 in.	1050 mm (41.54 in.)
45 in.	1125 mm (44.29 in.)
48 in.	1200 mm (47.24 in.)

Following the same system, following would be wall cabinet heights and depth:

Present dimension	Converted dimension
12 in. depth	300 mm (11.81 in.)
12 in. height	300 mm (11.81 in.)
15 in. height	375 mm (12.76 in.)
18 in. height	450 mm (17.72 in.)
24 in. height	600 mm (23.62 in.)
30 in. height	750 mm (29.52 in.)
33 in. height (custom)	825 mm (32.48 in.)

Base cabinet height and depth need standardization for appliance compatibility. Key dimensions are those to the top of the countertop and depth to the front of the countertop. The height currently is 36 inches, and the depth currently is 25 inches. On this basis:

Present dimension	Converted dimension
36 in. height	900 mm (35.43 in.)
25 in. depth	625 mm (24.61 in.)

This formula approach of using 300 mm in place of one English foot was devised by Mr. Kimmel, and has a lot going for it. It is a hard conversion, which is desirable, but the difference from previous size is so slight, only about 2 percent in the extreme and only about 1/16-inch for every 4-inches of current dimension, that it is easily accommodated mentally in a transition period. It accommodates also the physical aspects of design and manufacturing, as well as the psychological aspects of marketing and consumer acceptance. It recognizes that the dimensions of a kitchen depend on the dimensions of home building and stock-sized materials, and two of the basic materials are plywood and particleboard panels and lumber studs. Since the Canadian lumber industry has gone to a 1200 mm x 2400 mm panel (47.24 inches x 94.49 inches), it means that the conventional 8-foot stud would become 2400 mm or 94.49 inches. Throughout, this is a change that would not obsolete literature and A/V materials currently in use by the cabinet industry or home builders or the lumber industry.

An interesting alternative stems from the research of Mr. Himelreich, which came from a different direction — adapting from Europeans and others.

From any point of view, there are objectionable features to either Canadian modules or European modules. The Canadians use a 100 mm module, which is not compatible now with U.S. compactor, oven and range dimensions. Europeans use 150 mm modules in some cases, 100 mm modules in others, and all were adopted to conform to appliance measurements far different from those in the U.S. In some cases, a European manufacturer will use 100 mm modules for smaller sizes, then switch to 150 mm modules for larger sizes. So there is no uniform European system to follow.

And from a production point of view, both Canadian and European systems have sizes which would make it impossible to get three cabinet sides from the generally accepted new 1200 x 2400 mm plywood or particleboard sheet.

Let's look at these various possibilities in the following charts. In doing so, the goal is to end up with a solution that will result in lower cabinet costs for the builder and for the cabinet manufacturer.

Comparison German, Dutch, Canada and Proposed U.S. Metric Kitchen Cabinet Sizes

	GERMAN		DUTCH		CANADA		U.S. Hard Similar To Canada		U.S. Hard Widths In 75 mm Incre.		U.S. Soft Conversion	
	mm	inch	mm	inch	mm	inch	mm	inch	mm	inch	mm	inch
Wall Height	370	14.57	350	13.78	350	13.78	350	13.78	350	13.78	356	14
	560	22.05	550	21.65	550	21.65	450	17.72	450	17.72	457	18
	690	22.17					600	23.62	600	23.62	610	24
	900	35.43	700	27.56	800	31.50	750	29.53	750	29.53	762	30
Wall Depth With Door	350	13.78	335	13.19								
w/o Door					300	11.81	300	11.81	300	11.81	305	12
Base Height w/o CT.			870	34.25	870	34.25	870	34.25	870	34.25	876	34.50
With CT.	900	35.43	900	35.43	900	35.43	908	35.75	908	35.43	914	36
Base Depth With Door					600	23.62	600	23.62	600	23.62	610	24
w/o Door	600	23.62	600	23.62								
Vanity Height w/o CT.							750	24.53	750	29.53	749	29.50
With CT.							788	31.02	788	31.02	787	31
Oven & Utility Height			2070	81.50	2100	82.68	2130	83.86	2130	83.86	2134	84
Cabinet Widths	300	11.81	300	11.81	300	11.81	300	11.81	300	11.81	305	12
	400	15.75	450	17.71	400	15.75	400	15.75	375	14.76	381	15
	500	19.69	600	23.62	500	19.69	500	19.69	450	17.72	457	18
	600	23.62	750	29.53	600	23.62	600	23.62	525	20.67	533	21
	700	27.56	900	34.43	700	27.56	700	27.56	600	23.62	610	24
	800	31.50			750	29.53	750	29.53	675	26.57	686	27
	900	35.43			800	31.50	800	31.50	750	29.53	762	30
	1000	39.37			900	35.43	900	35.43	825	32.48	838	33
					1000	39.37	1000	39.37	900	35.43	914	36
					1100	43.31	1100	43.31	975	38.39	991	39
					1200	47.24	1200	47.24	1050	41.34	1067	42
									1200	47.24	1219	48

Chart shows comparison of German, Dutch, and Canadian metric systems for cabinets, plus a U.S. hard conversion similar to Canada's system, a U.S. hard conversion in 75 mm increments, and a U.S. soft conversion. For any who might still be unfamiliar with the terms, "soft" conversion is merely translating our inches into metric language, whereas "hard" conversion involves an actual change of dimensions.

In the German sizes, we would have trouble getting 900 mm sides out of any standard sheet without excessive waste, and in addition it is a size now approximated only by custom cabinet manufacturers. In the Dutch, most sizes are acceptable, although the 700 mm is a bit low for standard cabinets. The Canadian 800 mm size is bad from a production standpoint because we cannot get three sides from a 94.5-inch sheet of plywood.

We can get good yield from all the sizes listed under U.S. hard conversion, and we reject the soft conversion because a lot of odd and fractional numbers would be hard to handle and defeat the simplicity of the metric system.

The German and Dutch depths include the door because most of their cabinets are made without face-frames and with slab doors. Their doors usually are about 3/4-inch thick, so with depths of 350 mm and 335 mm they get 13-1/4-inches and 12-3/4-inches net depth. Again, the 47-1/4-inch-wide panel won't yield four sides.

Bathroom vanities are included in the chart because most U.S. vanities are produced by kitchen cabinet plants. Our 350 mm-high wall cabinet can be fitted above a refrigerator.

Comparison of Numbers of Doors, Drawer Fronts & Cabinets

	U.S. METRIC (1) 75 INC. 44.5 STILE 89 MULLION	U.S. METRIC (1) 100 INC. 38 STILE 76 MULLION	U.S. METRIC (1) 100 INC. 38 STILE 38 MULLION	CANADA METRIC (1) 100 INC. 38 STILE 76 MULLION	CANADA METRIC (1) 100 INC. 38 STILE 38 MULLION
DF 150	9	9	12	9	12
DF 206	4	4	4	4	4
TOTAL	13	13	16	13	16
DOOR 350	4	4	4	4	8
480					
450	7	6	8	6	
550				5	6
600	8	8	11	8	11
630					7
750	7	7	10	7	11
800				7	11
TOTAL	26	25	33	37	61
CABINETS	72	69	69	63	63

(1) Vanity bottom rail 68 mm   (2) Vanity bottom rail 38 mm

Here is a comparison of the number of cabinets, doors and drawer fronts needed for a single metric line in the various systems. There are more cabinets in the 75 mm-increment system simply because it is a 3-inch module instead of 4-inch. But because of possible interchangeability due to the double-size mullion, there is only one more door needed than for a U.S. 100 mm module with double-size mullion, and seven less than for the 100 mm module with mullion the same size as the stile.

This is for a single line. But assume a cabinet manufacturer has two colors and five different styles. Then he has 10 lines, and differences in number of cabinets doors and drawer fronts become significant. The difference of 25 doors (for col. 2) and 61 (for col. 5) is 360 more doors to manufacture and keep in stock.

Comparing the Commonest Measurement Units

Approximate conversions from Customary to metric and vice versa.

	When you know:	You can find:	If you multiply by:
LENGTH	inches	millimeters	25
	feet	centimeters	30
	yards	meters	0.9
	miles	kilometers	1.6
	millimeters	inches	0.04
	centimeters	inches	0.4
	meters	yards	1.1
	kilometers	miles	0.6
AREA	square inches	square centimeters	6.5
	square feet	square meters	0.09
	square yards	square meters	0.8
	square miles	square kilometers	2.6
	acres	square hectometers (hectares)	0.4
	square centimeters	square inches	0.16
	square meters	square yards	1.2
	square kilometers	square miles	0.4
	square hectometers (hectares)	acres	2.5
MASS	ounces	grams	28
	pounds	kilograms	0.45
	short tons	megagrams (metric tons)	0.9
	grams	ounces	0.035
	kilograms	pounds	2.2
	megagrams (metric tons)	short tons	1.1
LIQUID VOLUME	ounces	milliliters	30
	pints	liters	0.47
	quarts	liters	0.95
	gallons	liters	3.8
	milliliters	ounces	0.034
	liters	pints	2.1
	liters	quarts	1.06
	liters	gallons	0.26
TEMPERATURE	degrees Fahrenheit	degrees Celsius	5/9 (after subtracting 32)
	degrees Celsius	degrees Fahrenheit	9/5 (then add 32)

U.S. METRIC WALL CABINET SECTIONS

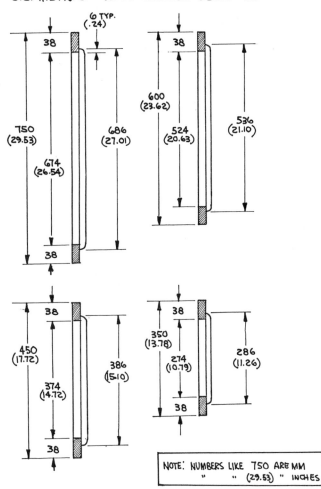

NOTE: NUMBERS LIKE 750 ARE MM
" " (29.53) " INCHES

U.S. METRIC - BASE SECTIONS

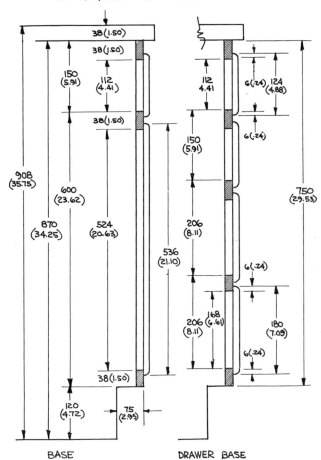

BASE   DRAWER BASE

These are the proposed four heights for U.S. wall cabinets. Rail sizes and door lap vary considerably from manufacturer to manufacturer, but this system proposes 38 mm rails (1-1/2 inch) and 6 mm door lap (.24 inch), both widely used. (The rail is the horizontal member of the face frame. Shaded areas are the top and bottom rails. The overlay doors protrude on the right.

In this base-section graphic, total height of the base cabinet without countertop is 870 mm. Subtract 120 mm for the toekick and you have 750 mm. This also is the height of the 750 mm wall cabinet, so a wall-cabinet front frame and door can be used as front frame and door for a base cabinet with no drawer. In inches, a 30-inch wall cabinet plus a 4-1/2-inch toekick is equal to a base cabinet without drawer, although drawers could be placed behind the door. If you check the height above the rail at the bottom of the drawer opening, 150 mm, which is the drawer opening plus the top rail, and subtract that and the toekick it leaves 600 mm, or the height of the 600 mm wall cabinet. So the same door can be used for both base and wall cabinets. These are production efficiencies that can mean cost savings.

Now look at the base cabinet with the four drawers, and note that it is divided below the top drawer space into 150 mm, 206 mm, 206 mm and the height of the bottom rail, 38 mm, or a total of 600 mm. This provides for a vanity, as we show in the next drawings.

U.S. METRIC VANITY SECTIONS

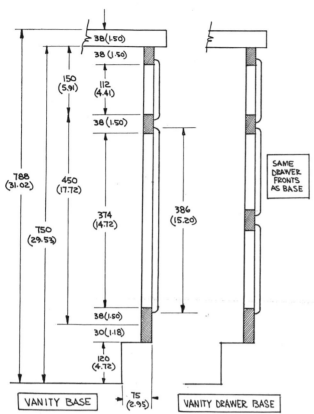

VANITY BASE

VANITY DRAWER BASE

U.S. METRIC
WALL, BASE & VANITY BASE CROSS SECTIONS
SHOWING MULTIPLE USE OF DOORS AND FRAMES

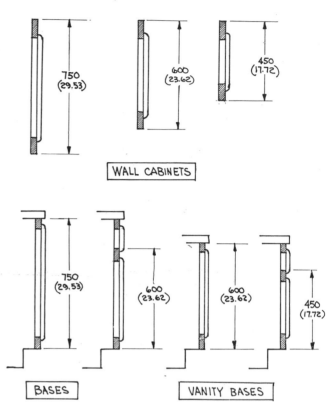

WALL CABINETS

BASES

VANITY BASES

Vanity base height without toekick is 600 mm plus 30 mm extra (added to the bottom rail) plus 120 mm toekick for an overall height of 31.09 inches plus top. This bottom rail for the vanity is about 2-5/8 inches, and this could be the size of all three rails, but it would make for many extra parts. Again, the 600 mm is the height of a wall cabinet, so vanities without drawers could use the 600 mm wall cabinet doors. The 150 mm at the top is the same as the drawer of the base cabinet, and the 450 mm is the same as a wall cabinet. So a 600 mm wall cabinet plus toekick is the same as a vanity without drawer, and a 450 mm wall cabinet plus a 150 mm drawer is the same as a vanity with a drawer. Now, looking back to the previous page of base sections, we see the reason for two 150 mm drawer spacings and two 206 mm drawer spacings. It gives us the flexibility to use the same cabinets for vanities.

To put those last three sets of drawings in a different perspective, this reviews the points. A 30-inch-high (29.53) wall cabinet plus a 4-1/2-inch toekick equals a base cabinet without a drawer. A 24-inch-high wall cabinet plus a 6-inch drawer equals a base cabinet without drawer. A 24-inch-high wall cabinet plus a 4-1/2-inch kickspace equals a vanity base without drawer, and an 18-inch-high wall cabinet plus a 6-inch-high drawer plus a 4-1/2-inch toekick equals a vanity with drawer.

U.S. METRIC - OVEN SECTION

U.S. METRIC - UTILITY SECTION

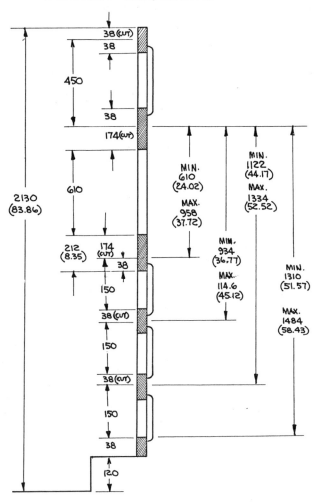

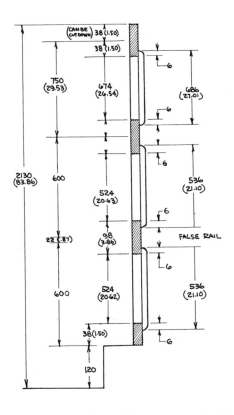

Built-in ovens are not as popular with builders now as they were in the 1960s, but they still are strong in the remodeling market and in much of the higher-priced new housing. The problem is that manufacturers offer, literally, hundreds of dimensional variations. Custom cabinet manufacturers determine the exact model number of the oven and then manufacture the oven cabinet so it fits. Stock cabinet manufacturers must make oven cabinets with enough latitude to be trimmed or cut so the oven will fit.

Presently, the oven cabinet comes to 84-inches from the floor. The proposed 2130 mm is 83.86-inches with a wide top rail that can be cut, and three similarly wide rails between the lower drawers that can be cut. Its top element is a 450 mm-high wall cabinet. Overall, it allows for varying oven heights from 24-inches to 58-inches by cutting rails or eliminating drawers. Thus it can accommodate anything from the small single-cavity oven to the big jobs that include two ovens and a warming drawer.

Like oven cabinets, utility cabinets are tall. They are fitted for various combinations of uses, such as Lazy Susan or other pantry arrangements, or broom closets, etc. This proposal shows a 30-inch-high wall cabinet door at the top, and the case should have no shelf behind the rail below the 750 mm spacing. The total lower spacing of 1222 mm could take a single door, and most cabinet manufacturers now make such doors, but they are not easy to make and can warp. The alternative is two doors of 600 mm wall cabinets connected with a false rail. Thus stock doors can be used and the warping problem is eliminated. It could be varied with a 450 mm-high wall cabinet door at top and a combination of two 750 mm-high wall cabinet doors.

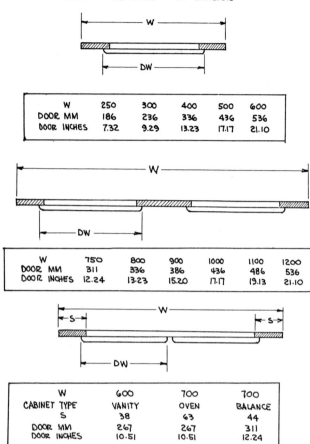

U.S. & CANADA METRIC CASE & DOOR WIDTH
100 INC - 38 STILE - 76 MULLION

W	250	300	400	500	600
DOOR MM	186	236	336	436	536
DOOR INCHES	7.32	9.29	13.23	17.17	21.10

W	750	800	900	1000	1100	1200
DOOR MM	311	336	386	436	486	536
DOOR INCHES	12.24	13.23	15.20	17.17	19.13	21.10

W CABINET TYPE	600 VANITY	700 OVEN	700 BALANCE
S	38	63	44
DOOR MM	267	267	311
DOOR INCHES	10.51	10.51	12.24

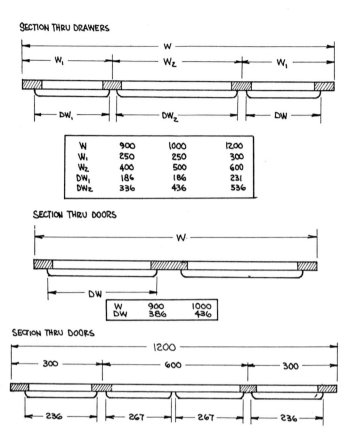

U.S. & CANADA -METRIC VANITY CASE & DOOR WIDTHS
100 INC - 38 STILE - 76 MULLION

SECTION THRU DRAWERS

W	900	1000	1200
W₁	250	250	300
W₂	400	500	600
DW₁	186	186	231
DW₂	336	436	536

SECTION THRU DOORS

W	900	1000
DW	386	436

SECTION THRU DOORS

These drawings show a family of cabinet and door widths based on the Canadian 100 mm increment, as could be used in the U.S., plus the needed 750 mm width and the 250 mm. Here the stiles (vertical members of the face-frame) are 38 mm, or 1-1/2-inches, with 76 mm mullions, twice the width of the stiles. An added 1/4-inch could be helpful in corners for pull or drawer clearance, but the 38 mm is adequate for standardization and, in addition, it is the same as the rails for less stock.

The mullion is twice as wide as the stile for an important reason: It makes possible the least number of door widths, as shown on page 48.

On the 600 mm vanity two doors are used, because a single door would be too wide to open in the normal bathroom. The wide stile on the 700 mm oven cabinet would make the minimum width of cutout the same as for the 600 mm oven cabinet, and might even obviate the need for the 600. A very small percentage of built-in ovens are wider and would need wider cabinets. These would normally be accommodated by custom cabinets, but the number is so small that specials could be made and the same doors could still be used on the cabinet.

All of the 700 series here use a 44 mm stile, or 1-3/4-inches, so the 750 doors can be used on the 700 cabinets with mullions.

These vanity sizes, again following the 100 mm increment, uses doors and drawers on the 900 series through 1200. To get two drawers in the 900 series we use a special 250 mm cabinet drawer. The other cabinets have standard doors and drawer fronts.

U.S. METRIC CASE & DOOR WIDTHS
75 INC - 44.5 STILE - 89 MULLION

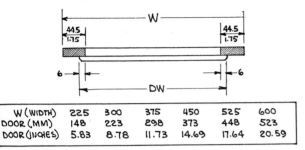

W (WIDTH)	225	300	375	450	525	600
DOOR (MM)	148	223	298	373	448	523
DOOR (INCHES)	5.83	8.78	11.73	14.69	17.64	20.59

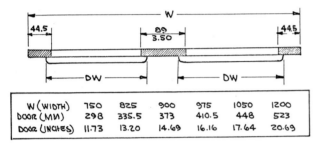

W (WIDTH)	750	825	900	975	1050	1200
DOOR (MM)	298	335.5	373	410.5	448	523
DOOR (INCHES)	11.73	13.20	14.69	16.16	17.64	20.69

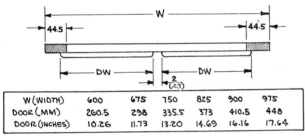

W (WIDTH)	600	675	750	825	900	975
DOOR (MM)	260.5	298	335.5	373	410.5	448
DOOR (INCHES)	10.26	11.73	13.20	14.69	16.16	17.64

This shows the 75 mm increment system, which the kitchen industry might prefer. It has 44.5 mm (1-3/4-inch) stiles and 89 mm (3-1/2-inch) mullions, although these widths are arbitrary. This stile width, however, gives better opportunity to design doors and hardware with clearance in the corners so no fillers would be needed. It is desirable to start using a mullion on the 750 series and wider, because it is easier for wider cabinets to get doors slightly out of line because of hinge sag or from cabinets getting racked in assembly or installation. When two doors nearly touch where they meet, any misalignment becomes very visible. But with a 2-1/2- to 3-inch space provided by a mullion, such misalignment is not noticeable.

U.S. CANADA METRIC VANITY SECTIONS
75 INC. 44.5 STILE 89 MULLION

SECTION THRU DRAWERS

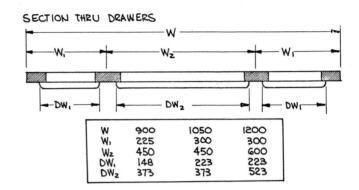

W	900	1050	1200
W₁	225	300	300
W₂	450	450	600
DW₁	148	223	223
DW₂	373	373	523

SECTION THRU DOORS

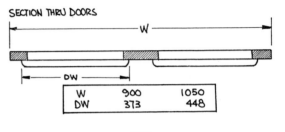

W	900	1050
DW	373	448

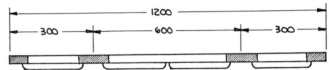

Here is the same 75 mm-increment line for vanities with 44.5 mm stile and 89 mm mullion. Here again, all standard doors and drawer fronts are used except that the 900 mm cabinet needs a special drawer in order to have two drawers in the cabinet.

5

Everything You Should Know about Kitchen Cabinets

Kitchen cabinets are manufactured in such a variety of sizes, shapes, styles, finishes, colors, and materials that classification becomes difficult. Perhaps we should stop calling them "kitchen" cabinets. Nearly all major cabinet manufacturers now manufacture and promote cabinet assemblies for nearly every room in the house. All of these other-room applications utilize standard or scaled-down "kitchen" cabinets with the fine "furniture finishes" that were developed in the 1960s.

Two types of cabinet manufacturers with whom the builder and architect may be involved may be identified: stock and custom manufacturers.

The stock cabinet manufacturer is most commonly used for new home construction, for several good reasons:

1. He manufactures to stock, to fill his own warehouse and the warehouses of his distributors. Delivery often is available almost immediately from local supply points.

2. Sales are usually handled through the local distributor. Although shipments are often made direct to the building site, particularly in large projects, the builder does have a direct local line to the factory through the distributor. The distributor will schedule shipments according to the progress of the building job and may even coordinate the various trades involved in kitchen installation, a chore most builders are happy to be rid of.

3. Stock manufacturers usually offer lines ranging from lowest to upper medium price, a range usually most consistent with new construction needs.

4. Stock cabinet manufacturers must, of necessity, tailor their lines along the broad lines of general customer preference. They follow the results of their own marketing research and of current developments in the furniture field. While there will seldom be a unique color or finish in a stock line, a speculative builder will find that all of these lines are "safe."

5. Freight or other damages are immediately rectifiable from local distributor stock.

The custom cabinet manufacturer is quite different from the stock manufacturer. He usually is local or regional, although some operate on a national basis. He does not start making cabinets until the kitchen floorplan is in his plant.

This normally means a delivery period of from six to eight weeks. Prices here range from upper medium to high. Sales to builders in the field are made through factory representatives (who are independent businessmen) or through local dealers who often act as representatives on builder jobs.

Custom home builders especially like the advantages of dealing with custom manufacturers because:

1. The quality ranges from very good to superb.

2. Exotic woods, style, finishes, and variations are available and can be specified for unique cabinets and kitchens. These manufacturers can supply teak, cherry, pecan, solid wood, or even a "five-quarter" door as opposed to the usual 3/4-inch or 7/8-inch thickness.

3. Many builders have gained real competitive advantages by using the design service of the local custom kitchen dealer.

The builder has a few other options, particularly if he is risk-oriented. He can build the cabinets himself, on-site. This used to be common practice.

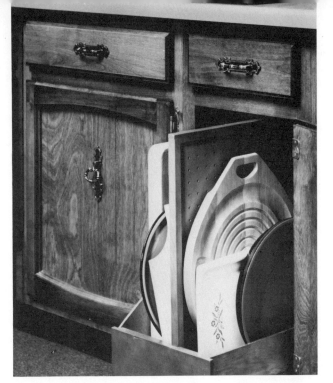

Clutter is kept off counter when drawers are outfitted with ventilated metal liners, as for bread and staples.

Storage problem of large flat items is solved with this lid and tray rack. Rack slides out so items can be placed or removed easily.

Lazy susan corner has revolving shelves, individually adjustable. This is for wall cabinet.

Pantry unit has adjustable, self-turning lazy susan rotating shelves.

DESIGN-A-WALL COMPONENTS

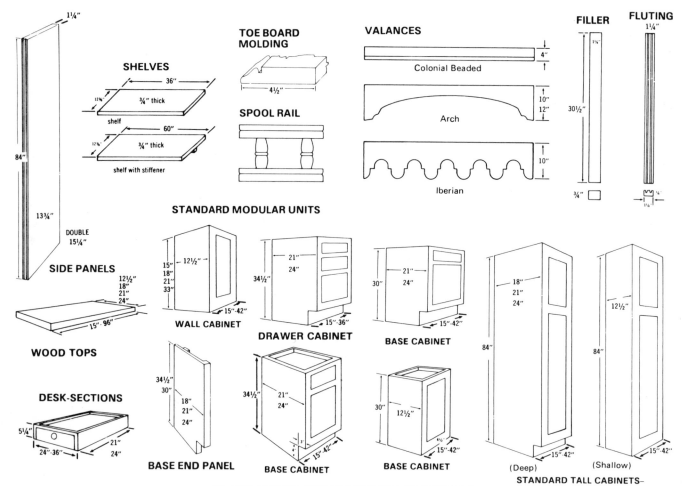

ALL BASE CABINETS AVAILABLE WITH FULL HEIGHT DOORS

Now only about 100,000 kitchens a year are built on this basis as more and more builders discover that they cannot afford this kind of work. Also, it can be very difficult to prove that site-built cabinets meet the new ANSI construction and performance standards without taking them through the established testing procedures at a recognized testing laboratory.

There also are numerous small plants and shops set up in various parts of the country specifically to serve the builder. Some may be very good. They usually are neither stock nor custom in the sense previously described. They often make an 8-ft. or 10-ft. run of wall or base cabinets as one unit for a specific builder floorplan, and turn them out by the hundreds with consequent economies. These cabinets may be good, but the builder must be sure

of what he is buying. When the housewife climbs up to put some plants on top of the wall cabinets and finds raw wood with nails sticking out, she will certainly be upset.

Cabinets set the kitchen style

There are four basic kitchen styles: Colonial, Traditional, Provincial and Contemporary.

There also are special styles such as Mediterranean, Oriental, Nautical, Pennsylvania Dutch, Swiss Chalet or others that the imaginative merchandiser might want to feature.

Whatever the style, basic or special, the motif is set by the cabinets. That means the style of the whole kitchen really is set by only two elements, the cabinet doors and the drawer fronts, since

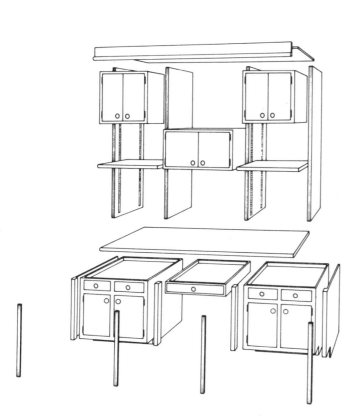

The term "kitchen cabinets" has become a mis-nomer as builders increasingly spread them throughout the house. Most manufacturers assist with components to adapt them. These pages showing adapting components and how to use them are from a booklet of Rutt Custom Kitchens. The photos that follow show what can be done with them.

these are the most visible elements in the kitchen.

Appliances are visible, but they have no particular influence on style. They simply "go with" the cabinets. Their colors might be varied to blend or highlight certain styles, but their role in kitchen styling always is either supplementary or complementary.

There is wide latitude in the definitions of styling. If a manufacturer wants to call his new line Colonial, Colonial it is, no matter how provincial or contemporary it looks.

With that in mind, let us review the various styles.

Traditional — This is the leader. More manufacturers offer it, and it accounts for 33 percent of all U.S. cabinet production. But many manufacturers include Colonial in this category because they are relating to American tradition.

Characteristically, traditional is a somewhat

dignified and conservative style featuring a recessed or a raised panel, or at least a false raised panel. Oak carries this style well.

Colonial — This might be called Early American or Country Western, or other similar names. A pegged, board-and-batten door possibly is the ultimate in this styling. V-grooves are common, but pegs alone are usually enough to establish the style even on an otherwise plain door. On the west coast and in the southwest, knotty pine is enough to establish the style, or knotty cedar where a redder look is desired. Colors will be mellow.

Provincial — This might be French or Italian, with the Italian being somewhat more ornate. Provincial is characterized by moldings on the face of door and drawer front, with arcs at the corners. In cost-cutting versions, the moldings are replaced by a routed groove. Routed grooves also are commonly used on plastic surfaced doors.

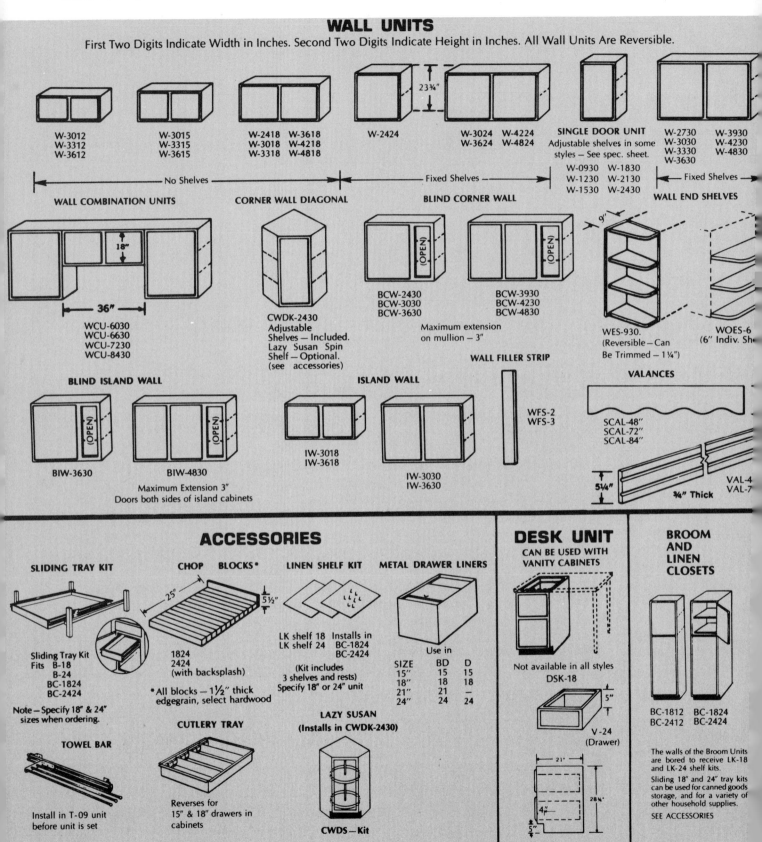

WALL UNITS

First Two Digits Indicate Width in Inches. Second Two Digits Indicate Height in Inches. All Wall Units Are Reversible.

W-3012
W-3312
W-3612

W-3015
W-3315
W-3615

W-2418 W-3618
W-3018 W-4218
W-3318 W-4818

23¾"

W-2424

W-3024 W-4224
W-3624 W-4824

SINGLE DOOR UNIT
Adjustable shelves in some styles — See spec. sheet.

W-0930 W-1830
W-1230 W-2130
W-1530 W-2430

W-2730 W-3930
W-3030 W-4230
W-3330 W-4830
W-3630

◄—— No Shelves ——► ◄—————— Fixed Shelves —————————► ◄— Fixed Shelves —►

WALL COMBINATION UNITS

18"

36"

WCU-6030
WCU-6630
WCU-7230
WCU-8430

CORNER WALL DIAGONAL

CWDK-2430
Adjustable
Shelves — Included.
Lazy Susan Spin
Shelf — Optional.
(see accessories)

BLIND CORNER WALL

(OPEN)

BCW-2430
BCW-3030
BCW-3630

(OPEN)

BCW-3930
BCW-4230
BCW-4830

Maximum extension
on mullion — 3"

WALL END SHELVES

9"

WES-930.
(Reversible—Can
Be Trimmed — 1¼")

WOES-6
(6" Indiv. Sh

BLIND ISLAND WALL

(OPEN)

BIW-3630

(OPEN)

BIW-4830

Maximum Extension 3"
Doors both sides of island cabinets

ISLAND WALL

IW-3018
IW-3618

IW-3030
IW-3630

WALL FILLER STRIP

WFS-2
WFS-3

VALANCES

SCAL-48"
SCAL-72"
SCAL-84"

5¼"

¾" Thick

VAL-4
VAL-7

ACCESSORIES

SLIDING TRAY KIT

Sliding Tray Kit
Fits B-18
       B-24
       BC-1824
       BC-2424

Note — Specify 18" & 24"
sizes when ordering.

TOWEL BAR

Install in T-09 unit
before unit is set

CHOP BLOCKS*

25"

5½"

1824
2424
(with backsplash)

*All blocks — 1½" thick
edgegrain, select hardwood

CUTLERY TRAY

Reverses for
15" & 18" drawers in
cabinets

LINEN SHELF KIT

LK shelf 18 Installs in
LK shelf 24 BC-1824
             BC-2424

(Kit includes
3 shelves and rests)
Specify 18" or 24" unit

LAZY SUSAN
(Installs in CWDK-2430)

CWDS—Kit

METAL DRAWER LINERS

Use in

SIZE	BD	D
15"	15	15
18"	18	18
21"	21	—
24"	24	24

DESK UNIT

CAN BE USED WITH
VANITY CABINETS

Not available in all styles
DSK-18

V-24
(Drawer)

5"

21"

28¾"

4"

5"

BROOM AND LINEN CLOSETS

BC-1812 BC-1824
BC-2412 BC-2424

The walls of the Broom Units
are bored to receive LK-18
and LK-24 shelf kits.

Sliding 18" and 24" tray kits
can be used for canned goods
storage, and for a variety of
other household supplies.

SEE ACCESSORIES

BASE UNITS

First Two Digits Indicate Width in Inches — Base Cabinet is 34½" High and 24" Deep from Face of Frame.
Single Door Base Units Reversible. Except Diplomat Style.

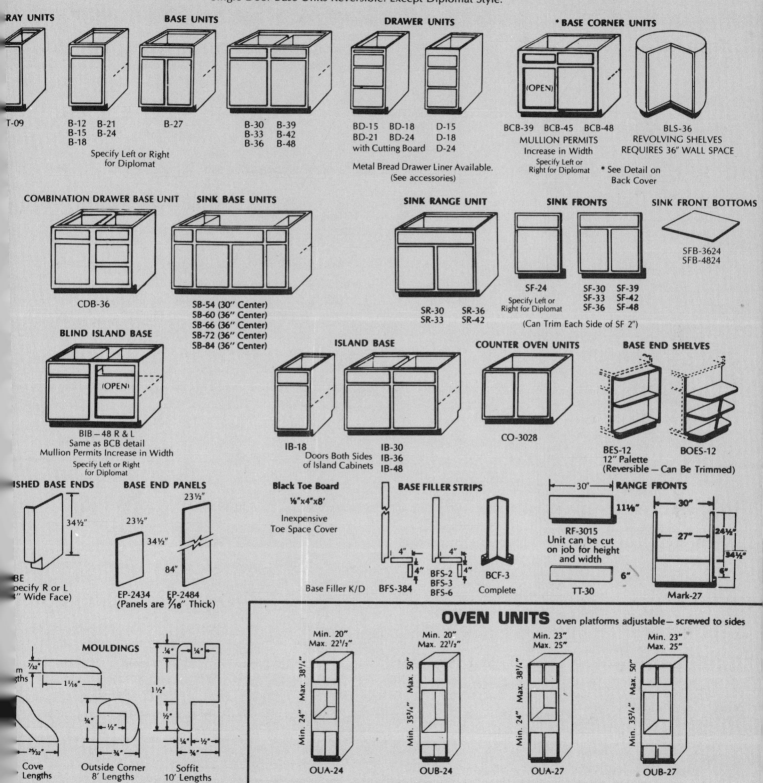

RAY UNITS

T-09

BASE UNITS

B-12 B-21
B-15 B-24
B-18

Specify Left or Right
for Diplomat

B-27

B-30 B-39
B-33 B-42
B-36 B-48

DRAWER UNITS

BD-15 BD-18 D-15
BD-21 BD-24 D-18
with Cutting Board D-24

Metal Bread Drawer Liner Available.
(See accessories)

* BASE CORNER UNITS

(OPEN)

BCB-39 BCB-45 BCB-48
MULLION PERMITS
Increase in Width
Specify Left or
Right for Diplomat

BLS-36
REVOLVING SHELVES
REQUIRES 36" WALL SPACE

* See Detail on
Back Cover

COMBINATION DRAWER BASE UNIT

CDB-36

SINK BASE UNITS

SB-54 (30" Center)
SB-60 (36" Center)
SB-66 (36" Center)
SB-72 (36" Center)
SB-84 (36" Center)

SINK RANGE UNIT

SR-30 SR-36
SR-33 SR-42

SINK FRONTS

SF-24
Specify Left or
Right for Diplomat

SF-30 SF-39
SF-33 SF-42
SF-36 SF-48

(Can Trim Each Side of SF 2")

SINK FRONT BOTTOMS

SFB-3624
SFB-4824

BLIND ISLAND BASE

(OPEN)

BIB—48 R & L
Same as BCB detail
Mullion Permits Increase in Width
Specify Left or Right
for Diplomat

ISLAND BASE

IB-18
Doors Both Sides
of Island Cabinets

IB-30
IB-36
IB-48

COUNTER OVEN UNITS

CO-3028

BASE END SHELVES

BES-12
12" Palette
(Reversible — Can Be Trimmed)

BOES-12

FINISHED BASE ENDS

34½"

BE
Specify R or L
(¾" Wide Face)

BASE END PANELS

23½"

23½"

34½"

84"

EP-2434 EP-2484
(Panels are ⅞₆" Thick)

Black Toe Board

⅛"x4"x8'

Inexpensive
Toe Space Cover

BASE FILLER STRIPS

4"

Base Filler K/D
BFS-384

4"
4"
BFS-2
BFS-3
BFS-6

4"

BCF-3
Complete

30"

RF-3015
Unit can be cut
on job for height
and width

6"

TT-30

11⅛"

RANGE FRONTS

30"

27"

24½"

34½"

5"

Mark-27

MOULDINGS

⁷⁄₃₂"

1¹⁄₁₆"

²⁵⁄₃₂"

Cove
Lengths

¾"
½"
¾"

Outside Corner
8' Lengths

¼" ¼"

1½"

½"

¼" ½"
¾"

Soffit
10' Lengths

OVEN UNITS oven platforms adjustable — screwed to sides

Min. 20"
Max. 22½"

Min. 24" Max. 38¼"

OUA-24

Min. 20"
Max. 22½"

Min. 35¾" Max. 50"

OUB-24

Min. 23"
Max. 25"

Min. 24" Max. 38¼"

OUA-27

Min. 23"
Max. 25"

Min. 35¾" Max. 50"

OUB-27

*Typical specifications sheet of cabinet manu-
facturer (in this case, Connor) shows cabinets available with nomenclature and sizes available. Line
drawing of each item helps eliminate confusion.*

Particleboard used for corestock is a finely engineered product relating little to the familiar floor underlayment. This demonstration by Georgia-Pacific shows its versatility and machinability.

Birch and maple are commonly used in provincial styling.

Contemporary — This style, often called modern, is characterized by clean lines and flush or overlay doors. This is the styling of most of the European cabinets now being sold in the U.S. market, and of the many U.S. copies of the European look. However, European cabinets generally are made without face frames and use six-way adjustable hinges for the doors to make up for any loss in rigidity. U.S. manufacturers prefer to keep face frames for added rigidity in installation.

In all other styles, lip doors are more common. Contemporary doors often have a reverse lip to eliminate the need for pulls or knobs, and are a predominant style for manufacturers of plastic-laminated cabinets.

Mediterranean — This is so popular that perhaps it is inaccurate to call it a special style. It is also difficult to define, because the Mediterranean region includes Greek, Italian, Moorish, French and many other possible styling influences.

Generally speaking, Mediterranean style is dark and heavy (although it might be light), and quite ornate (although it might be simple). Some

builders simply use a dark-toned avocado woodgrain plastic laminated cabinet and call it Mediterranean.

Other special styles, such as Oriental or Nautical, are good for model homes where the kitchens are being merchandised. They get talked about and they can draw crowds. But it isn't good business to install them before a home is sold, because the more special the style the more it cuts down the number of prospects. When the customer desires a special kitchen style, builders usually give the customer the kitchen allowance and refer him to a local kitchen specialist who handles it on a separate contract.

Wood, steel or plastic — and which plastic?

Wood cabinets lead in popularity with home buyers. Plastic laminated cabinets are making slow, steady gains. Steel, a strong leader in the mid-1950s, is no longer a major factor in the residential market although it continues to show some strength in apartments. In fact, at least one widely-respected custom manufacturer still specializes in steel (with wood and plastic options for the doors and drawer fronts).

New plastics are making some impact. These include foamed polyurethane for bathroom vanities and polystyrene for kitchen cabinets. Polystyrene is suitable only for the larger manufacturers because of high mold cost. These materials are finished like wood, and are hardly detectable from wood.

SOFTWOODS are more popular in the west and southwest. They include:

Pine — most common, creamy white and very workable. Both Ponderosa and Sugar varieties are used.

Fir — Douglas variety is most widely used, but western cabinet manufacturers also use White.

Knotty pine — again, either Ponderosa, Sugar, or Idaho, but characterized by numerous knots for distinctive styling.

Knotty cedar — quite similar to pine, but reddish in color.

Hemlock — a variety of spruce.

HARDWOODS are more numerous in variety and much more common in cabinetry in the east and midwest where most nationally distributed cabinets are made. They include:

Birch — the traditional leader for many years, although now challenged by oak. Birch is heavy, strong, with great variety of texture, and is inexpensive. White, red and European woods are used.

Oak — now rivaling birch in popularity, and consequently becoming much more expensive. It has great appeal to homeowners, is used in all styles but is especially good for traditional. While the wood itself has a wide color range, it increasingly is finished medium to light.

Maple — an excellent, straight-grained material but often with good markings and widely used in colonial styles.

Walnut — strong, with varied patterns, almost always finished medium to dark, but quite expensive.

Birch, beech, alder, ash, cherry, pecan, hickory and red or white lauan (often called Philippine mahogany) are used to varying extents by an appreciable range of manufacturers.

Before moving on to other materials, it should be noted that some of the prettiest leaks and sandalwoods you'll ever see are not that at all, but birch.

Some manufacturers take an inexpensive birch and print an exotic finish on it. Some do the same with a good, industrial-grade particleboard or medium-density fiberboard. This printing is done with big 4-color presses that print full rich coloring on drab materials and impress the grain markings. The technique also is widely used for stereo and television cabinets. It requires very expensive tooling, but the end result is the appearance of exotic woods at bargain-basement prices. The price, naturally, must be a function of volume.

PLASTIC LAMINATES are particularly favored by apartment developers, especially those who keep the property as an investment, because of their great durability, cleanability and visual attractiveness.

They nearly always are wood-grained and the variety is almost infinite. A builder can choose, for example, not just a walnut but from a dozen different walnuts in almost any of the major brands. Or he can choose any exotic woodgrain and it will be almost as true as the natural wood. It should, because it will be precisely printed from an actual color photograph.

The "high pressure" plastic laminates, more or less familiar to builders for the last 25 years, actually are made up of several sheets of heavy Kraft paper, the top sheet printed with the woodgrain or other pattern, and then covered with a transparent melamine plastic which gives the material its great hardness. Traditionally this has been 1/16" thick, and in this thickness it is by far the most common material for kitchen countertops.

Responding to a charge of "over-engineering" (which means "too expensive"), the laminate manufacturers have offered a 1/32" material specifically for vertical surfacing. This is less expensive and highly suitable for kitchen cabinets as well as for walls and table or desk tops that do not receive the wear of a kitchen countertop.

Wood lovers charge that these laminates can never really look like wood because of their uniformity of pattern. This is right, perhaps, when one looks at a full 5 x 12 sheet of plastic laminate, but in a finished cabinet door very few people can tell the difference.

For the high-pressure plastic laminate manufacturers, competition is coming not so much from woods as from what might be called "poor boy" laminates. These include rigid vinyls, which come in sheet or roll form and which are a much more finely engineered product than the vinyls of several years ago, with great vitality in the woodgrain printing, and low-pressure melamine laminated stock. There are also polyesters and other films used for upgrading the appearance of lower-grade woods; the better vinyls are now considered quality materials.

All of these plastic laminates must be adhered to a substrate, or corestock. The substrate might be plywood, styrofoam, or even a honeycomb paper, but more often it will be particleboard. Particleboard as a corestock is not the rough material familiar to builders as floor underlayment. It is a superbly engineered combination of wood particles and resins, almost infinitely variable (to spec) for surface smoothness, weight, screw-holding quality and any other characteristics the cabinet manufacturer might order.

Plastic Laminates for Durability

All of these plastic laminates are good materials for cabinets, as are all of the corestocks mentioned, but there are some traps the builder must avoid.

Any plastic laminated cabinet door needs a backing sheet. Otherwise, the construction is out of balance and warping can follow. The flocking or cheap paint sometimes applied to the back will not do the job.

Also, in any market area there always is a peripheral assortment of suppliers who prey on the builders who want the cheapest price. These are the ones who will offer unbalanced doors. Their vinyl surfacing often does not have proper adhesives. The result of this is that the vinyl, which has been molded to the door with heat, attempts

c

Colonial styling is exemplified here by, upper right, Provincial Type C by George C. Vaughan and Sons, *and below, Colonial by Scheirich, left, and Williamsburg by Wilson, right.*

a

b

a

b

Provincial is characterized by the curves at the corners of the design. Shown here are Royal Coach

by Grabill, left above, and Mission Oak by Boise Cascade, right above.

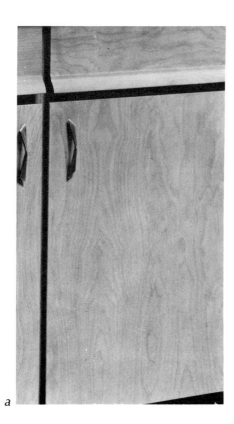

a

b

Contemporary styles are clean, uncluttered, often have no knobs or pulls on doors and drawers, as with the drawers of the first example here. Left,

Luxuria by Long-Bell; right, Contemporary Walnut by Wilson.

to revert back to its original form. This is called "creep," a term a housewife might also use to describe the builder when she sees the vinyl shrinking from the corners of her cabinets and leaving the wood exposed.

This was a common problem, because vinyl had been so inexpensive that it attracted the kind of cabinet makers who like to cut corners. Recently adhesive manufacturers have virtually eliminated the problem with adhesives developed specifically for vinyl, notably epoxy.

In recent years, the texture of high pressure plastic laminates has been expanded to true 3-dimensional surfaces. Nevamar pioneered this development with a "Cameo" pattern, and now several manufacturers offer 3-dimensional slate patterns in either white or black.

The 3-dimensional feature always has been available with the other laminates. A great advantage of vinyl, for example, is that it can be vacuum-formed to conform to any mold. In this process the sheet of vinyl is heated to a point of pliability, then sucked down by vacuum not only to cover the mold but to surround it. This yields a shell that is fully edged with corners turned, all one piece with no joining problem. This shell then needs only to be slipped over the corestock, adhered, and backed for balance.

The mold might be a specially carved or built-up wood master. It might be the cabinet door of a competitor that is being copied. Whatever it is, if the vacuum-forming is done properly the resultant vinyl shell will be a precise copy, mirroring all 3-dimensional aspects. Since the woodgrain or other pattern will already have been printed in the underside (so it will be protected against scratches by the vinyl on top) the door will need no further finishing except for the back.

This practice of printing the woodgrain or other pattern on the underside is called "reverse printing." Its only disadvantage is that the adhesive that bonds the vinyl shell to the corestock does not grip the vinyl itself, but the ink on the underside of the vinyl. Modern adhesives and bonding techniques make this a minor problem. But it does mean the job must be done right.

Some vinyls are surface-printed, so the bond is direct from corestock to vinyl. This helps the bond, but makes the surface more susceptible to scratching. Some suppliers now are solving both of these problems by surface-printing the vinyl and overlaying it with another sheet of clear vinyl. It solves the problems, but raises the cost.

Reneer Films developed a new vinyl product, Rendura, specifically to solve all these problems. It has a clear acrylic top ply that is ultra-violet cured, eliminating scratch problems, while epoxy-bonding eliminates adhesion problems.

Some cabinet manufacturers take different options. They buy prelaminated stock from their suppliers, then cut this to size for their cabinets. The prelamination can be done by various other methods, even to impregnating the corestock with a melamine plastic to make what might be called a fully plasticized board.

Low-pressure melamine board is the newest material of this type, consisting of particleboard or fiberboard substrate with the low-pressure melamine surface bonded permanently at the time of manufacture. Typical are Formica's MCP (for Melamine Component Panel) and a similar board by Funder America. This has many of the high-performance qualities of high-pressure melamine.

STEEL, as has been mentioned, is no longer a major factor in residential kitchen cabinets. As of this writing, there is only one quality custom steel manufacturer in the field, and there are several others who specialize in the apartment market. The apartment market, of course, is a price market.

Low-priced steel cabinets find it very hard to compete on a price basis with low-priced wood cabinets.

At the expensive end of the steel market, cabinet manufacturers offer a strong steel framework with options of steel, wood, plastic laminated or all-plastic doors and drawer fronts.

At the other end of the market there is a steel framework with steel doors, but sometimes the steel doors have vinyl plastic inlays to give them a semblance of wood. These inlays not only make the cabinets more acceptable to homeowners, they also permit modernization of the doors in later years through exchange of the inserts for new ones.

Steel is structurally rigid, strong, durable, and warp-free. Everything good that the steel people say about steel as a cabinet material is true.

Anyone who thinks plastic looks like plastic can try their eyes on these examples of plastics and plastic laminates: (a) and (b) are high-pressure melamine, Formica's Mozambique and GE's Spectographic Pine; (c) is Reneer vinyl film in Westchester Elm pattern, a planked look for furniture and cabinets; (d) is Formica's Silver Slate, a metallic laminate, and (e) a Union Carbide laminate; (f), (g), (h) and (i) are examples of foamed polyurethane doors, with regular wood finishes.

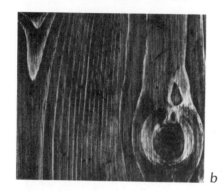

a

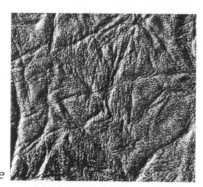

b   c

d   e

f

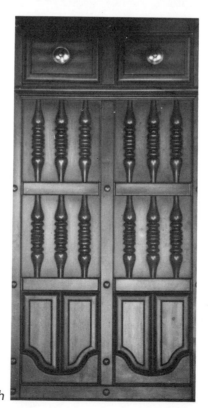

g   h   i

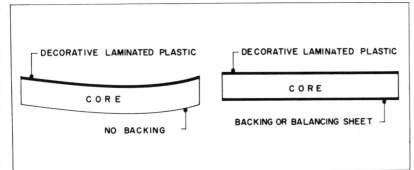

Plastic laminate, when used for cabinet doors or any other unsupported application, must have a backing sheet to balance the substrate for dimensional stability. Otherwise it will warp. Countertops do not need backing sheets because they are held stable by the base cabinets.

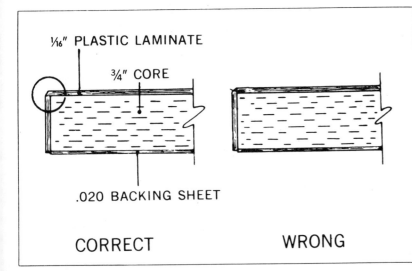

When self-edging is used, it should be applied first, before top surface, so top surface covers the edgeband.

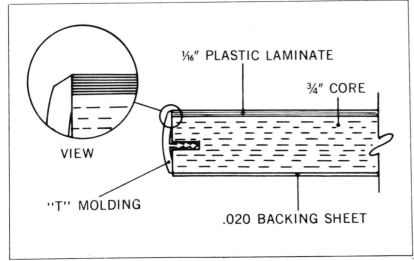

If T-edging is used it is applied after top surface. It must be precisely indexed with top of laminate.

There is nothing wrong with steel, except that most customers want wood.

THE NEW MOLDED PLASTICS have just commenced their invasion of the cabinet market. They include, primarily, polystyrene and polyurethane, but there might be more at any time. These materials are formulated in the Research & Development labs of the petrochemical companies, which develop combinations of resins and binders and then start scrambling for applications. In the scramble, the cabinet market always shows up because it offers a potential annual market of well over 100,000,000 cabinet doors, plus drawer fronts.

Generally, polyurethane is best for relatively short runs because the inexpensive mold materials won't hold up for lengthy runs. It is, therefore, most often used for bathroom vanities where five or six molds can cover an entire line. Polystyrene takes very expensive molds which also are very durable, so a larger cabinet company can use it for a single line of cabinets. (A different mold is needed for every different size and style, running to several hundred thousand dollars in tooling for just one line.)

Quality of the end product is excellent for both of these materials.

True value of these plastics is in the stylistic effects that can be achieved at a reasonable price.

If considered as a price product, they cost about 50 percent more than birch. Styles that would be impossible with any wood because of dimensional instability, such as in an interwoven cane door, can be achieved easily with any of these molded plastics with realism that defies detection. When the difference is only about $1 per door, the high style of the cane often is desirable.

These plastics are finished like wood, using the same equipment and materials. They are getting to be very common on bathroom vanities, because only four or five molds can supply an entire vanity line. Their success has been more limited in kitchen cabinets because the mold needs multiply. It is not unusual for a cabinet manufacturer to have as many as 400 or 500 variations in size and style, and this would mean that many different molds for a plastic line.

Marriages of wood and plastics are becoming

common — plain wood doors are decorated with plastic moldings to create Provincial, Mediterranean, or other styles. This is a low-priced way to get a highly-styled cabinet.

CABINET CONSTRUCTION varies among manufacturers to some extent, but it is fairly well standardized for stock cabinets.

The main components are *front frames, doors, drawers and drawer fronts, end panels, backs, bottoms, shelves* and *hardware*.

Horizontal members of the *front frame* are called *rails*. Vertical members of the front frame are *stiles*. Interior horizontal framing members are *subrails*, and interior vertical framing members are *substiles*. A kick rail at the bottom of the base cabinet, recessed 3" behind the front frame, is called the *toe kick*.

Front frames are usually made of 1/2" to 3/4" hardwood, and the rails and stiles usually are doweled or mortise-and-tenoned, with both glue and staples added for rigidity.

End panels are usually constructed of hardwood plywood, 3/16" or 1/4", glued to 3/4" side frames. Sometimes a 1/2" or thicker end panel is used without a side frame, and usually tongue-and-grooved into the front frame.

Doors typically are 3/4" or 7/8" but this is subject to wide variation. They might be hollow or have cores of particleboard, wood, high density fiber, plastic, paper honeycomb, or other material. As mentioned before, doors set the style, and drawer fronts match the doors, so this is the area where manufacturers are creative.

Backs usually are 1/8" hardboard or 3-ply plywood, and the backs have *mounting rails* or *hanging strips* at top and bottom for screwing cabinets to the wall.

Tops and *bottoms* generally are made of 3-ply or 5-ply hardwood plywood, 1/4" to 1/2" thick, dadoed into the sides and interlocked into the hanging strips of wall cabinets.

Shelves are 1/2" to 3/4" thick and might be lumber, plywood or particleboard. Increasingly they are vinyl-laminated for easy cleaning. They usually are adjustable.

Conventional *drawers* have hardwood lumber sides and backs with plywood bottoms. Sides usually are connected to the front and back with a lock or rabbeted joint, although more expensive cabinets go to multiple dovetailing. Drawer bottoms are dadoed into the sides, front, and back.

Some cabinet companies now are using molded polystyrene drawers, all one piece except for the front, with rounded corners for easy cleaning.

A few companies offer cabinets unfinished, but most are finished, some in very sophisticated equipment systems. Fundamentally, all surfaces are well sanded before a penetrating stain is applied. After the stain is dry, one or more coats of sealer are applied and then all nail holes are filled with a suitable putty. A thorough sanding follows, and then one or more finish coats. In finishing, some factories use spray gun systems, some use curtain coaters which lay on the finish in controlled mil thickness, while others use immersion systems. Finishing lines usually are conveyorized with the lines carrying finished parts directly through heat tunnels for drying.

TYPES OF CABINETS can be grouped into three categories: *Base, wall* and *miscellaneous*. The standard base cabinet is 34-1/2" high, so the addition of the countertop will bring it to an even 36". Depths vary from 23" to 24-1/2", depending on the manufacturer. Base cabinets are offered in 3" modules from 12" to 24" for a single door cabinet, and 27" to 48" for a double door cabinet. Special cabinets for the sink or a built-in cooktop range from 24" to 48" wide. Also relatively standard is a sink base combination with four doors and a drawer over the door on either end, with the center section blank, of course, for sink or cooktop, and these vary from 54" to 96" in width.

The standard *wall cabinet* is 30" high and 12" or 13" deep, depending on the manufacturer. Wall filler cabinets, designed to fit above the refrigerator or window or for other special purposes, might be 12", 15", 18" or 24" high. There also are wall combination cabinets with 30" doors on the ends and 18" doors in between, or other combinations made especially for builders. All of these match the widths of the base cabinets.

Two other fairly common cabinets are revolving-shelf (or lazy susan) corner cabinets, base or wall, and blank corner cabinets. The revolving shelf cabinets require 21", 24" or 27" along each wall for the wall cabinet, or 33", 36", or 42" along each wall for a base cabinet.

Blank corner cabinets are for turning a corner where another run of cabinets will join at a right angle. They are blank (no door or drawer) in the area where the other cabinets must butt up against them. Base blank corner cabinets might be 24", 36", 39", 42", 48", 60", 66", 72" or 84". There is one door and drawer in sizes over 24", multiple doors and drawers at 60" and over. Wall blank corner cabinets run in 6" modules from 24" to 48" and from 60" to 84".

Miscellaneous cabinets include:

A *refrigerator cabinet*, 36", 39" or 42" wide with the opening varying according to the size of the refrigerator;

An *oven cabinet* for built-in ovens, in widths of 24", 27", 30", or 33", with cutout sizes that must vary according to the countless specifications of oven manufacturers;

Utility or broom cabinets in widths of 24", 30" and 36", and depths of 12", 13" and 18" as well as standard base depths.

All of these come in the standard 84" height, but oven cabinets also come in 66" height without doors at the top. The broom cabinets also are often outfitted with hardware for lazy susan shelves or special fold-out pantry cabinets.

Base cabinets may be obtained without drawers, with one drawer, or with all drawers and no door. Sink or range fronts also are available, without full cabinets. Both wall and base cabinets are available with doors on both sides for entry from either side, for use in peninsulas such as between the kitchen and the dining or living area.

INTERIOR FITTINGS are to cabinets what accessories are to cars — all the little options that add function, organization, utility, and convenience and that make the difference between ordinary and great. Unfortunately, builders pass them up because they add to cost and homeowners never know about them.

These fittings are much more widely used in Europe. Builders, architects and homeowners often return from abroad raving about these little kitchen conveniences and wondering why U.S. kitchens don't copy them. Actually they always have been available here from both stock and custom cabinet manufacturers, and there are indeed many, many options.

There are towel racks, sugar bins, flour bins, vegetable bins, vertical tray storage cabinets, bread drawer liners, pan racks, slide-in table tops that disappear into the cabinetry, lazy susan assemblies for both base and wall units, electric mixer shelves counterbalanced with springs to pop up into place, slide-out maple cutting boards, to name just a few. There are even wheeled serving carts that roll into the cabinet run where they look like just another cabinet, silver drawer organizers, cup and plate storage organizers, in-cabinet or under-cabinet spice racks, and bar organizers, etc.

All of these are fitted into the cabinets or into the drawers by the cabinet manufacturer. In some cases he provides a special cabinet or special shelving for them, in other cases it is a matter of finding appropriate hardware and correctly installing it. In all cases these fixtures add special appeal to the kitchen and make it much more convenient for the housewife who will use it.

HARDWARE, generally, is a tremendously varied part of the kitchen cabinetry that performs many functions, both utilitarian and decorative.

Some of the possibilities of utility hardware are indicated in the previous section on options. There are many more. For example, drawers of low cost cabinets often operate with wood sliding on wood. They will work all right when new, but will be far less than satisfactory when humidity is high or as they get older.

In contrast, both simple and elaborate slides are available. These might have nylon sliding on nylon, low-priced but with excellent results, or finely engineered ball-bearing wheels in metal channels. It is a small part of the total kitchen, but a big factor in customer satisfaction as the years go by.

The pulls and knobs, and sometimes the hinges on cabinet doors, are decorative as well as functional. In fact, one hardware manufacturer calls its line "Cabinet Jewelry." And it is.

Knobs and pulls, for the drawers and doors, usually are metal and might be finished as brass, bronze, brushed chrome, antique pewter, or enamel. Some knobs and pulls are ceramic while others are plastic. The latter usually are finished to resemble ceramics. They might be solid colors or they might have delicate inlays. One hardware manufacturer has a "Mod" line with colored knobs

CATEGORIES

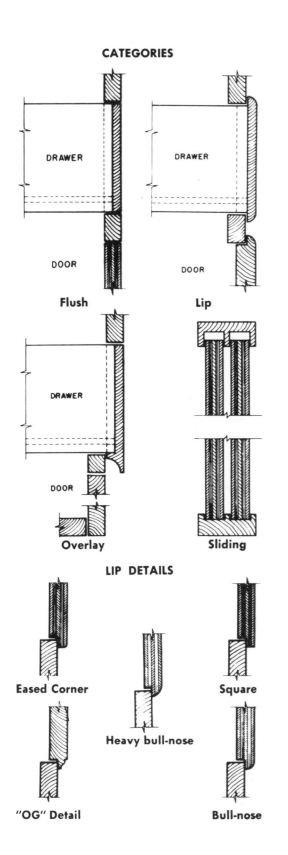

Flush **Lip**

Overlay **Sliding**

LIP DETAILS

Eased Corner **Square**

Heavy bull-nose

"OG" Detail **Bull-nose**

Detail drawings show the different ways cabinet doors might be constructed. Drawings are by the Southern California Assn. of Wood Cabinet Manufacturers.

DOOR STYLES

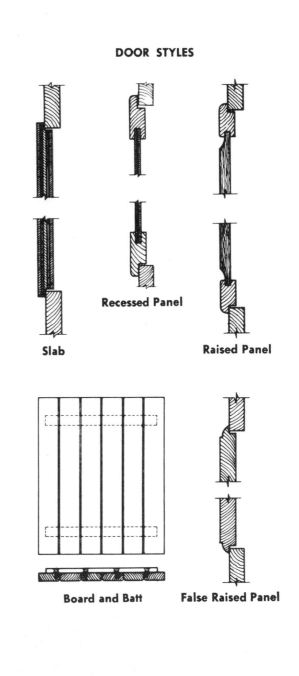

Recessed Panel

Slab **Raised Panel**

Board and Batt **False Raised Panel**

with square or circular backplates with Mondrian designs, geometrics, or swirls. These can work chromatic magic in brightening up a run of cabinets that otherwise might be dull.

Cabinets usually come with standard hardware selected by the manufacturer. However, the builder, architect or customer can ask to see options, and usually some options are available at no extra cost. In some cases the hardware is an integral part of the cabinet design, and the cabinet manufacturer will be reluctant to change it. In these cases, the manufacturer usually is right. He has spent a lot of money developing a design and he doesn't want to see it changed.

CABINET INSTALLATION is the true key to success in any kitchen.

If installed properly, the cheapest cabinets available give better service than poorly installed expensive cabinets. Proper installation is the one nonvarying essential, and as a precept it also is the most abused.

Cabinets must be installed level, plumb and true.

This means the walls and floor must be checked for high spots and low spots, and corners must be checked for square. High spots sometimes can be sanded down. Low spots must be shimmed.

If, on installation, one corner of a cabinet is pulled into a low spot in the wall, the cabinet will be racked and the door will hang crooked. If it is a cabinet with multiple doors, all of the doors will be crooked.

Cabinets should be installed always from a corner, never toward a corner. C clamps should be used to hold them aligned perfectly as they are screwed to each other. They must be attached to the wall with screws, never with nails, and the screws must go into the studs.

Wall cabinets should be installed first, although many cabinet manufacturers recommend that base cabinets be installed first because it then makes it easier to install the wall cabinets.

But if a wall cabinet should be dropped — it happens sometimes — and the base cabinets are already in place, it could damage both cabinets. There are many ways base cabinets can be damaged when they are installed first, so it is better to play it safe.

However, if base cabinets are installed first, the countertop should be installed next, and then it should be protected using the cartons the base cabinets came in.

(Note: Some inexperienced installers know that a kitchen always is *designed* starting with the sink, which usually is in the center of a run of cabinets. This is one reason why they sometimes try to install them that way, but this is wrong.)

Again, make sure the installers are expert at their work. Poor installation can ruin the highest-quality cabinets, and a bad kitchen can make it a bad house.

Simple, roomy kitchen is fully carpeted, gains extra distinction with wood treatment at window to match cabinets. This is Centennial line marking 100th anniversary of Connor Forest Industries.

Hardware is available for a wide variety of interior fittings for kitchen cabinets. These are only a few that bring much greater convenience to the new kitchen.

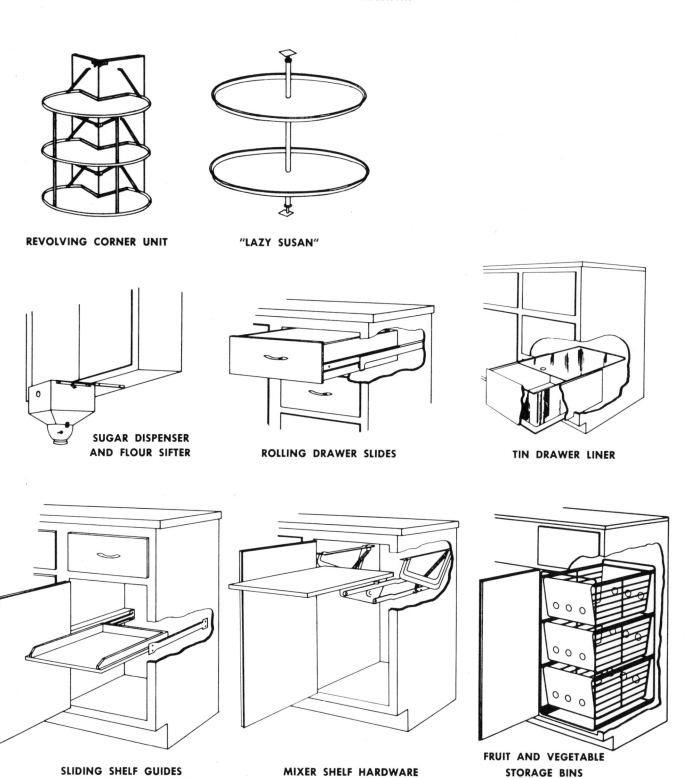

REVOLVING CORNER UNIT

"LAZY SUSAN"

SUGAR DISPENSER AND FLOUR SIFTER

ROLLING DRAWER SLIDES

TIN DRAWER LINER

SLIDING SHELF GUIDES

MIXER SHELF HARDWARE

FRUIT AND VEGETABLE STORAGE BINS

SHEET BUILD-UP

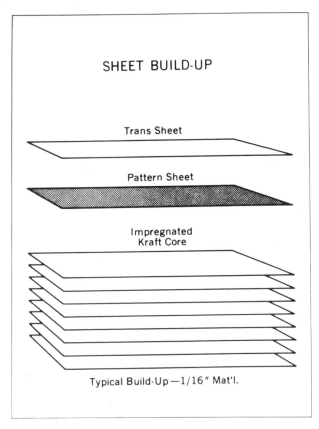

Trans Sheet

Pattern Sheet

Impregnated
Kraft Core

Typical Build-Up—1/16″ Mat'l.

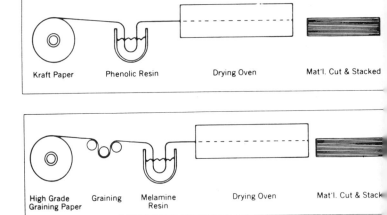

Kraft Paper   Phenolic Resin   Drying Oven   Mat'l. Cut & Stacked

High Grade   Graining   Melamine   Drying Oven   Mat'l. Cut & Stack
Graining Paper   Resin

High pressure plastic laminates gain their durability from a transparent sheet of melamine resin on top. A pattern sheet is just underneath, which might be woodgrained or have some other pattern printed on it, and the bulk (thickness) then comes from several sheets of Kraft paper underneath.

Sketches show manufacturing process for making high pressure plastic laminates, used for cabinets, wall paneling and the most common material for countertops. The decorative paper which gives the pattern or woodgrain is grained (printed) for the appearance that shows through the transparent sheet on top. Other layers of paper are resin inpregnated, but there is no need for graining.

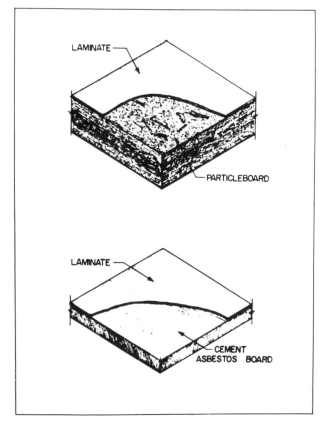

LAMINATE

PARTICLEBOARD

LAMINATE

CEMENT ASBESTOS BOARD

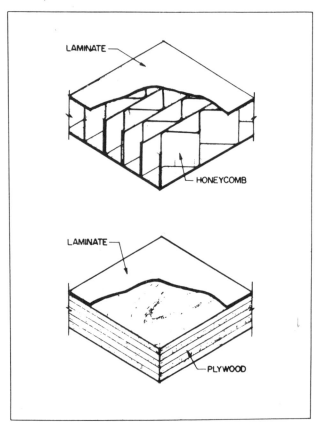

LAMINATE

HONEYCOMB

LAMINATE

PLYWOOD

Most common substrate for high pressure plastic laminate is particleboard. But other materials are used, such as paper honeycomb, plywood or even foamed plastics.

1

5

Cabinets must be attached to studs for full support. Studs are usually located 16″ on center. Locate studs with stud finder, tapping with hammer or nail driven through plaster at height that will be hidden by cabinets. Cabinets must always be attached to walls with screws. **Never use nails!**

On the walls where cabinets are to be installed, remove baseboard and chair rail. This is required for a flush fit.

2

6

Cabinets must be installed perfectly level — from a standpoint of function as well as appearance. Find the highest point of floor with the use of a level.

Start your installation in one corner. First assemble the base corner unit, then adding one unit on each side of the corner unit. This — as a unit — can be installed in position. Additional cabinets are then added to each side as required.

3

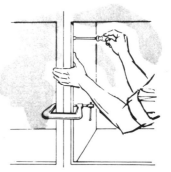

7

Using a level or straightedge, find the high spots on the wall on which cabinets are to be hung. Some high spots can be removed by sanding. Otherwise, it will be necessary to "shim" to provide a level and plumb installation.

"C" clamps should be used in connecting cabinets together to obtain proper alignment. Drill 2 or 3 holes through ½″ end panels. Holes should be drilled through to adjoining cabinet. Secure T-nut and secure with 1½″ bolt. Draw up snugly. If you prefer you may drill through side of front frame as well as "lead hole" into abutting cabinet, insert screws and draw up snugly.

4

Using the highest point on the floor, measure up the wall to a height of 84″. This height, 84″, is the top height of wall cabinets, oven and broom cabinets. 84″ cabinets can be cut down to 81″.

The most expensive cabinets made will be failures if not properly installed. And the cheapest cabinets can give good service if they are installed right. Cabinet manufacturers realize this, and all give

detailed instructions for installation. The accompanying sequence is from the installation manual of Kitchen Kompact, the giant of the industry. (Also overleaf)

8

Each cabinet — as it is installed to the wall — should be checked front to back and also across the front edge with a level. Be certain that the front frame is plumb. If necessary, use shims to level the cabinets. Base cabinets should be attached with screws into wall studs. For additional support and to prevent back rail from "bowing," insert block between cabinet back and wall. After bases are installed cover toe kick area with material that is provided.

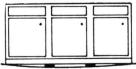

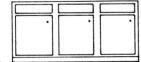

9

Attach counter top on base cabinets. After installation, cover counter tops with cartons to prevent damage while completing installation.

10

Wall cabinets should then be installed, beginning with a corner unit as described in step #6. Screw through hanging strips built into backs of cabinets at both top and bottom. Place them ¾" below top and ¾" above bottom shelf from inside of cabinet. Adjust only loosely at first so that final adjustments can be made.

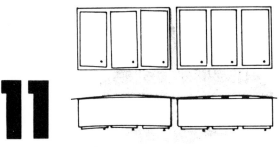

11

Wall cabinets should be checked with level on cabinet front, sides, and bottom to insure that cabinets are plumb and level. It might be necessary to shim at wall and between cabinets to correct for uneven walls or floors. After cabinets and doors are perfectly aligned, tighten all screws.

Problem Doors:

There are very few "perfect" conditions where floors and walls are exactly level and plumb. Therefore, it is necessary to correct this by proper "shimming" so that the cabinet is not racked or twisted and so that cabinet doors are properly aligned.

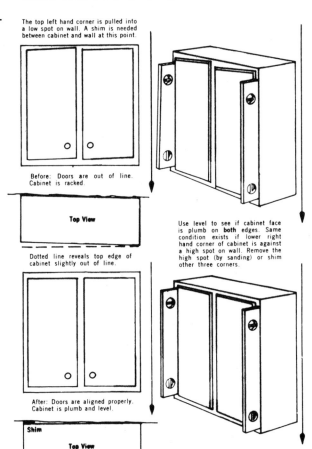

The top left hand corner is pulled into a low spot on wall. A shim is needed between cabinet and wall at this point.

Before: Doors are out of line. Cabinet is racked.

Top View

Dotted line reveals top edge of cabinet slightly out of line.

Use level to see if cabinet face is plumb on **both** edges. Same condition exists if lower right hand corner of cabinet is against a high spot on wall. Remove the high spot (by sanding) or shim other three corners.

After: Doors are aligned properly. Cabinet is plumb and level.

Shim

Top View

6
Major and Minor Appliances

By definition and by function, the major home appliances are the range, the refrigerator, the freezer, the dishwasher, the washer, and the dryer.

The latter two are not kitchen appliances, although they sometimes are placed in the kitchen. More properly they belong in a utility room or a basement or, ideally, in the main bathroom if space permits.

Other very important appliances that belong in any modern kitchen are a ventilating hood over any cooking appliance, and a garbage disposer.

There are some other appliances that can add greatly to homeowner convenience and lift a kitchen far above the ordinary. These include the microwave oven, built-in warming drawer or other food warmer, built-in mixing center, toaster, can opener, and under-the-counter ice maker. There also is the barbecue grill, which might be integral with the range or cooktop or, better, separated from the main cooking area as an added appliance.

And there are, of course, the trash compactors. These are rapidly getting to be standard appliances, but they still are relatively new.

Some communities have challenged them on an ecological basis, fearing that their community incinerating facilities may not be able to handle their compacted "bricks" of trash, and have even gone so far as to legislate against their use.

On the other hand, the compacted trash makes excellent landfill. So where a builder runs into a local incinerator problem, there are alternatives he can investigate.

There's no question on consumer attitudes. They like compactors. And as a family grows to four or more, this appliance becomes much more significant.

There are other areas to be watched on a month-to-month basis. Some water purification systems are already on the market and others might come out at any time. Also check air purification and humidity control systems. As new appliances are introduced, they must be weighed for value, utility, and customer appeal.

Every category of appliances presents its own range of choices and decisions. In this chapter we will consider the available options, category by category.

Ranges

No other category of kitchen appliances offers the variety of configurations, sizes and features that you get from cooking appliances. Configurations are:

Free-standing — a range that stands by itself, independent of the wall or cabinets on either side. It can be a single oven model, with broiler, or a double-oven with eye-level oven or broiler, even with a microwave oven. These come now with squared sides so they fit neatly against adjacent countertops. The common size is 30" wide, but choices range from 19" to 40". They can be gas or electric, with or without backsplash, with controls in the front, on top along the side, or on a backsplash.

Built-in — again either single or double cavity for the oven which must be fitted into a wall cabinet built for this purpose, with or without a microwave component. Companion to the wall oven is the built-in cooktop, and these also are offered in a wide variety of configurations, gas or electric, and many sizes. The built-in system offers the greatest flexibility in kitchen design. However, it entails cutting precisely-sized holes in the oven cabinet and the countertop according to specifications for the particular model being installed, so great care must be taken to check the specs against the model numbers. There are about 60 manufacturers of built-in cooking equipment, each with from two to a dozen models, and specs vary widely.

Slide-in — this is basically a free-standing range, but with the side panels left off and engineered to fit snugly against the countertop, or even overlap it, for a built-in look. Nevertheless, it rests on the floor. It is popular with builders and in less-expensive modernization, and sizes range from a minimal 19" to a more standard 30". It can have one or two ovens and can be either basic or deluxe. It might fit under or against a backsplash that is continuous with the countertops, and some are made to be fitted to the cutout backsplash of the countertop on either side.

Drop-in — a variation of the slide-in, the drop-in does not rest on the floor. Flanges rest on the countertop on either side, and it is supported from there. Special cabinets are available to fit under it for a more built-in look, although it might extend all the way down to the kick space.

Stack-on — a type that might not always be on the market at a given time, the stack-on consists of a built-in cooktop and superstructure with an eye-level oven. Although configuration limits the range to a single cavity oven, one manufacturer has had great success by combining a stack-on with a matching built-in dishwasher that fits directly beneath it, an innovative space-saver.

The specials — There are other models which could be fitted into the foregoing categories, but they have differences that require special mention.

Modern Maid, for example, offers a "Cook and Clean Center" which incorporates an eye-level oven, a cooktop, and a dishwasher in the base. This is all one unit.

Jenn Air can be either built-in, free-standing or slip-in, but it has built-in down-draft ventilation so it needs no ventilating hood. Venting goes down beside the oven cavity, but inside the range (which is 30 inches wide), and then it can be ducted along the kickspace to an outside wall, or straight back through an outside wall, or through the floor into the basement and thence out through the basement window. The fan used for venting also is used for convection cooking, which speeds up oven cooking by 40 percent.

Another is the Fasar cooktop, a dramatic system that cooks by magnetic induction. A magnetic field heats the metal pan and that, in turn, cooks the food, but the Fasar unit has no heat and stays cool. With this you might place ceramic tiles at random in the countertop, each of them a burner.

CONVENIENCE FEATURES of cooking appliances are as plentiful and varied as the configurations.

Cooktops, which might come with from two to six burners, often have thermostatic controls on at least one burner.

Cooktops can be purchased with griddle and grill inserts, which might be in the center or along the side.

They feature varying degrees of cleanability. Some detach completely to leave only a smooth-surfaced pan to be cleaned. Many feature top surfaces that can be raised, with a drop bar to hold them upright for cleaning underneath.

Automatic timers are common. It should be noted, though, that many less-expensive models have built-in timers that will signal a lapse of time, but do not control the cooktop or the oven.

Some ovens feature simultaneous over-and-under broiling. Some have their own built-in exhaust systems. Most have optional rotisseries and temperature-sensing probes.

The real aristocrats of ovens will have such complete automatic controls that a housewife can put her meal in the oven, set a time for it to start cooking hours later, set a time for it to stop cooking, and from then on it will hold a keep-warm temperature (about 170 degrees) until she and her family return home in the evening.

The cook-and-hold feature is available even without the more elaborate start-and-stop controls described.

SELF-CLEANING is probably the greatest oven feature to be developed in recent years. Through the years, cleaning the oven has been the housewife's most-abhorred kitchen chore. Now ovens clean themselves.

There are two types of self-cleaning ovens, pyrolytic and catalytic, and they should be explained.

In the pyrolytic system, invented by GE, the oven is heated to a temperature range between 900 and 1,000 degrees and the mess in the oven is incinerated. This leaves only a fine ash to be wiped off.

The catalytic system employs a coating on inside surfaces which, in effect, lets the oven clean itself in normal cooking ranges through action of the catalytic coating. This system usually is referred to as "continuous clean," or "stay clean."

The pyrolytic system adds about $100 to the selling price of a range. The catalytic system adds only about $25. But there are many other considerations besides cost.

The pyrolytic system, in its infancy, placed serious design demands on the range manufacturer, particularly for gas ranges.

Simply stated, it requires raising interior temperature to the 900 to 1,000-degree range for a period of from 30 to 90 minutes. The heat-up and cool-down time, however, makes this a period of from two to four hours. The time depends on soil density.

Free-standing ranges now have squared corners so they look more built-in, fit flush against cabinetry. Many also have microwave cooker at eye-level, as in this model by General Electric.

Slide-in ranges might come with or without side panels. Squared corners give built-in look, and in this Hotpoint the flanges actually fit over counter-top. This has glass ceramic cooktop, self-clean oven.

Drop-in ranges must rest on cabinet at bottom or hang from flanges that fit over ountertop, as does this Frigidaire "Touch-N-Cook" with computerized cooking controls.

Jenn-Air model, bottom, has built-in down-draft ventilation so needs no hood. It comes as a drop-in, but special kit adds bottom compartment and backsplash to convert to free-standing. Cooking elements slide out also to convert to glass tops, conventional electric burners or grill on either side.

Built-in installations have most design flexibility, such as this Jenn-Air cooktop (with downdraft ventilation and interchangeable cooking units) and Thermador wall oven with combination microwave and thermal cooking and self-cleaning. Here the cooktop goes in an island with wall ovens nearby, but ovens could go out of work triangle for design purposes if necessary. These unusual cabinets are by Allmilmo.

The heat must be raised and the burning must take place under fully-controlled conditions, and this means the oven must be brought to full-heat slowly. This is first a matter of safety, and second, a matter of preventing thermal shock to the porcelain which would result in crazing and loosening.

Also, the burning process requires a controlled input of air for proper oxidation. This is done usually through control of the air space under the oven door, or air passages in the lower part of the door. If too much air is admitted the temperature will rise too fast. This is why all pyrolytic oven doors become locked when the temperature is over 625 degrees. Any opening of the door after that point would permit a dangerous inrush of oxygen.

Pyrolytic ovens also have to be made somewhat smaller than others. This is because the usual organic binders in common insulation break down at pyrolytic temperatures. Inorganic high-temperature binders are needed, and this makes the insulation package bulkier.

Conventional control systems will not work in pyrolytic ovens, either. Most common control systems use an organic, oil-type fluid in hydraulic tubes, and expansion or contraction of the fluid in response to heat activates a thermostat. This fluid will not stand up over 750 degrees. This has been solved with matched resistance systems, with inert gas or by utilizing the different expansion properties of dissimilar metals.

There also must be some method of eliminating the smoke that results from the burning of the oven soil.

And as a matter of safety, the manufacturer must insure that the oven cannot be turned on accidentally.

Gas range manufacturers had to solve different kinds of problems in addition. For example, gas combustion requires much air, and in a gas pyrolytic oven there would be about 720 cubic feet of air and gas going through the oven. That is about 12 cubic feet per minute, which at 1000 degrees, cannot be exhausted into a kitchen.

It took a lot of engineering ingenuity, but all of these problems have been solved satisfactorily and pyrolytic ovens are now part of our lives.

In the catalytic process, interior oven surfaces are coated with a porcelain frit that contains a catalyst. This gives the surfaces a porosity that enables them to retain oxygen. At higher (baking) temperatures this results in a slow oxidation that disposes of the oven soil.

Much oven cooking, however, is not baking, so obviously the system does not work as totally and automatically as indicated. Nevertheless, the oven can be set for "bake" for a few hours after cooking is completed, and then it will clean itself.

With either system, excessive food spillage should be wiped up before cleaning.

Both systems are available from most range manufacturers, but because of the lack of design problems and because of the price advantage, the catalytic system probably offers a greater variety of choices among models.

THE NEW SMOOTH GLASS COOKTOPS are an exciting development in cooking appliances. They are attractive, totally uncluttered, effective, and reduce surface cleaning to a minimum.

Actually, the idea of a smooth cooktop is not new. It was common in grandmother's day when much cooking still was done with wood and coal. The only breaks in the smooth metal top of the range were for the slots into which a lifter was placed to remove the burner covers.

Deluxe microwave oven cooking center by Hotpoint shows different kind of installation in run of base and wall cabinets. This features a lower self-cleaning oven and an upper microwave cooker controlled by time or temperature.

These GE cooking appliances show deluxe glasstop cooktop at lower right, and conventional free-standing range with night-light ventilating hood.

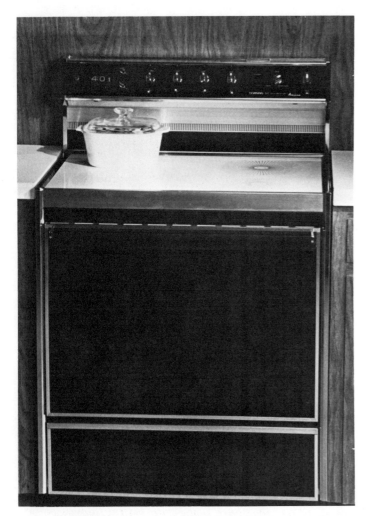

Corning range, now made by Amana, was first of the glasstops. This newest version has three temperature-controlled burners, and one for use when temperature control isn't critical. It has self-cleaning oven. Black glass doors are popular now in appliances.

Corning Glass brought the idea up to date with the development of a glass ceramic, Pyroceram, in 1957. There now are different versions by several other manufacturers.

The material has interesting features. For example, it transmits heat vertically to the cooking vessel, but heat does not migrate horizontally through the glass ceramic material. While the area of the burners can be hot enough for all cooking operations, at the same time the areas immediately surrounding the burners remain cool to the touch.

As a safety factor, heated areas over the burners turn a yellowish color to warn against careless touching. This coloration disappears as the glass cools. While some critics have expressed the fear that a hot surface might be touched accidentally by a child, there really is no more danger of this than there is from a conventional electric range burner.

Other critics have worried about breakability. But Corning is so confident of the strength of its unit that it has gone to a single sheet of glass over the full 30-inch width of the range. Other manufacturers, in deference to the worriers, put a separate sheet of glass over each burner so that, in the unlikely event of breakage, only that one part would have to be replaced.

In actual use, the main difference between the Corning product and all others is that Corning provides a matched set of cooking vessels, also of Pyroceram, with bottoms that are perfectly flat and ground to mate with the smooth surface of the cooktop. The recommendation is that no other cooking vessels be used.

The primary reason for this is control. All materials have temperature limitations, and this includes metals as well as glass ceramics. And while these limitations are subject to change according to the progress in the R&D departments, at this writing the limits are around 600 to 700 Celsius (degrees Centigrade.)

A bright aluminum saucepan with a wavy bottom could easily raise the rangetop temperature above the limit, particularly at times when the housewife forgets and lets it boil dry.

Corning uses temperature control on each of the four elements, with a sensor cycling the heat on and off according to the setting. The precise control requires excellent thermal contact with the cooking vessel, hence the special vessels which insure this contact.

The top will cook with other vessels, including metal, but if the bottoms are not flat for good contact, there could be a control problem.

The Corning range division now is owned by Amana, but Corning makes the glass cooktops for many manufacturers.

MICROWAVE COOKING is not the newest marvel in the kitchen but it certainly is one of the most exciting. These microwaves are electromagnetic waves of energy, similar to radio waves, light

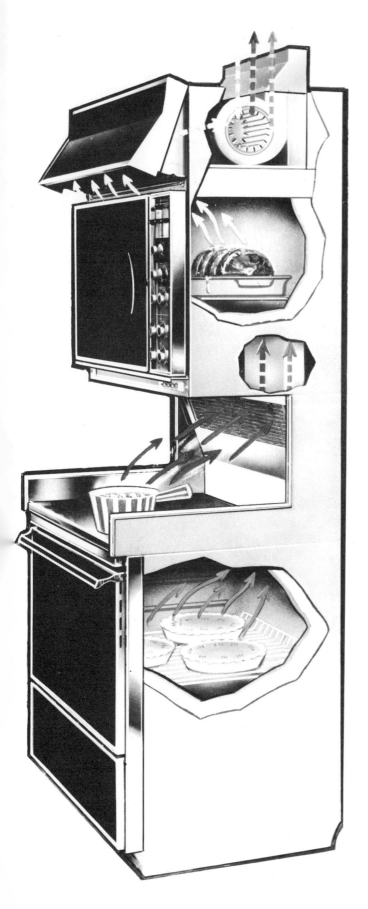

Cleanability of modern cooktops is demonstrated with this Modern Maid model. Top flips up exposing only a shallow pan to be wiped.

Catalytic continuous-cleaning is demonstrated by applying special frit on one side, not on other, then setting oven to baking temperature for a couple of hours.

Drawing shows how blower at top can vent entire Modern Maid range. Hood at top tilts out when in use.

"Cook-n-Clean Center" by Modern Maid solves the space problem in another way. Center includes eye-level oven, a super-thin cooktop and dishwasher below.

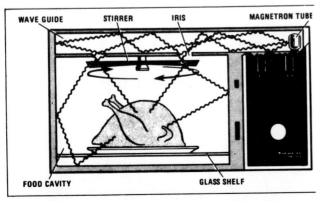

Sketch showing operation of microwave oven.

waves, or radar. Microwave cooking was, in fact, discovered in the 1940s by a radar technician who inadvertently left some uncooked popcorn exposed to radar waves. When the corn started popping a whole new system of cooking was conceived.

There are many microwave ovens on the market in countertop, built-in, and free-standing configurations.

Why is it exciting? Because it is instant cooking. Four strips of bacon that take 23 minutes to cook conventionally take four minutes in a countertop microwave. Roast beef medium takes about eight minutes per pound and frozen shrimp is cooked in six minutes.

It is cooking without pots and pans. Cooking can be done on a paper plate or a glass or plastic dish, and these materials do not heat up except from the heat of the food itself.

Modern microwave cookers bear little resemblance to the units first introduced to the residential market by Tappan in 1955, or popularized by Amana's countertop unit in 1967. Now they have microprocessor chips for control at a touch. You can tell them when to start themselves, when to slow down or speed up, or to start cooking after they defrost the food, and if you guess wrong on the timing they'll shut themselves off and call you. These are really the forerunners of the coming home computer.

You also can get a microwave and conventional oven combined in the same cavity, for a wondrous mixture of microwave speed and conventional browning; afterward, the oven cleans itself.

For more on how microwave works, see Chapter 3.

Refrigerators: "Old Faithful" of the Kitchen

There is probably no other manufactured product that gives as much for the consumer dollar as the refrigerator. It stays on duty every minute of every day and night, often for as long as 15 or 20 years, controlling its own temperature, recycling itself on and off, with very infrequent need for service.

It is such a great appliance that it is unfortunate that it is such a monstrosity. Refrigerators are very handsome per se, but they are too big and inflexible to really fit in with kitchen design. In many cases it's almost like parking your car in your kitchen. The car might be beautiful, but it just doesn't belong.

The best treatment for a refrigerator is to design it into a cabinet run and then use available trim kits to install cabinet paneling to match the cabinets, or plastic laminate to match the countertops, or even wallpaper or fabric. This raises the cost, but it helps integrate the design.

Mechanically, the refrigerator consists of a compressor, or pump, which pumps the refrigerant; an evaporator, or plate, which gets cold and cools the cabinet, and a condenser that transfers heat from the cabinet.

Basic features to be found on any model include shelving, crispers, ice cube trays, a freezing compartment, and light. Special features on better models would include rollers, a 7-day meat keeper, a butter conditioner, an ice maker, egg holders, and convertible doors.

There are some deluxe models that also offer ice cubes and ice water through the door. This, of course, and any ice-maker model, also requires a cold water line. Some models are available that provide for later installation of an ice maker, a good feature for the builder who wants to cut his costs without totally precluding the convenience.

There are four types: the single door, the 2-door top-mount, the 2-door bottom-mount, and the side-by-side.

The *single door* model is the lowest priced, and a spring-type door inside gives access to a freezer compartment that will be 10 to 20 degrees above the desired 0 degrees. So it is not a true freezer.

All other models have two doors with a solid barrier between freezer and refrigerator. So the freezer will hold at 0 degrees while the fresh food compartment will maintain a temperature of between 37 to 40 degrees.

Top-mount models have the freezer above the regular food compartment, and bottom-mounts have the freezer below. *Side-by-sides* have gained fast popularity by eliminating all the bending and stooping, and their gains have been directly in proportion to losses for the bottom-mounts.

Refrigerators may be free-standing or built-in. The built-ins are best from a design viewpoint, and they usually have wood fronts to match the cabinets. They require a refrigerator cabinet,

Microwave countertop units usually crowd the counter too much, and building them in is solution. This Hotpoint comes with sleeve kit for building in.

Side-by-side refrigerators are gaining in popularity, and so are the "through-the-door" features such as ice and water. This Whirlpool has a new feature, an extra door in the refrigerator door for quick access to foods commonly used without opening the big door and the resultant loss of cold. This is called "Serva-Door."

Multiple choice of cycles is shown by many push-buttons in this deluxe GE dishwasher. These cost more, but can save energy and/or water or do extra heavy duty. The "economy" model is shown below, in contrast, with no pushbuttons, one dial for control.

Another dishwasher solution in kitchens with small space is this special General Electric model which will fit under a sink with a 6-inch-deep bowl. There's still room for disposer, as shown at right.

adding to the cost.

There also are many "compact" refrigerators, which might be free-standing or built-in. These usually are found in mobile homes, vacation homes, recreational vehicles, offices, motels, and apartments, but they also are fine for the home as a luxury touch — for the den, rec room, master bedroom, or even to store cold drinks for the kids by the outside door to keep them out of the kitchen traffic patterns.

Conventional refrigerators must be defrosted, usually about once a month. Automatic models have separate freezer and fresh food compartments, and the latter will defrost itself but the freezer must be defrosted about once a year. No-frost models have dual controls for the two compartments and neither compartment should ever need defrosting. This runs about a penny a day more in operating cost.

A separate freezer, which might be upright or chest type, is good for large families or families that like to cut the frequency of their shopping trips. It is good for the budget-conscious person because it permits economies such as buying a half a hog and a half a steer which a butcher would carve up into the appropriate cuts and package and label for storage in the home freezer.

But there must be a place to put a freezer. This should not be in the kitchen. The basement, utility room, or garage would be better, but fewer houses are being built with basements, and, on the average, houses are getting smaller. Space, then, could be a problem.

Where there is a separate freezer, there is no need to have more than a conventional refrigerator except as a luxury.

Dishwashers: Cheap at Twice the Price

Washing dishes is the easiest task in the home. It is just a simple matter of applying a little hot water and soap to a succession of plates and glasses, requiring no skill, strength, or concentration, and thus there is little need for an expensive appliance to do the job. Ask any husband.

Home Economist Retta Presby, however, struggled through massive calculations to determine that any average American who lives to the age of 70 will have consumed 150 head of cattle, 2400 chickens, 225 lambs, 26 sheep, 310 pigs, 26 acres of grain, and 59 acres of fruits and vegetables.

Multiply that by the number of people in the family and break it down to the number of plates, dishes, glasses, pots, pans, etc., it takes for individual servings, and communicate it to The Great American Husband. Now he is beginning to wonder about giving the best years of his wife to this senseless job.

Dishwashers are no longer luxuries, they are essentials. It is difficult to rent an apartment that does not have a dishwasher. Builders are including them in their new-home appliance packages. A housewife who gets used to one in her first apartment will never go back to the old method, nor should she.

Dishwashers can be top-loading or front-loading. Top-loaders are "portable," which means free-standing. Front-loaders are built-in or convertible. A convertible comes on wheels, but can be installed under the counter later when the consumer has more money or moves to what she considers her permanent home.

Standard width for a built-in is 24 inches. All other dimensions are standardized to fit under the standard kitchen countertop with the base cabinets. Cabinet manufacturers offer dishwasher fronts to match their cabinets, so they can be made to blend in with kitchen design.

Some manufacturers of related kitchen products have cooperated to make dishwashers feasible even for very small kitchens.

One sink manufacturer, for example, makes a special double-bowl sink with one bowl deep, the other shallow enough to fit over an undercounter dishwasher. Another manufacturer offers a matching family of cooktop, eye-level oven, vent hood and dishwasher below, so all four fit in 30 inches of space.

One manufacturer makes a different kind of dishwasher that can be sunk into a countertop, over a dead corner, for example. This product is water-powered and therefore needs no electrical hookup.

In operation, a dishwasher is more economical than most people think. In a normal full cycle of two washes and three rinses, the housewife hears the spraying and roiling of about 800 gallons of water. But actually only about 15 gallons of water

While there are big differences in disposers, their method of operation is substantially the same. Here a cutaway shows interior of Waste King grinding mechanism.

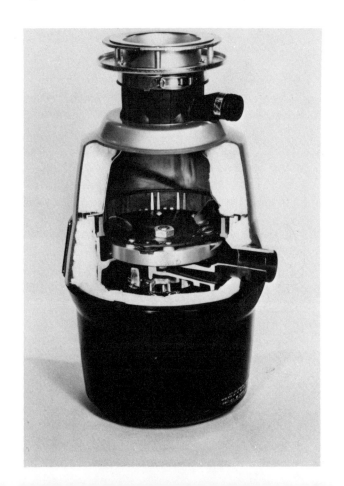

are consumed, less than she would use when washing by hand. In a dishwasher the water is used, filtered and recirculated, over and over.

In her apartment, the housewife always has had the builder model, the economy model. She turned the knob and it did the job.

The lower-priced single-control dishwasher will do an excellent job. All the fancy pushbutton models will do a lot more, however. They do add to performance.

For example, one pushbutton might be for warming plates for dinner. Another might be for fragile dishes that aren't very dirty, giving gentler action with less water and detergent.

Still another would boost water temperature in the final rinse for greater sanitation. Other buttons would be for pots and pans, or to give dishes a quick rinse after which it automatically waits for her to get the other dishes loaded. And then, of course, there's the regular cycle, the equivalent of the single control on the economy model.

For effective dishwasher operation, water temperature must be between 140 and 160 degrees. The increasing impurities in and hardness of water have not been much of a problem because dishwasher detergents are formulated to cope with a wide range of water conditions. But in some areas of excessive water hardness, a water softener might be needed.

Garbage Disposal — A Real Grind

Most of us in today's world have mental pictures of women, their noses wrinkled in distaste, emptying garbage from the sink into paper bags to be carried out to a garbage can.

Those mental pictures are justification enough for the modern garbage disposer, an appliance that takes a small bite of electricity, a long drink of water, and then chews up all the garbage you feed it into tiny particles that wash down the drain with the waste water.

There are two types of disposers.

The batch-fed type has a locking cover that also serves as a switch. To operate this type you fill it with waste (just put it in, don't pack it in), lock the cover in place, and the disposer operates.

The continuous-feed type has a separate switch, usually on the wall over the sink. To operate this

type the water is turned on, the switch turned on, and food waste is simply fed in until it all is gone.

Both must be operated with running cold water. Both will do the job with the same efficiency. Neither has any advantage over the other. It is a matter of personal preference.

There is, however, another way to categorize disposers, and this way the difference is vast.

There are cheap ones and there are expensive ones.

Buying a cheap disposer is like buying a cheap parachute. It is made of different materials that won't wear nearly as long, performance will not be as good, noise will be worse, and you will be lucky to get more than two or three years of use out of it.

A good one might cost three times more, but it will last dependably for 10 years, will install more easily and operate much more quietly.

Anyone who has had an unhappy experience with a disposer in the past should be aware of those big differences. Disposers that builders put into housing developments almost always are bought on a price basis, and that means the consumer gets a cheap disposer. You should be aware also that these "economy" disposers are made by the same manufacturers who make the very finest, so don't condemn a good brand name just because you got stuck with one of their cheapies 10 years ago.

Good disposers will dispose of bones, and fruit pits, and corn cobs, and some will even take normal household quantities of paper napkins and towels. They have trouble with food wastes that are particularly fibrous, such as corn husks or avocado leaves. They will handle these, but it will take longer because of the stringiness, so often it is easier to dispose of such waste with other kitchen trash. Celery and coffee grounds are no problem.

Metal should never be dropped in a disposer, not even small bits like the staples on tea bags.

There was a time when disposer repairmen would drop glass pop bottles into an operating disposer to clean it. This was a good way to clean the disposer, but the glass particles would collect in the plumbing lines, catch food particles and eventually clog the lines. Therefore, glass is not recommended. Bones and fruit pits will do the same cleaning job.

Ventilating hoods have become decorative as well as functional. These, the Chuck Wagon series by Broan, have various optional straps and plaques that apply with adhesive and can be changed. These take big dual squirrel cage blower rated for cfm and sones—air movement and sound level. They have solid state controls for light and power.

Incidentally, there are about 100 cities in the U.S. that require, by ordinance, disposers in all new residential construction. These cities benefit from improved sanitation and from considerable economies in garbage collection.

And, for those who are not in cities, any septic tank system which meets HUD Minimum Property Standards can handle the slight added load from a disposer.

Ventilating Hoods — For Indoors Ecology

A ventilating hood provides the gift of fresh air in the kitchen. It stops airborne cooking odors at their source, traps grease and soil that otherwise would end up on walls, ceilings and draperies, and should be considered one of the essentials over every cooking appliance. That means over both the cooktop and wall ovens when these are built-in, over both the cooking surface and the oven in an eye-level range, and over either a microwave oven or barbecue grill when these are present in the kitchen.

There are many things you should know about vent-hoods that affect their performance. There are

Another built-in appliance that helps organize kitchen and eliminate problems is the built-in mixing center. The two shown here are by Ronson (above) and NuTone (below). Both take full range of attachments, and storage of all these and bowls is right at point of use.

different types, and performance features, and they must be powered in relation to their distance above the cooking appliance. All vent hoods manufactured by members of the Home Ventilating Institute have performance ratings, and they also have sone ratings that measure their noise levels.

As for types, there are ductless and ducted vent hoods.

Ducted types are better. They filter the air as it enters the hood, and then they have ductwork to exhaust it to the outside. Because of the ductwork, their fan units can be remote, out of the kitchen, to minimize noise, and they can have more powerful fan units for greater air movement.

But there are some places where ducted hoods are not practical; in apartments, for example. Here a non-ducted hood is much better than none. These have excellent filter systems that gather the air, clean it and then exhaust it back into the kitchen, commonly from vents in the top that direct it upward. Thus the heat and moisture of cooking is exhausted back into the kitchen rather than being vented to the outside, but grease and odor have been removed.

Some expensive wall ovens are made with attached vent hoods. These are designed to match the ovens. They pull out to protrude a few inches when in operation during cooking, then can be pushed in to fit flush with the oven at other times.

Hoods come in many shapes, colors, and sizes. Some are squared, some angled, some curved. They come in colors to match major appliance colors — mainly the earth colors, such as avocado and harvest — or in white, chrome, or other options.

Some are manufactured with three finished sides to project over kitchen peninsulas, or with four finished sides for kitchen islands. One brand has modular sections so it can be made larger or smaller on-site. While most are made of steel, at least one brand is constructed of fiber glass.

In addition, most custom cabinet manufacturers offer custom hoods of wood to match the cabinets, and most kitchen dealers have local sheet-metal sources for making custom hoods.

The perfect vent hood in one kitchen might be unsatisfactory in another kitchen because the layout of the kitchen can affect the performance of the product. For example, a certain cfm rating

Infrared heating lamps are incorporated in this Trade Wind hood, so it serves as a food warmer while it vents.

And ventilating fans aren't what they used to be, as these pictures prove. The ceiling model is by Emerson. The wall model is by NuTone. They suck in air around the perimeter. All of these fans and hoods have HVI power and sone ratings.

The "clean-up trio" by GE includes Potscrubber II dishwasher, left, with pushbuttons for heavy-duty, energy-saving and other cycles, the food waste disposer mounted in sink, and trash compactor, right.

in a hood over a built-in cooktop that is installed against a wall might be inadequate over a cooktop installed in a peninsula or island, because of cross-drafts in the kitchen. Added duct run from a peninsula also would require greater power.

In order of importance, there are these four considerations in selecting a vent hood:

1) *Be sure of enough power.* A hood must take out smoke, odors and grease as fast as they are produced, and it must have power to overcome the resisting pressure of the length of duct run with its elbows and end caps. Look first for a Home Ventilating Institute rating. Otherwise, be wary of suspiciously low prices for any power rating.

2) Then consider *noise level.* Again, check HVI sone ratings.
3) Select the right product then on the basis of *style, service,* and *workmanship.*
4) Then consider *price.* There will still be price variations, big ones, even after the first three considerations, but to put price ahead of those other considerations would be a disservice to the housewife who must live with the product.

As for performance, the FHA and the HVI both require a minimum of 40 cfm per foot of hood length. So a 140-cfm fan would be minimum for a 42-inch hood. Most of these are fan type and have retail prices well under $50, but this type is for minimum performance.

For fair performance, a 200-cfm fan could qualify, but it would not get the job done when the cook is using all burners or cooking something exceptionally smoky. Fan type vent-hoods in this range still usually retail for about $50 or less but might be noisy. A centrifugal blower would be more quiet for only about $5 or $10 more.

For good performance, think in terms of 300 cfm and up. These will have several speeds, or with solid state control an infinite range of speeds. You will seldom see a fan-type here. Most will have twin centrifugal blowers (often called "squirrel cage") which will be quiet and might sell at retail for as low as $75 or up to twice that.

In tightly constructed houses, a window might have to be opened slightly to permit a vent hood to do its job. A hood should be 24 inches to 30 inches over the range.

Little Extras for Big Differences

The appliances described so far are the routine equipment that might be found in any new kitchen. There might be extra margins of quality — the extra features interpretable into extra convenience or extra function — but still, they are basics.

There are many other appliances that can be built in and that can add up to a super kitchen.

When a housewife moves into her new home, for example, she must go out and buy a toaster, and an electric mixer, blender, and perhaps a knife sharpener. She will go to a housewares department and look for some sort of box that her husband can hang on a wall or attach under a wall cabinet to dispense her foil and plastic wrap and paper towels.

Whatever she buys, she has to find space for the item, both in use and when she wants to put it away. She has a shining new kitchen, but every time she buys something for it she finds she has bought a problem.

It doesn't have to be that way. All of these items can be designed into the kitchen in the first place. No storage problem. No countertop space problem. Here are a few examples.

Built-in toasters are available. They can be wired and recessed into the wall, tilting out for use and then pushing back to their flush position.

Two different manufacturers offer two different built-in mixing systems, combining all mixing, blending, juicing, and other such functions. In both of these, the motor is mounted under the counter, which helps minimize noise, and all attachments go in a base cabinet directly under the appliance, at the point of use. In one of these systems only a small stainless steel plate shows above the counter, and when lifted it exposes the drive shaft onto which all attachments fit. The other system has a small control panel that protrudes above the counter in use, and snaps down flush afterward.

There also are built-in can-openers, electric-powered, that recess into the wall, and built-in knife-sharpeners.

There are either electric or hydronic heating units engineered to recess into the kick space under a base cabinet.

There are different types of food-warming appliances. One is a slide-out drawer, similar to those used in restaurants but designed for the modern residential kitchen. Wood trim kits are available for these so they accept paneling to match the cabinets. Another food warmer is a wired rectangular glass-ceramic plate that recesses into the countertop. This has the added advantage of providing a place to put hot pans from the cooktop. Other food warmers use infrared radiation and mount under the wall cabinets, and one ventilating hood incorporates this warming feature.

There are water purification systems that become more relevant in these days of bottled drinking water. One can be mounted on the wall or recessed into the wall near the sink, or mounted on a wall cabinet near the sink. These need a cold water line, of course. There are several others in the developmental stage.

There are musical-intercom systems that can put music throughout the house from a master panel in the kitchen, which also monitor other rooms (such as the baby's bedroom) and incorporate burglar and fire alarms.

Paper caddies can be recessed into the wall. Automatic ice-makers are available and can be free-standing or can be built-in under the counter. There are also instant hot water dispensers.

Trash compactors can be free-standing or they can replace a 15-inch base cabinet under the counter. One model, under the Thermador or Waste King name, is only 12 inches wide. They require a 3-wire line and should take a separate 15-amp fuse. But there are a dozen different brands, so specifications will vary and might be changed.

7
Sinks and the Counter-Revolution

Kitchen countertops are playing an increasingly important role in the modern kitchen. Years ago when the sink was recessed in the only countertop in the kitchen, they were called sinktops. Gradually, new materials and new ideas changed this ordinary part of the kitchen. In the middle 1950s, high-pressure plastic laminates were popular as a surfacing for these countertops, but it was difficult to mate sink with sinktop in a way that would prevent moisture seepage and consequent rotting. To answer that challenge a clamp-down rim, the "Hudee" rim, was developed.

At around the same time the technique known as postforming became popular. This is the technique that gives a clean seamless sweep of plastic surface from the front of the countertop to the back, curving up at the back to cover a 4-inch backsplash or more.

And then sink manufacturers started wondering why sinks had to be so ordinary. They started improving their surfaces and materials. They added lights and soap dispensers. They became innovative in configurations.

All of these factors led to the counter-revolution. Sinks and countertops became things of beauty and previously-undreamed-of function. They became parts of the new kitchen concept.

In more recent years, new adhesives and sealants have led to a return of the "self-rimming" sink that does not require a Hudee-type rim. Now either type can be trusted for long years of use.

The most popular sink is of stainless steel. The most inexpensive is made of porcelain-on-steel, often called pressed steel. A more expensive type

is porcelained cast iron. The newest material is molded plastic, or artificial marble, commonly used for bathrooms but not kitchens.

Both porcelain-on-steel and cast iron sinks now come in glamour colors and with innovative configurations. But the former can chip easily. The latter is very durable but more expensive.

Stainless steel costs more than either, but its prices vary according to gauge of the steel and nickel and chrome content. Some are shiny, some are not.

All of these differences are more or less academic in new homes where the sink is provided by the builder. The kitchen sink, after all, is a small part of a kitchen and most housewives will accept anything the builder provides.

But the differences are significant in custom homes and in kitchen remodeling, where the housewife is shown the options for added beauty and utility. In stainless steel, she will have a definite preference for either the satin or brilliant finish, and she should be given the opportunity to choose. She might want the bright color of a porcelain finish, or the futuristic design of a particular brand. She might want a deluxe model with three compartments, a fluorescent light attached, soap and lotion dispensers, a separate pull-out spray, a purification device for the drinking water, an instant hot water device for instant soups and beverages, and built-in compartments for ice or for placement of a built-in small appliance.

The new designer styling has pretty much done away with standard measurements in kitchen sinks. Most still are 21 or 22 inches from front to back

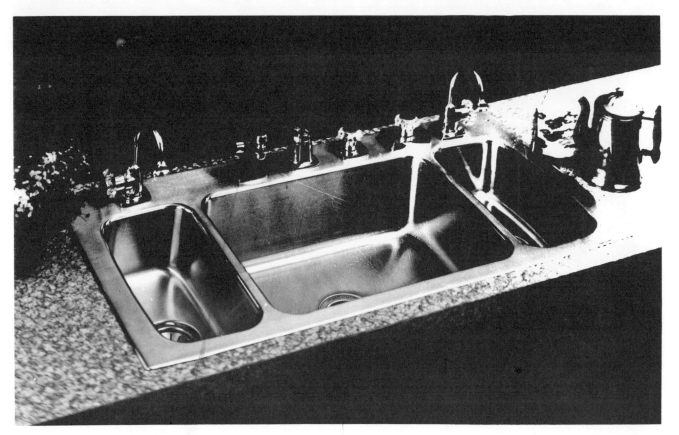

How classy a kitchen sink can be is proven by this, the self-rimming stainless steel "Cuisine Classique" by Elkay. With the glamorous name go glamorous functions, even to a color-coded temperature control. Back ledge features, from left, include: Separate goose-neck faucet for disposer compartment; pull-out spray; single main faucet; water supply knob; color-coded temperature-control knob (from blue to red, for cold to hot), and then another goose-neck faucet for vegetable-cleaning compartment.

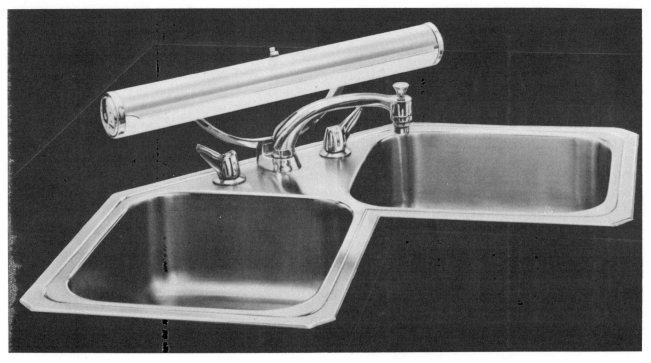

Another example is pie-cut for corner installation and with a fluorescent fixture mounted behind the faucet. This also is by Elkay.

Decorator colors characterize sinks of porcelain-on-steel or cast iron. This cast iron model by Kohler is the Trieste, with two big working bowls and one in the center to take the disposer.

Kohler's urbanite is unique in that it combines a disposer compartment in a single bowl sink to meet space limitations. It's only 25x22".

because the depth of the countertop is standardized, and the bowl itself usually is 16 inches from front to back. But these dimensions vary according to brand and style.

While the usual depth of the bowl is 7-1/2 inches, this too can vary widely. A triple-bowl sink might have a small vegetable sink between two larger bowls, and this might be only 3-1/2 inches deep. It also might be round, and it might be the ideal place for the disposer. A 3-1/2-inch depth for one bowl of a double-bowl sink allows the housewife to sit while cleaning or preparing vegetables and salads.

While there are many round and oval sinks, they normally are used in bathrooms or hospitality areas rather than in the kitchen.

For corner installation, sink manufacturers offer double-bowl sinks in a pie-cut configuration. For kitchens where space is at a premium, there also are special depths (5-1/2 inches) to permit one bowl to fit over a built-in dishwasher.

Sinks may come with faucets and other attachments, or simply with punched holes so faucets can be purchased separately.

In the latter case, options are limited by the number of holes punched. But it will always be possible to accommodate either the traditional pair of faucets — hot and cold — or the more modern single-handle faucet.

A single-bowl sink is adequate if the kitchen is equipped with a dishwasher. Even with a dishwasher, the double-bowl is desirable.

Stainless steel sinks come in 18-gauge and 20-gauge. The 18-gauge is heavier and much more satisfactory. Two other figures that require interpretation refer to the mix of the alloys. For example, 18-8 would mean 18 percent chrome content and 8 percent nickel content. Chrome relates to the sink's ability to stand up and keep its finish over the years. Nickel gives the steel the ability to withstand corrosion.

There are three basic surfaces for kitchen countertops.

The standard utility surface is decorative high-pressure plastic laminate, such as the well-known Formica. It should be 1/16-inch thick for horizontal applications in the kitchen. The thinner 1/32-inch vertical grade material is not recommended, although it often is used as a cost-cutting measure.

The other two basic materials are for use in conjunction with high-pressure laminates. One is laminated hardwood, the familiar "butcher block," for cutting operations. The other is tempered glass ceramic (or ceramic tile, stainless steel, or marble) used as a counter insert for hot pans direct from the range, or for cutting.

This is not to say that all, nor even that most, kitchens actually have these three types of surfaces. Most have only the plastic laminate surfacing.

And as a consequence, the woman who must take a hot pan from the oven and put it down quickly must put it in the sink, or on the range top if there is a space there. And she cuts bread or meats or vegetables on the plastic laminate and, in the course of only a couple of years, puts thousands of tiny cuts in it. If, in an emergency, she puts a hot pan down on the unprotected countertop, permanent damage can result. Then the top must be replaced, or a kitchen specialist or top fabricator can cut out the damaged part and replace it with the counter insert that should have been there in the first place.

In the far west, ceramic tile is widely used for the entire kitchen countertop. This is an excellent and beautiful material. But it also is much noisier, its hard surface dulls knives, and dishes break more easily on it. The same is true of marble and of the newer artificial marbles so widely used as bathroom vanity tops. Stainless steel is a good material, but it can be dented, it dulls knives, and the scratches and stains on this surface are difficult to remove.

One artificial marble is different enough to get special mention, and is proving itself excellent for kitchen countertops. This is DuPont's Corian, and it differs from all other cultured marbles in that it is machinable and workable with woodworking tools. It is a homogeneous material, the same all the way through, so nicks or scratches can be "wiped" off with a Scotchbrite pad. It can take any sink, or it can be ordered with integral sink bowl, all one piece of the same material. It also is available with integral bar or vegetable sink. Its only drawback is a limited color range — white or gold or with faint marbling.

Plastic laminated tops have 1/16" high pressure plastic laminate adhered to particleboard. Close-ups show no-drip edge at front, accomplished with plastic T-mold inserted in particleboard and under laminate.

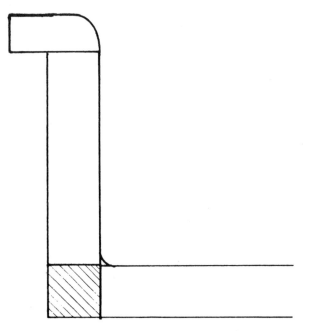

Other end of a postformed top shows how cove stick is placed for 90-degree angle. Small void at radius is not undesirable.

Many kitchen designers will plan whole sections of laminated wood into the countertop, along with a glass ceramic section or insert. Many like to include custom stainless steel sinks in the design with stainless steel drainboards or extensions for the hot pan problem.

Forget linoleum. It went out with running boards and rumble seats and, in fact, is no longer made in this country. Vinyls, low-pressure laminates and other plastic alternatives are also poor choices. They are fine for vertical surfaces and good for table tops, but not for kitchen counters.

Since high pressure plastic laminated tops are the standard, from this point on we'll simply call them tops. Two types of tops can be identified: self-edged and postformed. Self-edged tops are flat. They have a square front and the edging is a separate piece of the same material, hence the term self-edged. The backsplash is a separate piece with a square inside corner, but firmly attached at the shop before delivery.

The backsplash can be any height, but the standard is 4 inches. The usual alternative is a backsplash that rises all the way to the bottoms of the wall cabinets, adding much to the overall cleanability of the kitchen. This high backsplash is seldom done with postformed tops because of equipment limitations.

Postformed tops present one clean sweep of plastic surface from the bottom of the front edge to the top of the backsplash.

In a modern postforming line, which can be fully automated, a sheet of corestock is fed in flat. The leading edge is machined and grooved for a T-molding, the under side is grooved in the backsplash area, contact adhesive is sprayed onto the corestock and onto a sheet of plastic laminate, and the plastic is indexed onto the corestock. Next the two go through a pinch roller which fuses the plastic to the core permanently. The plastic is then heated along the leading edge and molded down and adhered, and the plastic is heated along the backsplash area. The machine bends it up 90 degrees, and finally a coving stick is inserted in the resultant gap in the core to hold it at 90 degrees. This process produces a fully formed top.

The top just described will have a waterfall leading edge. If a T-molding is inserted in the

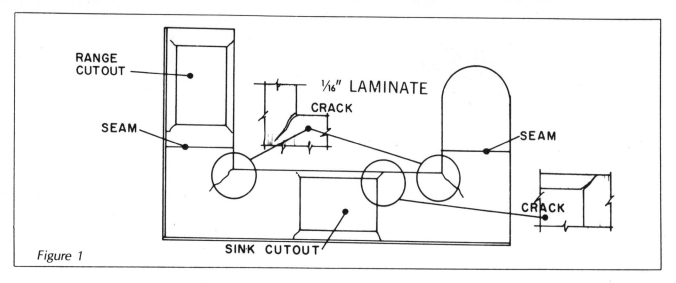

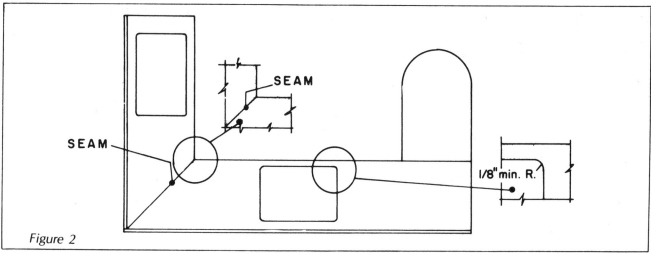

Improper placing of laminate seams can cause cracks. When seam is mitered from front to back corner it avoids stresses that come with no miter. Figure 1 shows wrong way, Figure 2 shows right way. All corners of sink or range cutouts should be radiused. Square corners in these places tend to crack. Formica Corp.

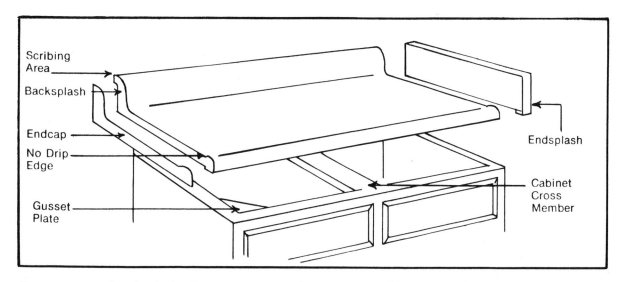

Components of a plastic laminate countertop (art courtesy of SUBA Manufacturing, Inc.).

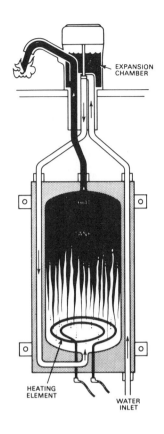

Here's how instant hot water dispensers work. Sketch by In-Sink-Erator shows how turning valve at top allows cold water to enter inlet at bottom right. Water passes through valve assembly, down and enters tank at bottom where heat is. Tank does not operate under pressure since valve controls inlet water, not instant hot water.

Corian countertop with integral sink bowl has Corian backsplash and cup ledge. This was routed along front edge to follow cabinet line, a unique advantage of Corian over other cultured marbles. It can be worked with woodworking tools.

Ceramic tile is used here for both countertop and backsplash. Tile is Monarch, comes in six colors including lemon, strawberry, avocado, kumquat, ginger and mandarin orange.

groove of the leading edge before the plastic sheet is laid on it, the result is a slight rise at the edge before the plastic is bent down. This is a no-drip edge.

Because of the automation, postformed tops, which are better and more attractive products in every way, are often available at about the same price as self-edged. But in high-production shops, self-edged tops can be made on a completely automated basis also.

However they are made, tops are one of the best bargains in the home.

Fabricators usually use 3/4-inch particleboard as a corestock, building it up around the edge with a double-layer to bring it to standard 1-1/2-inch height. This 1-1/2 inches is necessary to bring the top up to height of slip-in or drop-in ranges. Depth of the top from front to rear would be about 25 inches, enough to extend up to 1 inch over the cabinets beneath.

Regular kitchen countertops, properly attached to the base cabinets, need no backing sheet for dimensional stability. The structure itself will prevent warping.

But peninsulas that extend several feet out from the base cabinets must have backing sheets.

Measuring for tops is critical. When a top is delivered to the home it is complete. There is no way to change it. It has to fit.

Kitchen specialists find a folding 6-foot rule is more accurate than a steel tape. If the measurements are going to be checked by a second person, each makes sure they use the same type and brand of rule. There are differences. Many specialists also check their rules against those being used in the shop where the countertops are fabricated.

Tops that must be positioned tightly between walls must be 1/4-inch to 3/4-inch short. A top that measures the same as the between-walls dimension will not go into position.

Out-of-square walls are always a problem. Theoretically, every wall meets another wall at 90 degrees. In practice it just doesn't happen. So, in practice, tops often must be slightly out-of-square.

The rule-of-thumb used by kitchen specialists on corner squareness is a simple formula: 3 ft + 4 ft. = 5 ft.

To use it, measure the base wall to a point 3 feet from the corner and mark the point. Then measure along the side wall and mark a point 4 feet from the corner. Now measure the direct distance, point to point. It should be 5 feet.

If it measures less than 5 feet, the side wall is coming in. If it measures more than 5 feet, the side wall is going out.

Communicate the precise measurements to the top fabricator and he can allow for it so that the top will fit.

8
Kitchen Planning and Design

The primary ingredient in good kitchen design is common sense. You've got to have places to put things. You've got to have places to put things down. It's better to store things near where you use them. You've got to have a little elbow room. And when you're working in the kitchen you don't want to have to step aside whenever somebody else in the house wants to go from the living room to the bathroom.

Those are the basics, but they raise several loaded questions.

For example, you've got to have a place to put things. But how many things? A 2-bedroom house presumes a family of two or three, maybe four. A 4-bedroom house presumes a family of five or six. Obviously a homeowner needs a lot more pots and pans and dishes and space for a family of six than for a family of two.

The concepts of "enough room" and "good kitchen layout" are matters of opinion for most people until they actually start storing foods and dishes and working in a kitchen. Kitchen experts through the years have formularized most kitchen planning principles to remove the subjective guesses and substitute objective facts and measurements that always will work.

The considerations are these:

1. Storage space that is both ample and logical. Ample means enough, but not too much. Too much would be wasteful both of money and of floorspace in the home. Logical means having enough storage space at the proper places.

2. Countertop space that is both ample and in the right places.
3. Well-planned placement and areas for each of the major appliances and their related activities.
4. Reduction of waste motion. (Few of us are naturally efficient, but our inefficiencies can be lessened greatly by good kitchen planning.)
5. Good lighting and good color-matching.

The best way to start planning to satisfy all of those considerations is to consider the activity areas. Each of these relates closely to a major appliance or the sink. And each requires its own cabinetry and work space. These are:

1. The food preparation center, which incorporates the refrigerator. This sometimes is referred to as the mixing center.
2. The cooking and serving center, which includes the range or, in built-in installations, at least the cooktop.
3. The clean-up center, which incorporates the sink. Major appliances found in this area include the dishwasher and disposer.

Many housewives also want an eating area in the kitchen, and there is a growing trend to include a planning center which serves as the housewife's "office." Such a planning center will include at least a desktop with some storage facility for household bills, notes and the like. Well-planned ones will also include a telephone and an intercom which provides communication throughout the house, monitoring of baby's sleeping or play areas, and even burglar and fire alarms.

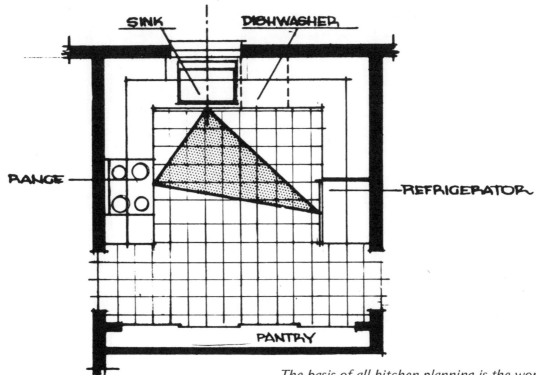

SINK   DISHWASHER

RANGE

REFRIGERATOR

PANTRY

The basis of all kitchen planning is the work triangle. It connects the food preparation center, which includes the refrigerator; cooking center, which includes the range; and the cleanup center with the sink and dishwasher. Total distance from middle front of sink, to range to refrigerator and back to sink, should be from 12 to 22 feet. Within these limits the housewife has sufficient freedom of action but doesn't have to cover tiring distances.

Other possible centers could include a bar, a hobby center, or sewing center, but these are functions of space.

The ground rule for arranging these three major centers is to form a triangle, and the straight-line distance between the front center of the sink, refrigerator and cooktop must not total more than 22 feet nor less than 12 feet.

That is called the work triangle, and it is the basis for all kitchen planning.

The distance from the sink to the refrigerator should be from 4 to 7 feet; from sink to range, 4 to 6 feet, and between range and refrigerator, 4 to 9 feet.

Any one-piece range fits into that triangle. A built-in installation, however, adds a fourth element, since there is a separate oven and cooktop. The guideline here is to put the oven outside the triangle since it is used least, although it often can be designed within the triangle.

Both the maximum (22 feet) and the minimum (12 feet) of the work triangle are important. More than 22 feet wastes steps, energy, and time. Less than 12 feet crowds the appliances and activities too close together.

Kitchen planning starts with the sink. A kitchen designer always locates it first, partially because good planning usually centers it with refrigerator to the right of it, or clockwise from it, and the cooking and serving area to the left of it, or counter-clockwise. In addition, the sink must go where the plumbing lines are, and location of the plumbing lines usually is determined by other factors, such as location of bathrooms.

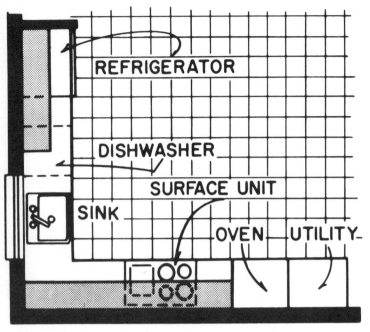

L Shaped

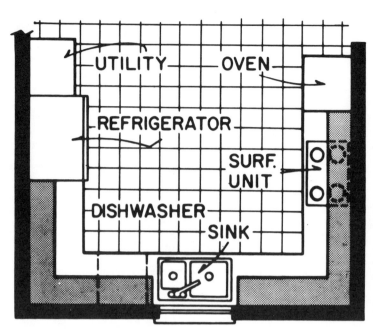

U Shaped

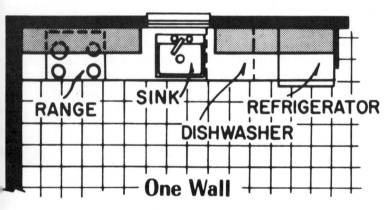

One Wall

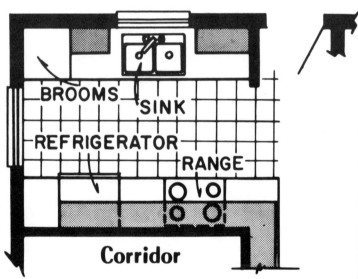

Corridor

The four basic kitchen configurations are the U shape, the L shape, the Corridor, and the One Wall. The U and the L usually afford efficient work triangles without cross traffic. A U or L broken by a door cuts efficiency by permitting cross traffic. If it is open, traffic cuts through. A central island or a peninsula often is used to help form the work triangle.

The sink is the center of clean-up activity before as well as after the meal. So plenty of counter space is required.

There should be 36 inches of counter space to the right of the sink, and there should be 30 inches of counter space to the left.

The dishwasher should be adjacent to the sink. If a dishwasher is not included, a 24-inch cabinet should be designed adjacent to the sink for later installation of a dishwasher.

If a dishwasher is not included, a double-bowl sink is needed. Even if there is a dishwasher, a double-bowl sink is desirable.

If fillers are required to make the run of cabinets fit flush to walls to left and right, the best place to put them is to the left and right of the sink cabinet.

Many kitchen activities relate closely to both refrigerator and range so, as stated before, the sink is best placed between those two other centers.

Storage must be provided near the sink for clean-up supplies, for fruits and vegetables that do not require refrigeration, for sauce pans, coffee pot and food preparation supplies, and for foods that require soaking and washing.

If the recommended counter space to the right (36 inches) and left (30 inches) of the sink cannot be provided, the absolute minimums would be 24 inches and 18 inches respectively. But don't be that stingy to the housewife.

A double-bowl sink with one shallow bowl will permit sit-down convenience for the housewife when she is cleaning vegetables or for similar tasks.

The sink does not have to go under a window. This is a matter of personal preference, and the idea that it enabled the mother to watch the kids playing has always been questionable. At best, it leaves a lot of gaps in the surveillance. If there is one window, it might be best to save it for a breakfast-lunch area.

We have referred to the area around the refrigerator as the food preparation area, or the mixing center. Some kitchen designers separate these in different ways, but the functions and needs are closely related.

It is good to localize various types of food storage here — cold foods in the refrigerator and its freezer compartment, canned goods in a pantry unit of some sort. Pantry units can be obtained 84 inches high or as wall or base cabinets, with fold-out vertical racks to hold a maximum number of cans, or with revolving shelves that are particularly good for corners.

The refrigerator door must open into the work triangle, not away from it. And there must be at least 18 inches of landing space where the refrigerator door opens. Side-by-side refrigerator-freezers tend to defeat this principle, but with these models it is the refrigerator door, not the freezer door, that should open to the landing space.

When the food preparation and mixing functions are included in this activity center, there should be 36 to 42 inches of counter space on the door-opening side of the refrigerator.

A maple insert in the countertop is particularly useful here. It could be as small as 12 inches wide, or it could be a whole section of countertop. Women use knives often when preparing food and it is next to impossible to keep from cutting the countertop.

The maple cutting board also can be a pull-out accessory of the base cabinet, positioned over a drawer.

Here, also, is the place for a built-in mixer, with a cabinet below for its many accessories.

The cooking center is the most active area of the kitchen after the sink and cleanup center.

The built-in cooktop should have at least 18 inches of counterspace on each side.

A built-in oven needs 24 inches of counter space.

A one-piece range needs at least the minimum 18 inches on each side, but it is much better to provide at least 24 inches on the inside of the work triangle.

Provide a counter insert of either stainless steel or glass ceramic near the range for placing hot pans. The plastic laminate of a countertop should never be subjected to heat over 270 degrees.

Since the oven is the least-used appliance in the kitchen, built-in installations can be out of the work triangle. However, it still will need its counter space.

In their specifications for every model, manufacturers of built-in ovens always list a height above the floor for the bottom of the oven cut-out.

A woman can work with least effort at an oven if the opened door is 3 to 4 inches below her elbow level. The usable range here is from 1 to 7 inches below elbow level. If there is a choice, relate the height of the opened oven door to the user's elbow level.

The cooktop usually will be 36 inches from the floor because it is cut into the countertop and that's the height of the counter. It could be dropped as much as 4 inches, and a lot of housewives would probably appreciate it.

Because both the built-in wall oven and the refrigerator are high appliances, a common design error is to put them together. This should never be done, because both need their own landing space. It does not help to have a landing space on either side when these two are together because that non-solution would put the landing space on the wrong side for either the refrigerator or the oven.

If the range corner of the work triangle is oriented toward the dining area, it might be combined with a serving center. This is common, although the serving center need not be in conjunction with any particular appliance.

The serving center needs storage space for the toaster, serving trays, ready-to-eat foods, platters, serving dishes, table linens, and napkins. There should be at least 30 inches of counter space.

Needless to say, the serving center should be near and accessible to the eating area. Since this is where the china and glassware are stored for serving and eating, it also can be considered as a china center.

Families like eating space in the kitchen, supplementary to a separate dining area, and most builders provide this space in most of their homes.

This adds another center to be included in the kitchen plan — the eating center.

This might be along a peninsula, an island, or it might protrude from a wall.

If it is a peninsula, island, or protrusion, allow at least 42 inches clearance from its end to the opposite wall. Do not put the refrigerator or wall oven on that opposite wall where an open door would block traffic.

Allow 24 inches of elbow room for each place for the lunchers.

For breakfast, the minimum depth should be at least 15 inches. For dinner, it should be 24 inches.

A table and chairs require at least 8 x 6-1/2 feet.

Tables and chairs are simpler and easier. Islands and peninsulas add much to the impact of the kitchen, and they are not complicated.

For about $400 or less a builder can design-in an island with a maple block top that can serve as a food mixing and preparation center on one side, a snack bar on the other. For approximately another $30 he can make this a beautifully textured brick island, then add a built-in barbecue unit and a cooktop.

The peninsula is different only in that it is connected to the cabinets along the wall, extending out into the room to add design interest, give extra storage and counter space, and keep traffic out of the work triangle.

The builder needs a run of 14 feet minimum for a peninsula, which would allow a minimum of 8 feet for the kitchen, including the 24-inch peninsula, and 6 feet for the dining area.

If the opposite side of the peninsula will provide a snack bar instead of a dining area, the 6 feet can be reduced. There must be at least 30 inches from the edge of the snack bar to the wall for seating, and this is a bit tight.

Standard height for island or peninsula would be 36 inches. The snack bar height would drop to 30 inches. If the snack bar is not dropped, high chairs or stools would be needed.

If the snack bar is 36 inches high, the top will have to be extended from 12 to 18 inches for knee space, depending on the type of seating.

If, however, the snack bar is dropped to 30 inches, the minimum for knee space is 15 inches.

The island or peninsula also can be an excellent place for the sink and clean-up center. Unfortunately, this usually will add to plumbing expense.

If possible, the kitchen should be laid out so there will be no traffic crossing any legs of the work triangle. This will not always be possible, but if compromises must be made, the range center should be kept most sacrosanct.

Avoid placing the refrigerator too close to an adjoining wall. If the door cannot be opened far enough, the crisper trays cannot be removed for cleaning.

As a rule of thumb, the kitchen should have at

least 10 feet (linear) of base cabinets and 10 feet of wall cabinets. These are absolute minimums.

Allow 27 inches of space along both walls to turn a corner. A base corner filler is the most economical way to turn the corner but gives only dead space. This insures full operation of adjacent doors and drawers.

Other better ways to turn a corner are (1) with corner units that give reach-in storage space; (2) with a lazy susan cabinet that makes all the corner space easily accessible, and which requires 36 inches along each wall; (3) with a sink or appliance cutting the corner on the diagonal, requiring varying amounts of wall space.

For turning a corner above the counter, a wall corner filler (with dead space, so not desirable) takes 15 inches along each wall. Diagonal wall cabinets can be used, or open diagonal shelving, or butted wall cabinets that have reach-in space. A diagonal wall cabinet takes 24 inches along each wall.

In the home-planning stage, the kitchen should be planned before house plans are finalized. Otherwise it can be costly to the kitchen. For example, a door placed in a corner of the kitchen must use both walls of that corner, with a resultant loss of 30 inches of valuable kitchen space. If this door is installed at least 30 inches from the corner, cabinets can be run all the way to the corner and the only loss is the dimension of the door itself, and its framing. And windows should be a minimum of 12-3/4 inches from a corner for the same reason.

In any inside corner of a cabinet installation, watch for clearances. Normally there will be doors and drawers along both sides of the corner. If they are butted precisely, there might not be clearance for the knob or pull. This would call for a filler to create the clearance. Minimum for clearance is 1/2 inch.

When blank base cabinets are used to turn a corner, the blank end of the cabinet does not have to fill the entire space where it is not exposed. In fact, it is better if it does not fill the space because it is very difficult to reach into such a corner and much of the space would, therefore, be wasted.

Diagonal corner cabinets can add much interest to the kitchen design. However, they use up a lot

of wall space. For example, a cabinet that has 20 inches of exposed surface along the diagonal requires 39 inches along each wall. A 30-inch diagonal cabinet requires 45-1/2 inches along each wall. (This presumes that the depth of adjacent cabinets is 24-1/2 inches.) This does not waste any space, because all space inside the diagonal cabinet is usable. But it uses wall space that, depending on overall kitchen dimensions, might be needed for other purposes.

For the above reason, kitchen specialists usually advise that no sink or appliance over 32 inches in width be used to turn a corner diagonally.

In a straight-wall assembly, the distance from the front edge of the countertop to the front edge of the sink is usually 2 inches. In a diagonal assembly, this distance must be increased to 3 inches so as not to intrude into adjoining cabinet area on each side.

Conventional cabinets can be positioned diagonally across corners. But this creates big pie-shaped dead spaces on either side, wasting kitchen space.

Putting it all together makes the kitchen — the cabinets, the appliances, the corners, the work centers, the activity areas — with the basic work triangle measuring from 12 feet to 22 feet.

This results in one of four basic configurations, or "kinds" of kitchens.

These are the one-wall kitchen, sometimes called straight-line; the corridor kitchen, sometimes called two-wall or pullman or parallel; the L-shaped kitchen which turns one corner, and the U-shaped kitchen which has two inside corners.

All of these have variations. If, for example, a door interrupts the continuity of an L or a U kitchen, it becomes a broken L, or a broken U. If an island or a peninsula is used to achieve the work triangle, it might be called an island kitchen or a peninsula kitchen.

In the one-wall kitchen, the work centers and the appliances are arranged along one wall. This means, of course, that there is no work triangle, and usually both storage space and counter space are much too limited for efficiency or convenience. It is, however, the most economical kind of kitchen, and the most easily installed.

For motels, vacation homes, offices and the like,

this configuration is available from about a dozen manufacturers in one manufactured piece, usually called a unit kitchen, or a compact kitchen.

A complete unit kitchen will include a sink, two surface burners (or more), and, underneath, an oven compartment and a refrigerator compartment. The smallest such unit is made by Douglas Crestlyn, fitting into only 19 inches of wall space. Larger units range up to six feet or more. Sub-Zero offers them as ornate consoles with furniture finishes, with tops and drawers that close so they look like a buffet.

A corridor kitchen adds the opposite wall, making possible a tight, efficient work triangle and added usable storage and counter space. Where the opposite wall is too distant, a peninsula or island can be added to create one side of a corridor kitchen, and in this case at least one of the work centers will be placed in the created counter space.

The only disadvantage of a corridor kitchen is that through traffic always cuts through two legs of the work triangle. In a family with active children this can be bothersome.

The L-shaped kitchen is the most popular, affords efficient work triangle, and is never bothered with through traffic. While the two sides of the L are usually along two walls of the room, in larger kitchens one leg of the L often is formed with a peninsula that affords a snack bar on the other side, outside the work area.

A U-shaped kitchen, as its name indicates, has three sides. Customarily these are three of the walls of the room, but often a peninsula is added to make a U out of what otherwise would be an L. The objective of a U-shape is to place a work area in each side, making a well-balanced equilateral work triangle.

U-shaped kitchens usually go into fairly good-sized rooms, but sometimes there is an effort to squeeze one into dimensions that are too tight. The base wall, or middle leg, of the U must be at least 9 feet to give the desirable 5 feet clearance in the middle after the cabinets are in.

Broken U's or L's are signs of failure in the house design. They happen when a door has been placed without allowing for the kitchen design. Kitchen design still can be good except for the basic flaw of interrupted work from cross traffic. Traffic through the kitchen always will cross two

legs of the work triangle.

As noted previously, islands and peninsulas can be used to form the work triangle, provide eating space in the kitchen, or added counter for work space.

Sometimes a peninsular eating area is nothing more than a countertop projecting from a cabinet line or a wall, with a supporting leg at the far end. These can be square, rectangular, kidney-shaped, free-form or in any shape desired. This is a simple, easy installation that, in effect, makes the dinette table a structural part of the house and relieves the homeowner of the need to buy a dinette.

Other peninsulas that also provide storage space are a bit more involved. Projecting from the cabinet line, they will consist of regular base cabinets, a counter which might also hold the sink or cooktop, and a line of wall cabinets overhead which would house the vent hood.

Both wall and base cabinets in such a peninsula can be ordered to open on either side of the peninsula, or on both sides. When they open on both sides it adds greatly to convenience, because then dishes or other items can be stored or removed from either side.

Here are a few pointers for these peninsulas.

The base cabinet at the end of the peninsula should have a kick space on the end side, as well as on the kitchen side, so a person can work at the end. Depending on the use of the peninsula, it might be necessary to have kick space on both sides of all the base cabinets.

The wall cabinet run should be shorter than the base cabinet run. This prevents head bumping and also contributes to a more open appearance to the kitchen.

When ordering wall cabinets for use in a peninsula, the buyer should specify that they are for peninsular use. The cabinet manufacturer will add extra reinforcing at the top of these cabinets — maybe. If they do not come with reinforcing, it will have to be provided by the installer.

The countertop at the end of the peninsula should have radiused corners for safety. Square corners will lead to bruised hands and hips forever.

All of these considerations apply also to islands.

If a cooktop is used in either a peninsula or an island it probably will need some sort of backsplash or other barrier to protect others from grease spatters, hot handles, and the like.

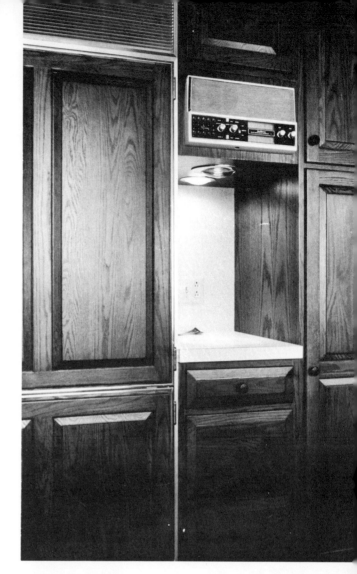

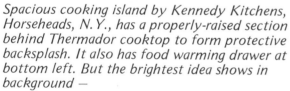

Spacious cooking island by Kennedy Kitchens, Horseheads, N.Y., has a properly-raised section behind Thermador cooktop to form protective backsplash. It also has food warming drawer at bottom left. But the brightest idea shows in background —

(above right) — This opening is the cabinet wall, beside the built-in refrigerator, has AM-FM radio-intercom at top, infra-red warming light recessed along with a matching white flood (because you can't really see by infrared) and even a convenience outlet at back.

Another bright idea in the same Kennedy Kitchen is this lowered work surface with maple block top. Kennedy studied some kitchen research at Cornell University, found that most work surfaces were too high for most women. That's a Trade-Wind built-in can opener in wall.

How to "Draw Up" the Kitchen Plan

Drawing a kitchen floorplan will seem too rudimentary for many professionals. But for the many who have never tried it, or for those going into remodeling, here are the steps.

Rule No. 1 is that you never fully trust the blueprint. It can be inches off in the final room even when followed, and often there are minor changes made between conception and execution.

So the first step is to measure the room, and measure it precisely to within 1/16 inch. Mark all of the measurements on the print or, if there is no print, make a rough sketch. Measure to door framing and to door opening, to window framing and to window opening, measure all heights including windows and framing, and measure the entire room, not just the part where cabinets or other kitchen components will go. Measure each entire wall, and make sure the figure corresponds with the sum of the parts. Where the cabinets will be, measure along the floor right next to the wall and then measure again 24 inches out from the wall. This will warn you in case the wall is bowed or the corner out of square, so you can use the smaller figure; otherwise, the cabinets won't fit. Do this for vertical measurements, too, for the same reason.

On the sketch, mark all electrical outlets and the plumbing rough-in, and give a thought to adequacy. Along a 10-foot wall over a countertop, a homeowner will want three double outlets, and there will also have to be outlets on the opposite wall and perhaps elsewhere. There should be wiring for a ceiling light as well as light fixtures to go under the wall cabinets to light the countertop, and there should be a 220 circuit for an electric range. Make sure all these are there now, because it can be too late once the kitchen is in.

If there is an owner present, discuss it. The owner might want rough-in for a dishwasher he has bought on his own, or that he will want to buy in a year or two. He might want an ice-maker in the refrigerator, and this will require installation of a 1/4-inch line for water.

Incidentally, to provide for a future dishwasher, the trick is to put a 24-inch base cabinet adjacent to the sink. It can simply be pulled out at a later date and replaced by the dishwasher.

Now take the sketch back to the office and transfer it all to 1/2-inch graph paper. The 1/2-inch to 1-foot scale is big enough for all your notations. A smaller scale would cramp your work.

Draw a floorplan to exact scale, marking in the figures and the locations of outlets and plumbing. Make dotted lines for things you must do, such as putting in new outlets. Along with the floorplan, make an exact to-scale elevation drawing of the walls with which you will be concerned.

Drawing in the kitchen plan often starts with the window because so many homeowners want the sink at the window, and this is where the plumbing rough-in will be. You will want to start with the sink, wherever it is, window or no window, because the plumbing is there and it can't move. You will have to know precisely what sink you are using so you can draw it in to scale and label it by model number.

Then draw in the dishwasher adjacent to the sink. You can work either left or right, but it is better not to have the dishwasher between the sink and the range because it could interfere with efficiency. If the dishwasher is to come later, put in a 24-inch base cabinet and mark it "Fut DW" for "future dishwasher."

Then continue around the kitchen drawing in the base cabinets, range, refrigerator, compactor if there is one, and microwave location. Mark each cabinet for size and type and drawer-swing. (For example, B18L2dr, for base cabinet, 18 inches, left door swing, 2-drawer). You might show the drawer swing as most kitchen designers do, simply by drawing in the hardware pull on one side or the other of each door.

Reminder: Your base cabinets extend 24 inches out from the wall, or four graph squares. Your wall cabinets will extend out 12 inches and can be marked either with a solid or dotted line.

When you complete your run of base cabinets, which in this case includes sink, dishwasher and probably range, be sure you come out precisely where you intended to come out. There is no way you are going to get 135 inches of cabinets into 134-1/2 inches space. You will not even get 135 inches of cabinets into 135 inches of space. You should allow an inch on a run that long. If you come up a bit short, fillers are available to extend the run, which you can fit in on either side of the sink cabinet for a good fit. If you are too close for fillers, the cabinets often have "extended stiles" that can be cut down to fit the wall. (The stile, remember, is the vertical member of the frame. An extended stile, simply, is a couple of inches wider than the cabinet so it can be trimmed.)

Follow the same procedure to draw in your wall cabinets. Their widths will match the widths of the base cabinets below them.

With the floorplan completed, you know everything will fit. The wall elevations help you check yourself on outlets, drawers available, etc. As you'll remember, you can get a base cabinet with no drawers or with one, two, three or four drawers. The elevations also will give you a good visual picture of what the kitchen will look like.

Paris Kitchens, Paris, Ontario, supplied the following artwork to show the steps in drawing a kitchen floorplan.

1. First measure the room carefully and make a rough sketch, on the spot. Then back in the office, draw it more precisely on graph paper, 1/2-inch scale, making sure all measurements are accurate to 1/16-inch. Don't rely on a blueprint for measurements.
2. Also draw a wall elevation to mark precise locations of windows, doors, electrical and plumbing. Do this for all walls that will be involved in the kitchen, and mark which wall it is.
3. In addition to measuring distances at the wall, measure total distance 24 inches out from the wall (the depth of base cabinets) to

Measure the room...

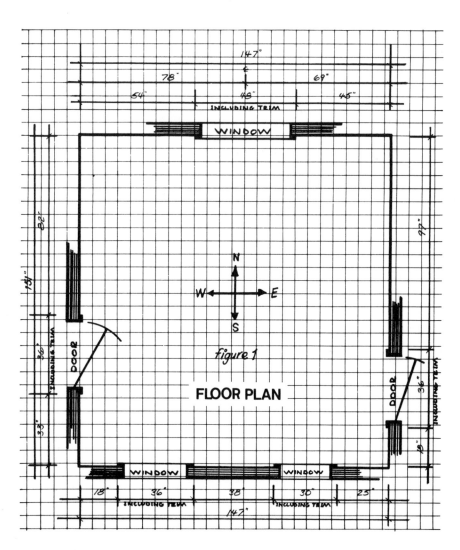

figure 1

FLOOR PLAN

make sure the wall is not out-of-square. Use the shorter measurement to be sure the cabinets and appliances will fit.

4. After designing the kitchen roughly to locate the various centers (preparation, mixing, cleanup, etc.) and the work triangle, start laying in the cabinets and identifying them, in the sequence of the block numbers. The base sink cabinet, 36 inches wide, is drawn in first, identified in the Paris catalog as "BSF36" (for Base Sink Front), and this is centered on the window. Using a subtraction method, note that the distance from window center to east wall is 69 inches; subtract half of the BSF, 18 inches; it leaves 51 inches of space to be filled. Best way to turn the corner here is with a lazy susan unit, the BLS36, which stands for Base Lazy Susan 36 inches wide along the wall. Now subtract that 36 inches from the 51 inches we had remaining and we see we need a 15-inch cabinet to fill in between sink and corner unit. The number 4 in the code B15-4 indicates a 4-drawer cabinet rather than a simple base cabinet with door and shelves. Drawers are usually needed near the sink.

Now looking to the other side, for simplicity and maximum use of the corner space we place another BLS36, and this leaves us the desirable 24 inches for a future dishwasher. We put in a 24-inch base cabinet here. Next we place the refrigerator, 36 inches wide, and subtracting the 36 inches of the BLS and the 36 inches of the refrigerator we find we need a 21-inch base cabinet to fill on the east wall. Similarly, we then take a 12-inch base cabinet to fill on the west wall, the base cabinet layout is complete. Direc-

tions of door-swings are noted here with a dot indicating the pull. NOTE ALSO that this drawing is for illustration of a method only. In practice, you would need an inch of leeway to get this full base assembly of 147 inches into 147 inches of space.

5. Going now to the wall cabinets, there is nothing to center over the sink, so we start with the right-hand corner. We have 45 inches to fill between the corner and the window trim. We start with a revolving shelf cabinet, the T2432CR. As listed in the Paris catalog, the T identifies it as a "top wall" cabinet, the 24 means 24 inches of wall space, the 32 means 32 inches high, and the CR is for "Corner, Revolving." Subtracting the 24 inches from our 45 inches of available space, we have 21 inches left, so we use a T2132. We then go to the opposite corner and fill in toward the window. Then go to the east wall and select a cabinet to match the width of the refrigerator, but only 18 inches high because of the height of the refrigerator, and subtraction tells us there are 33 inches left between the two cabinets already placed. We could match the base cabinets with a 12-inch wall cabinet over the one side of the BLS, and a 21-inch wall cabinet over the 21-inch base cabinet; this matching is something that should always be considered. But in this case we use the 33-inch wall cabinet because one larger cabinet is always cheaper than two smaller cabinets. Going then to the west wall we match the width of the range with a 30-inch wall cabinet 22 inches high (allowing extra space over the range) and then fill in with the 24-inch standard-height cabinet.

Show the exact locations...

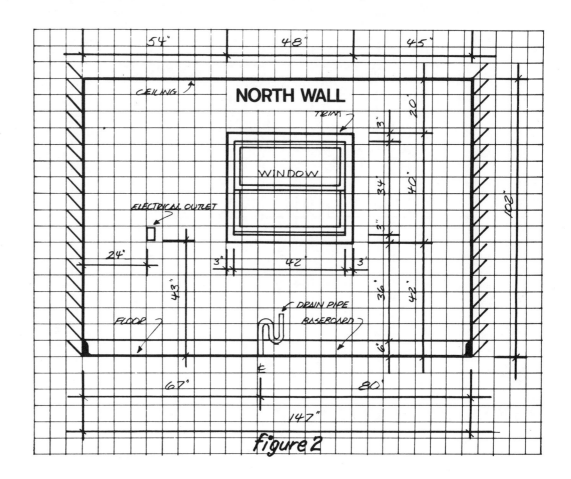

figure 2

Verify your measurements

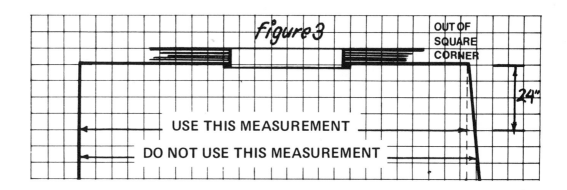

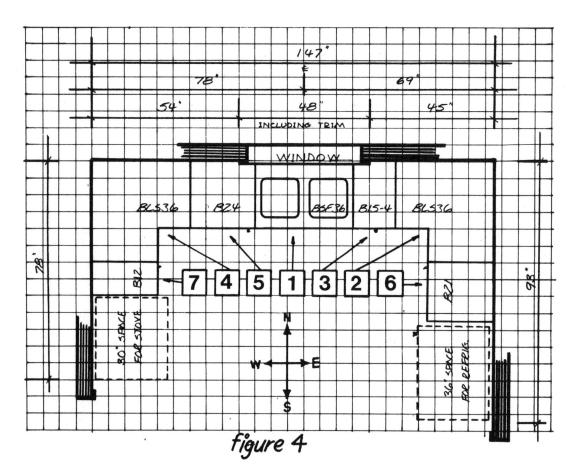

figure 4

Turning the corners

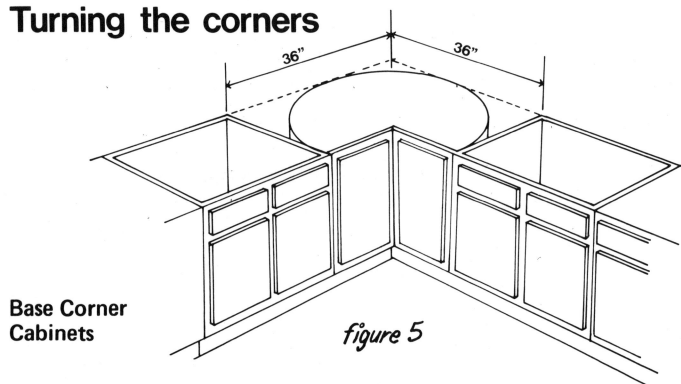

Base Corner Cabinets

figure 5

Selecting Top Wall Cabinets

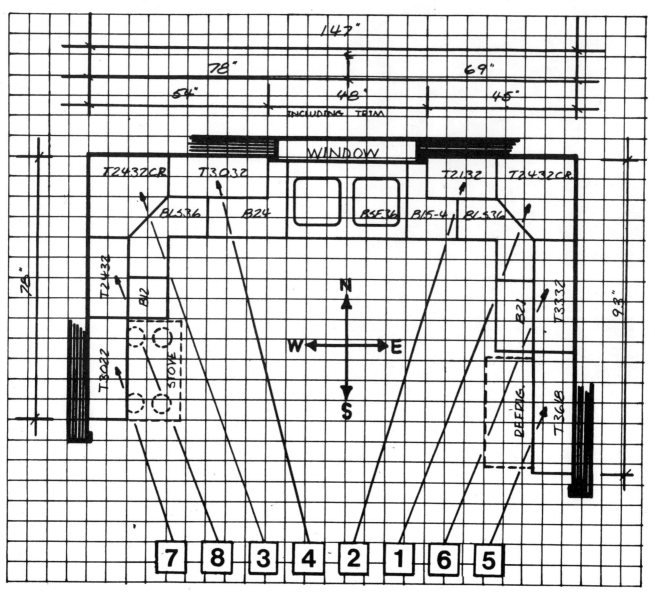

figure 6

Bisulk Kitchens, Garden City, N.Y. used Dacor artificial brick for this cooking wall with Waste-King double wall oven. Designer put the wood beam across cooking alcove to hide vent equipment and lighting, made the crisscrosses on base cabinets himself to add to ambience.

60 Successful Kitchen Floorplans

The Kitchen Design Studio of General Electric Company and Hotpoint has designed at least 25,000 kitchens for builders and architects in the last 15 years, kitchens which have been installed in hundreds of thousands of new homes.

Specifically for this book, Design Manager William J. Ketcham, CKD, selected 60 floorplans that represent good design principles well worth emulating.

All are drawn to 1/4" scale.

In some cases extended areas of the house are included because of the way the kitchen inter-relates. In one case, two different floorplans are included for the same kitchen, one in Corridor and the other in L-shape configuration, showing how variations are possible for cause. In this case, the Corridor kept all cross-traffic out of the kitchen, but the L permitted access to the bathroom from the kitchen.

In many cases the laundry area is included in the floorplan. The laundry is never recommended in the kitchen, but it often is wanted near the kitchen, with access.

Floorplan abbreviations: REFR — refrigerator; DW — dishwasher; RA — range; COMP — trash compactor; W — clothes washer and D — dryer.

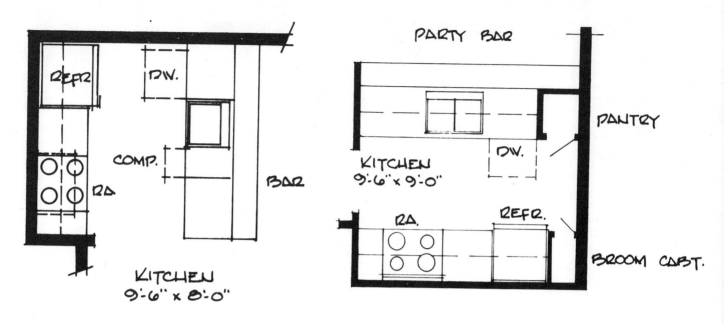

REFR.

D.W.

COMP.

RA.

BAR

KITCHEN
9'-6" x 8'-0"

1.

PARTY BAR

KITCHEN
9'-6" x 9'-0"

D.W.

PANTRY

RA.

REFR.

BROOM CABT.

2.

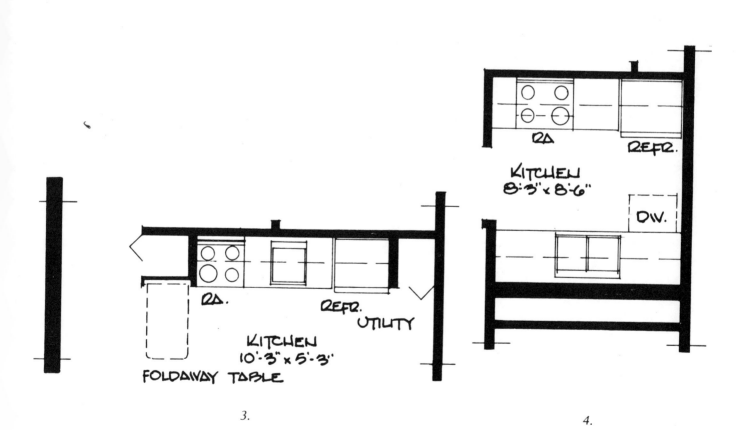

RA.

REFR.

UTILITY

KITCHEN
10'-3" x 5'-3"

FOLDAWAY TABLE

3.

KITCHEN
8'-3" x 8'-6"

RA.

REFR.

D.W.

4.

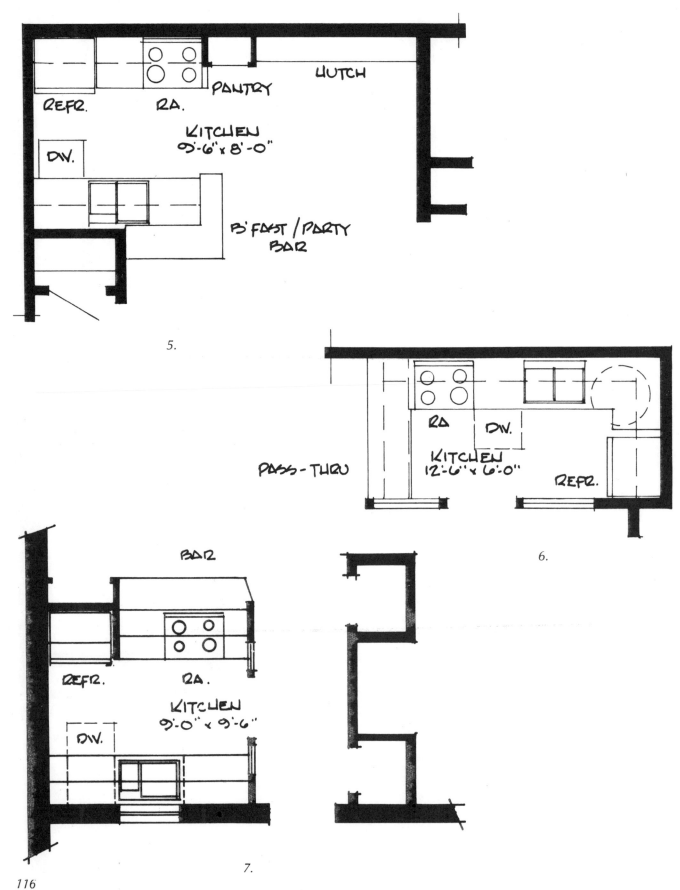

REFR.   RA.   PANTRY   HUTCH

KITCHEN
9'-6" x 8'-0"

DW.

B'FAST / PARTY
BAR

5.

PASS-THRU

RA.   DW.

KITCHEN
12'-6" x 6'-0"

REFR.

6.

BAR

REFR.   RA.

KITCHEN
9'-0" x 9'-6"

DW.

7.

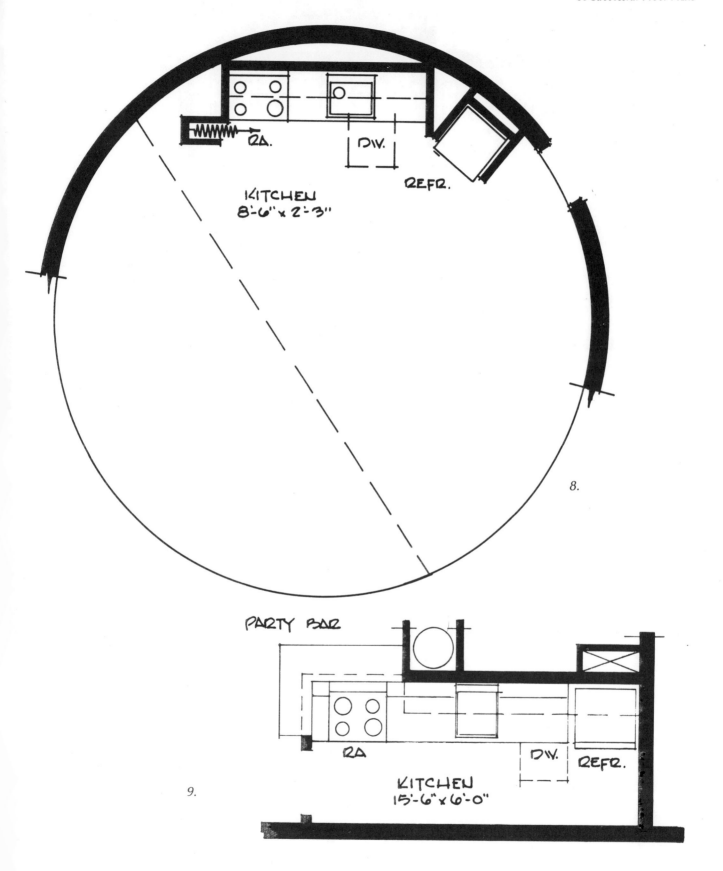

KITCHEN
8'-6" x 2'-3"

RA.

DW.

REFR.

8.

PARTY BAR

RA

DW.

REFR.

9.

KITCHEN
15'-6" x 6'-0"

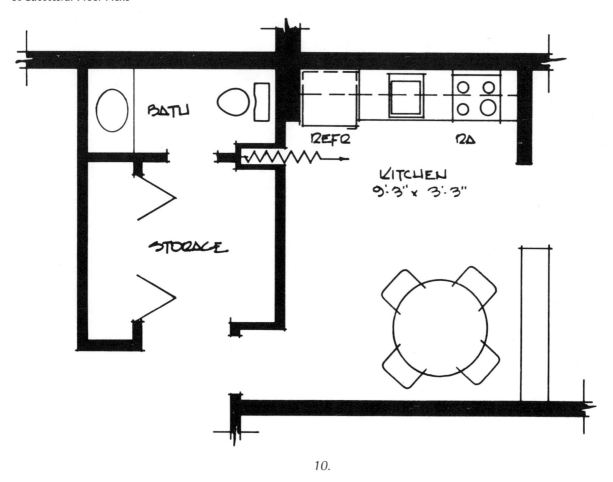

BATH

STORAGE

REFR

RA

KITCHEN
9'-3" x 3'-3"

10.

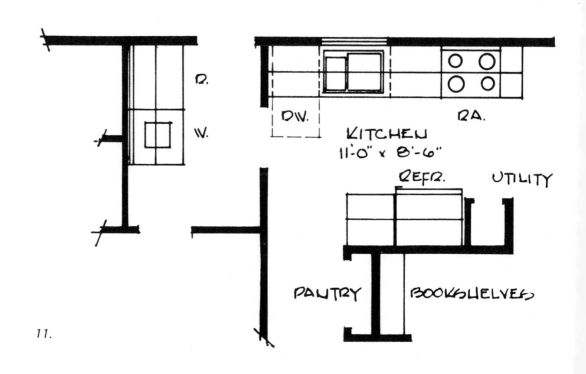

R.

W.

DW.

RA.

KITCHEN
11'-0" x 8'-6"

REFR.

UTILITY

PANTRY

BOOKSHELVES

11.

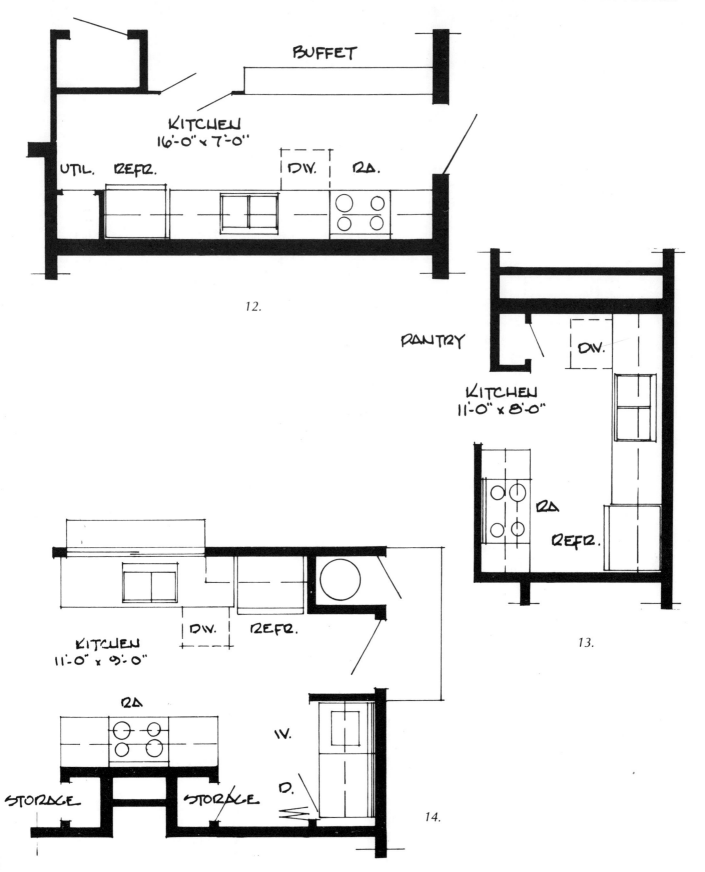

BUFFET

KITCHEN
16'-0" x 7'-0"

UTIL.   REFR.   DW.   RA.

12.

PANTRY

DW.

KITCHEN
11'-0" x 8'-0"

RA

REFR.

KITCHEN
11'-0" x 9'-0"

DW.   REFR.

RA

13.

W.

D.

STORAGE   STORAGE

14.

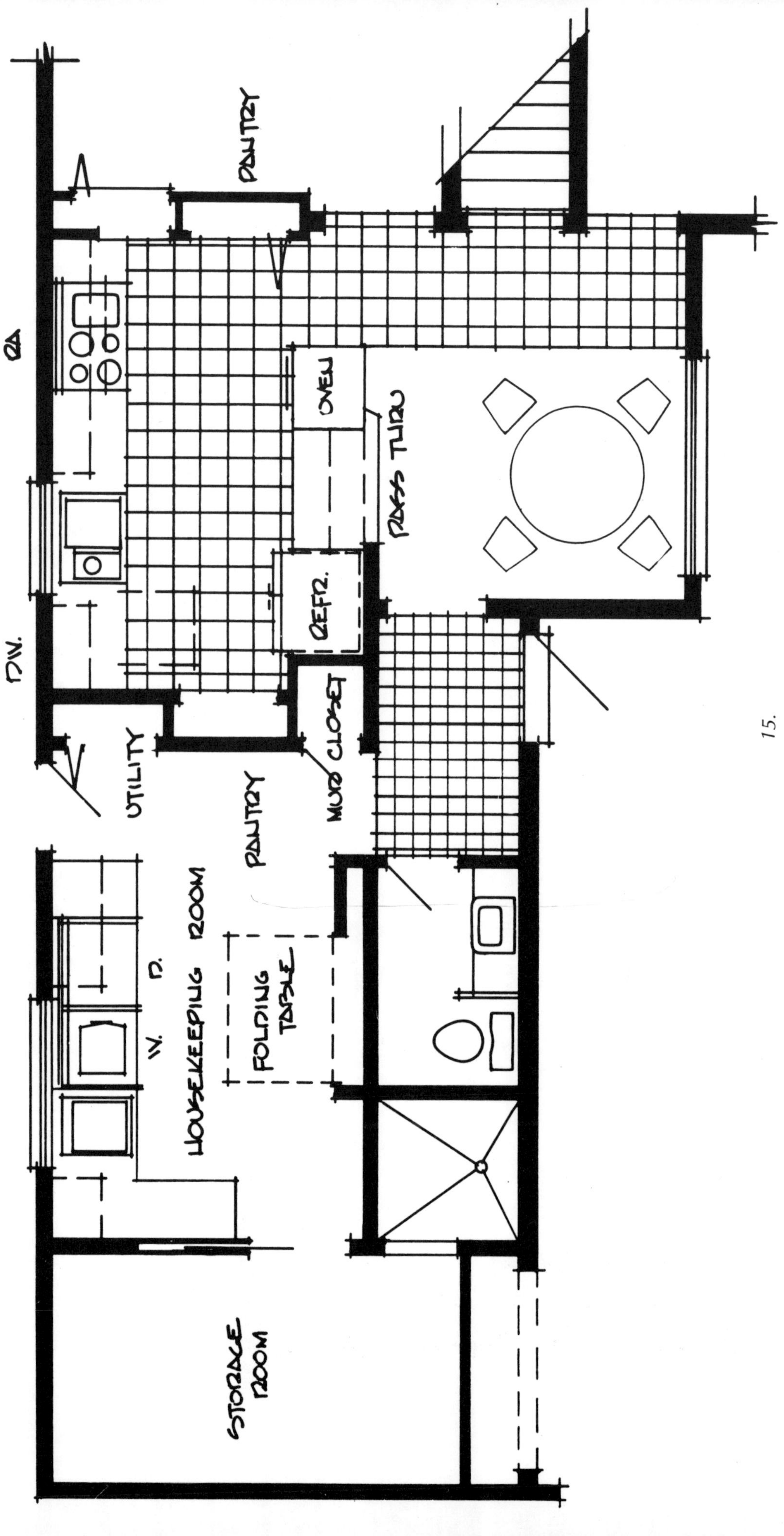

KITCHEN
12'-6" x 9'-0"

PANTRY

OVEN

PASS THRU

REFR.

DW.

UTILITY

PANTRY

MUD CLOSET

HOUSEKEEPING ROOM

W. D.

FOLDING TABLE

STORAGE ROOM

15.

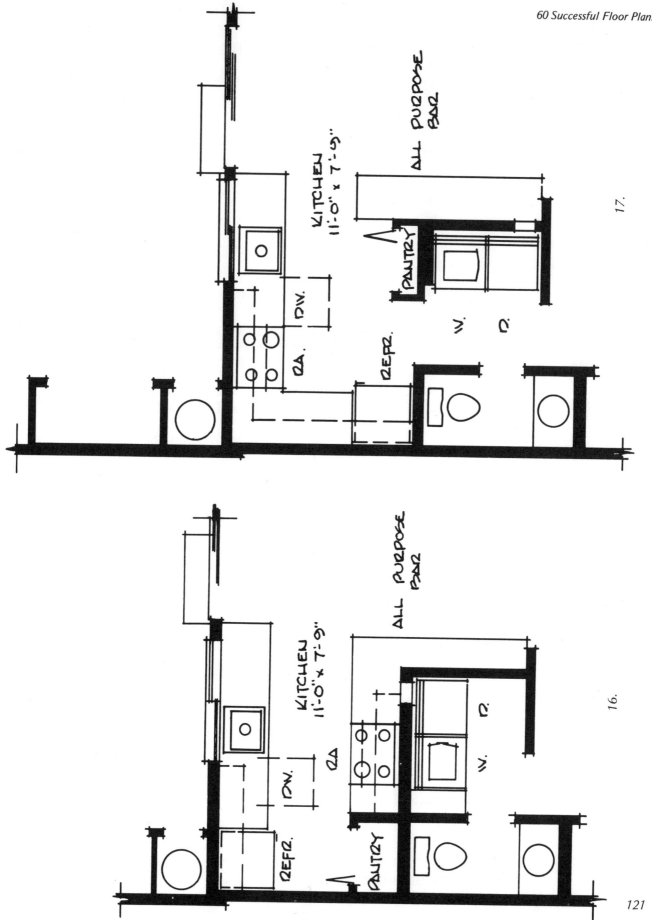

KITCHEN 11'-0" x 7'-9"

ALL PURPOSE RM

PANTRY

REFR.

DW.

17.

KITCHEN 11'-0" x 7'-9"

ALL PURPOSE RM

REFR.

DW.

PANTRY

16.

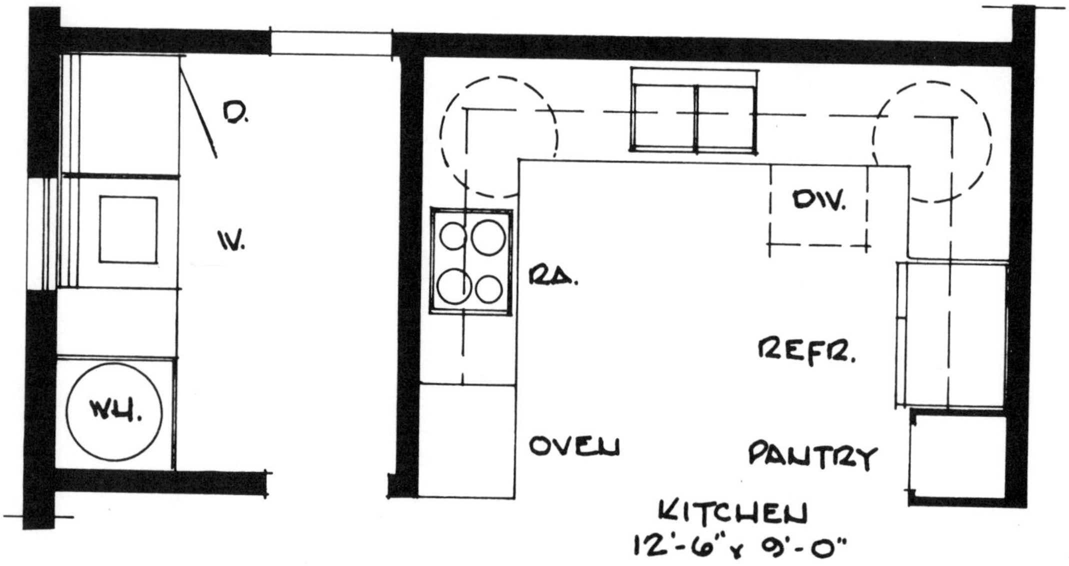

D.

W.

W.H.

RA.

DIV.

REFR.

OVEN

PANTRY

KITCHEN
12'-6" x 9'-0"

18.

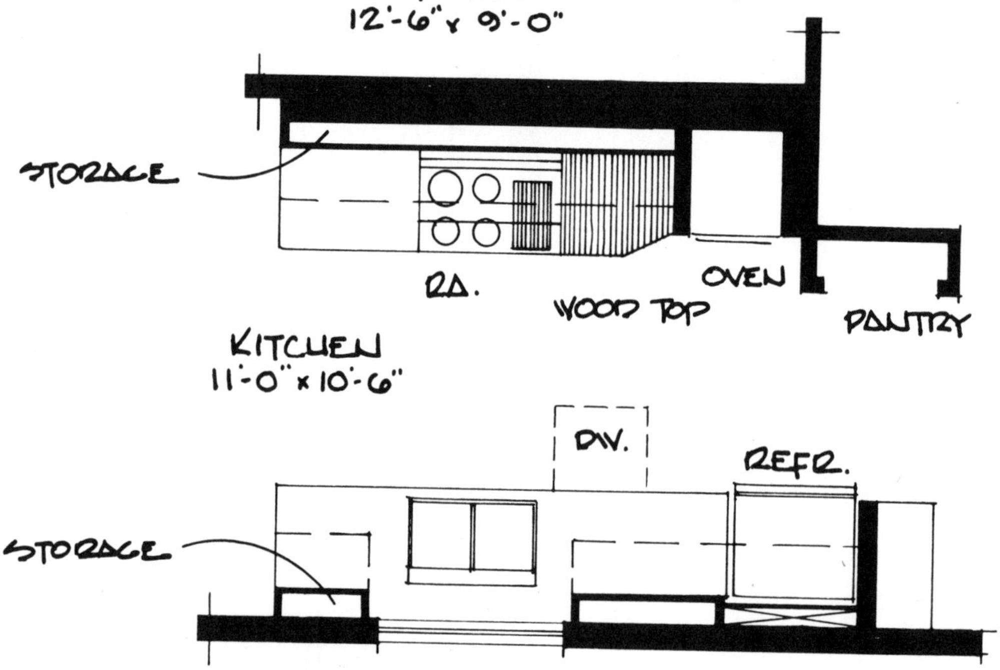

STORAGE

RA.

WOOD TOP

OVEN

PANTRY

KITCHEN
11'-0" x 10'-6"

DIV.

REFR.

STORAGE

19.

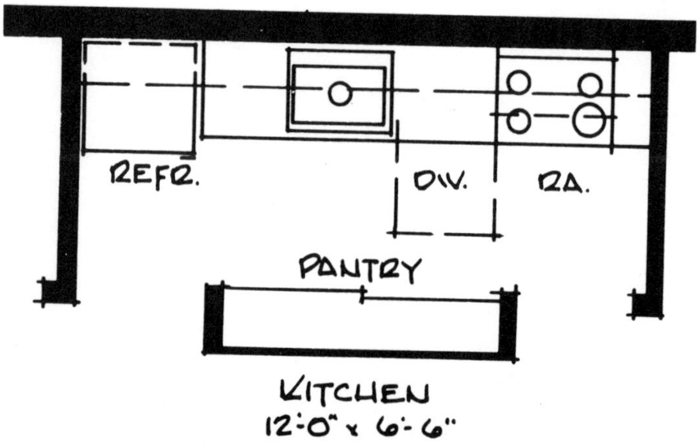

REFR.

DIV.

RA.

PANTRY

KITCHEN
12'-0" x 6'-6"

20.

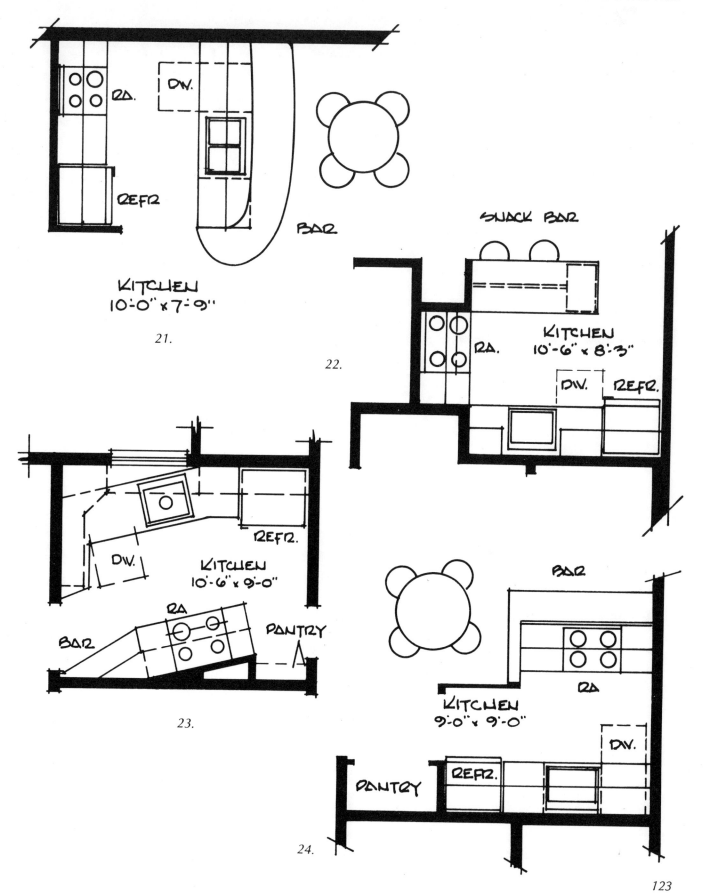

KITCHEN
10'-0" x 7'-9"

21.

SNACK BAR

KITCHEN
10'-6" x 8'-3"

DW. REFR.

22.

BAR

KITCHEN
10'-6" x 9'-0"

RA PANTRY

BAR

23.

BAR

KITCHEN
9'-0" x 9'-0"

RA

PANTRY REFR. DW.

24.

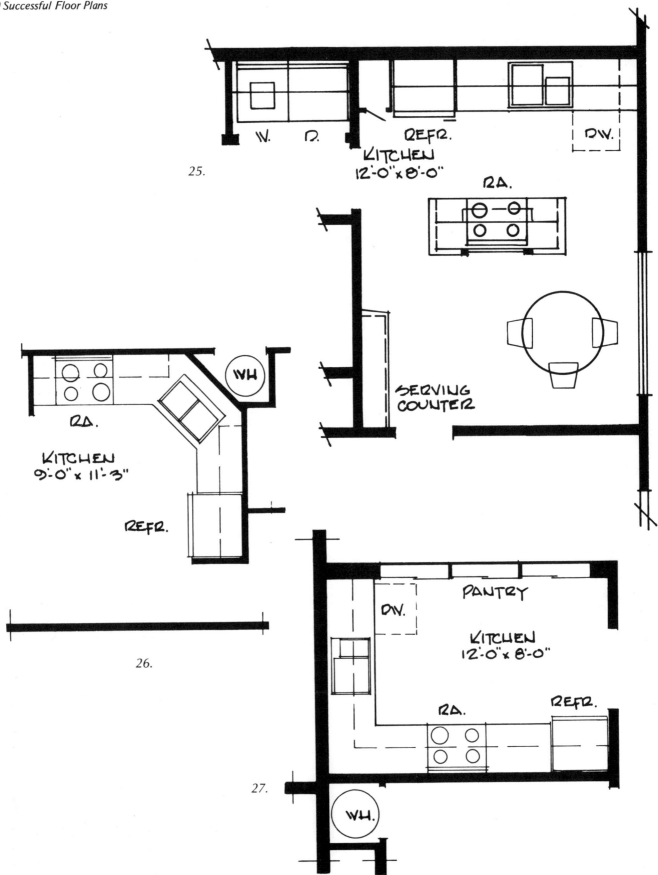

W. D. REFR. DW.

25.

KITCHEN
12'-0" x 8'-0"

RA.

SERVING
COUNTER

WH

RA.

KITCHEN
9'-0" x 11'-3"

REFR.

26.

PANTRY

DW.

KITCHEN
12'-0" x 8'-0"

RA. REFR.

27.

WH.

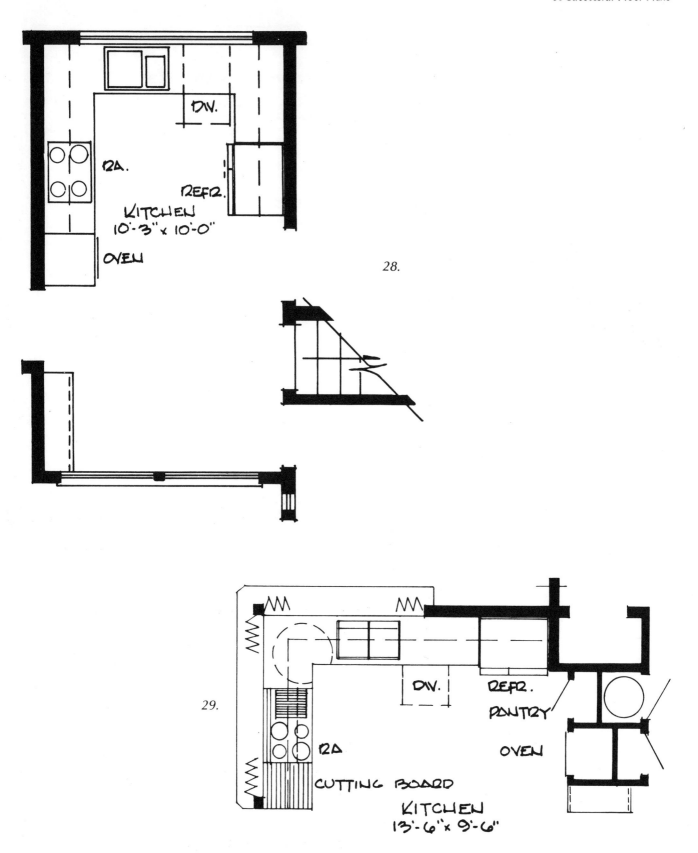

RA.

DW.

REFR.

KITCHEN
10'-3" x 10'-0"

OVEN

28.

29.

DW.

REFR.

PANTRY

OVEN

RA

CUTTING BOARD

KITCHEN
13'-6" x 9'-6"

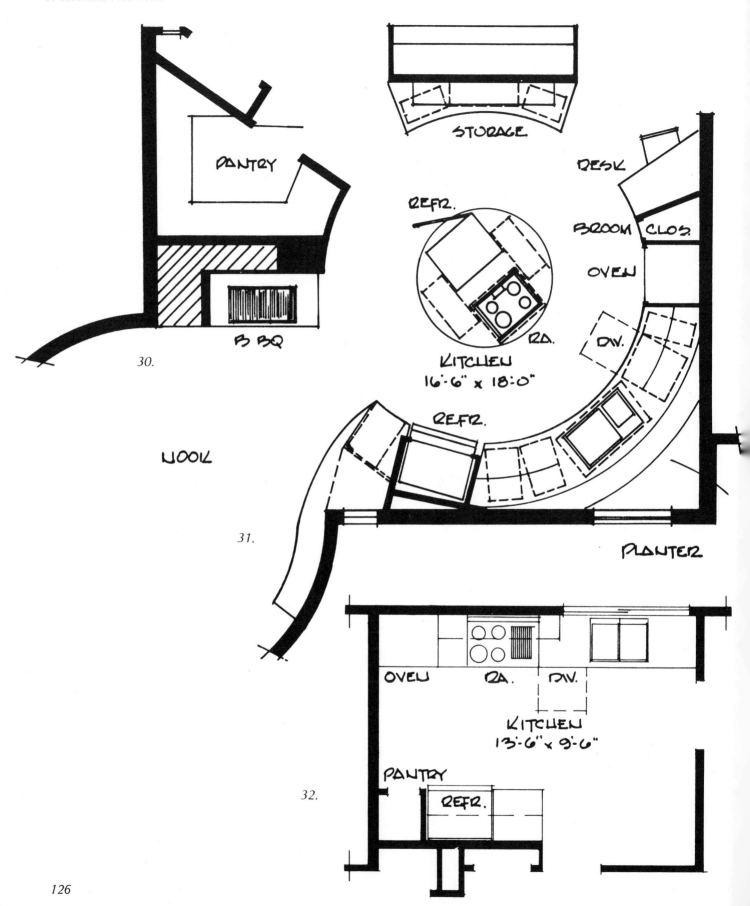

PANTRY

BBQ

30.

STORAGE

REFR.

KITCHEN
16'-6" x 18'-0"

RA.

DESK

BROOM CLOS.

OVEN

DW.

NOOK

REFR.

31.

PLANTER

OVEN

RA.

DW.

KITCHEN
13'-6" x 9'-6"

PANTRY

REFR.

32.

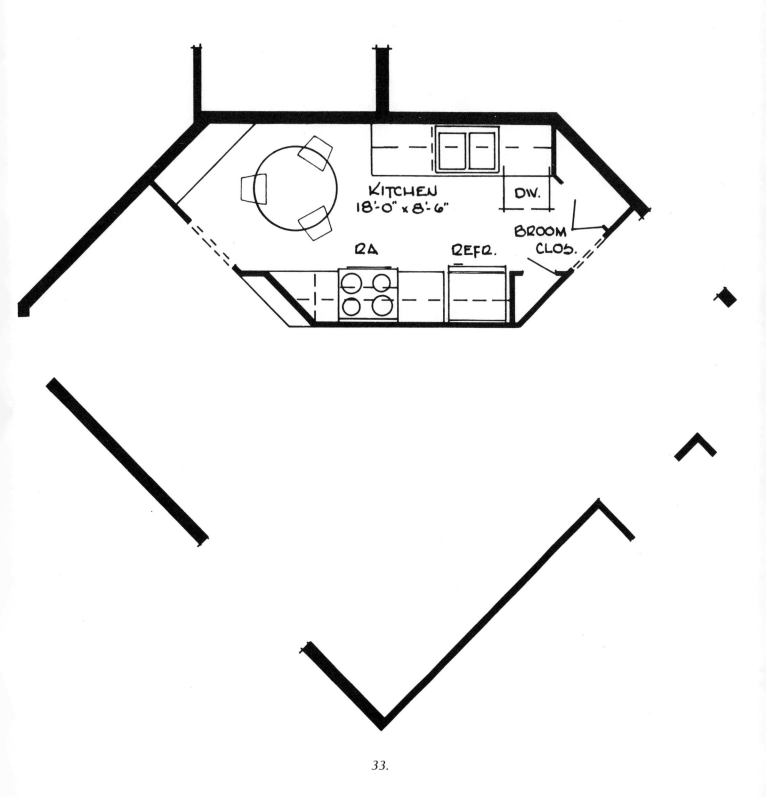

KITCHEN
18'-0" x 8'-6"

DW.

BROOM
CLOS.

RA

REFR.

33.

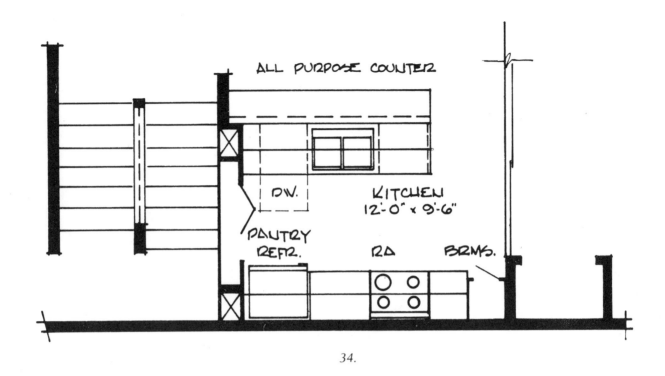

ALL PURPOSE COUNTER

DW.

KITCHEN
12'-0" x 9'-6"

PANTRY
REFR.

RA

BRMS.

34.

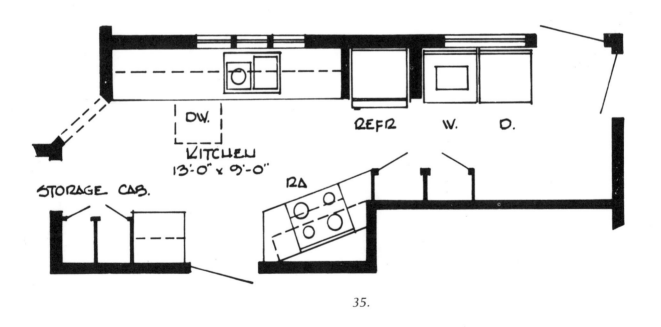

DW.

KITCHEN
13'-0" x 9'-0"

REFR

W.

D.

STORAGE CAB.

RA

35.

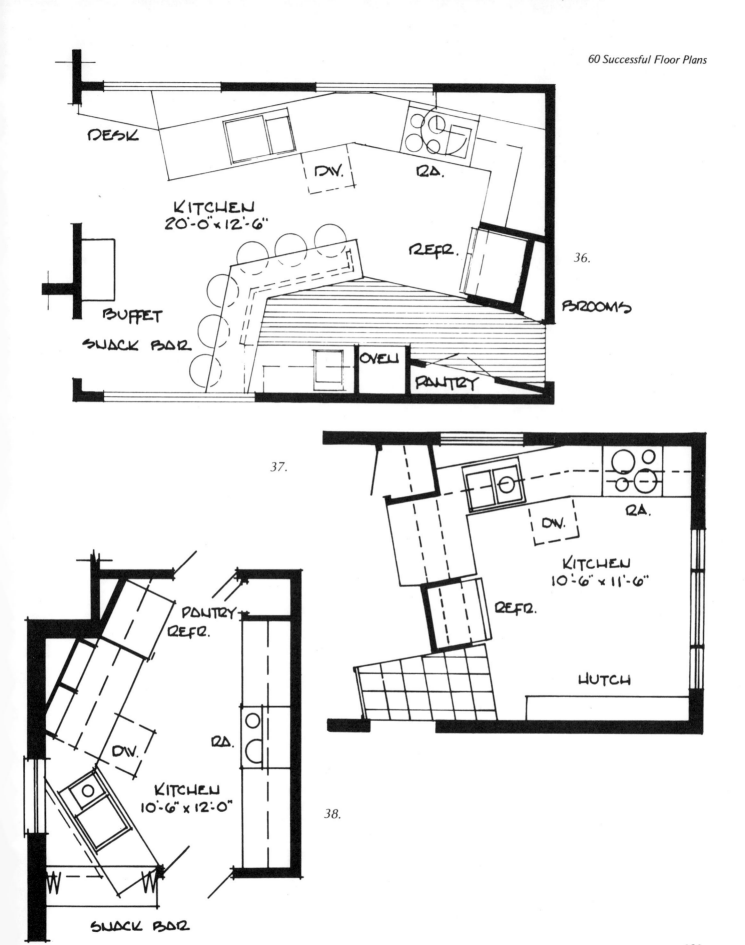

DESK

KITCHEN
20'-0" x 12'-6"

DW.

RA.

REFR.

BROOMS

36.

BUFFET
SNACK BAR

OVEN

PANTRY

37.

PANTRY
REFR.

DW.

KITCHEN
10'-6" x 12'-0"

RA.

SNACK BAR

38.

DW.

RA.

KITCHEN
10'-6" x 11'-6"

REFR.

HUTCH

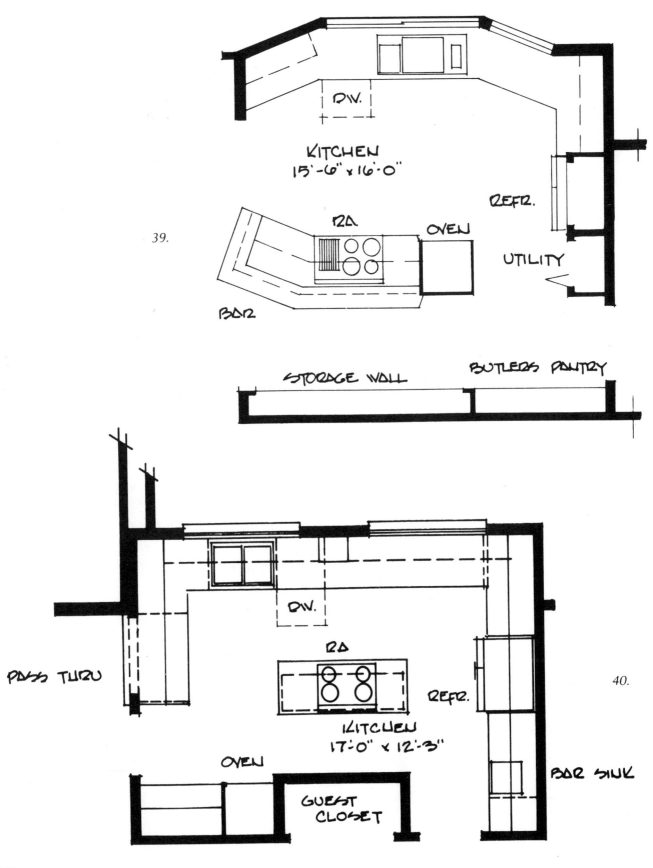

KITCHEN
15'-6" x 16'-0"

D.W.

RA

OVEN

REFR.

UTILITY

39.

BAR

STORAGE WALL

BUTLERS PANTRY

PASS THRU

D.W.

RA

REFR.

KITCHEN
17'-0" x 12'-3"

OVEN

GUEST CLOSET

BAR SINK

40.

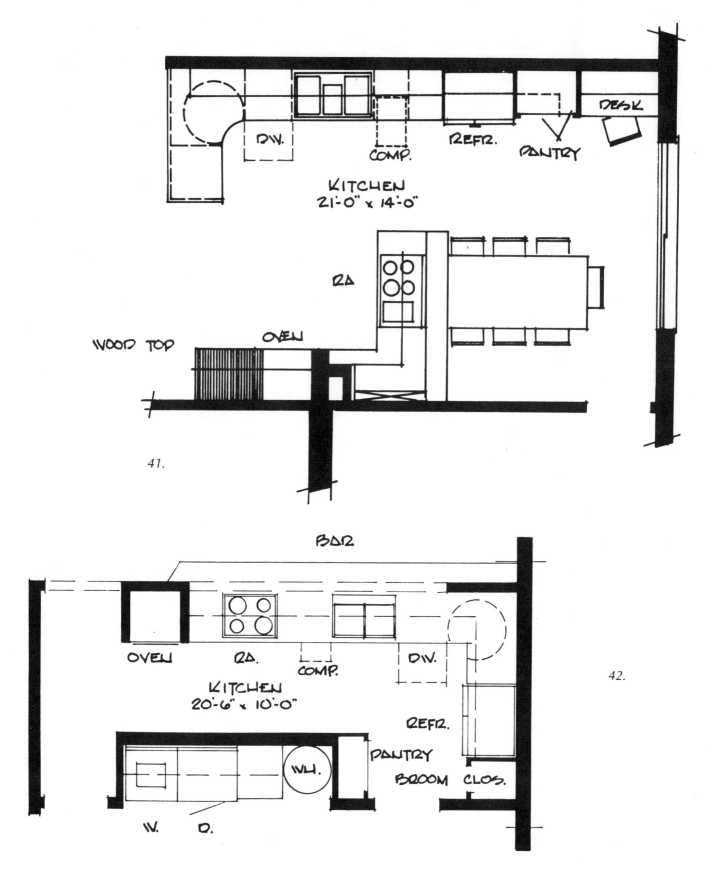

KITCHEN
21'-0" x 14'-0"

D.W.

COMP.

REFR.

PANTRY

DESK

RA

WOOD TOP

OVEN

41.

BAR

OVEN

RA.

COMP.

D.W.

42.

KITCHEN
20'-6" x 10'-0"

REFR.

PANTRY

BROOM CLOS.

W.H.

W.   D.

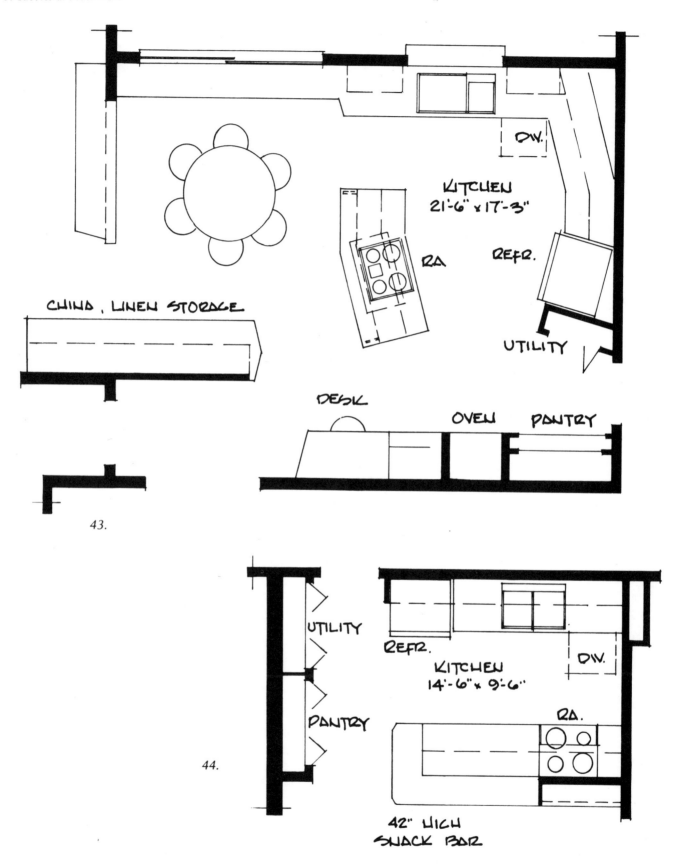

CHINA, LINEN STORAGE

KITCHEN
21'-6" x 17'-3"

RA

REFR.

D.W.

UTILITY

DESK

OVEN

PANTRY

43.

UTILITY

PANTRY

REFR.

KITCHEN
14'-6" x 9'-6"

D.W.

RA.

44.

42" HIGH
SNACK BAR

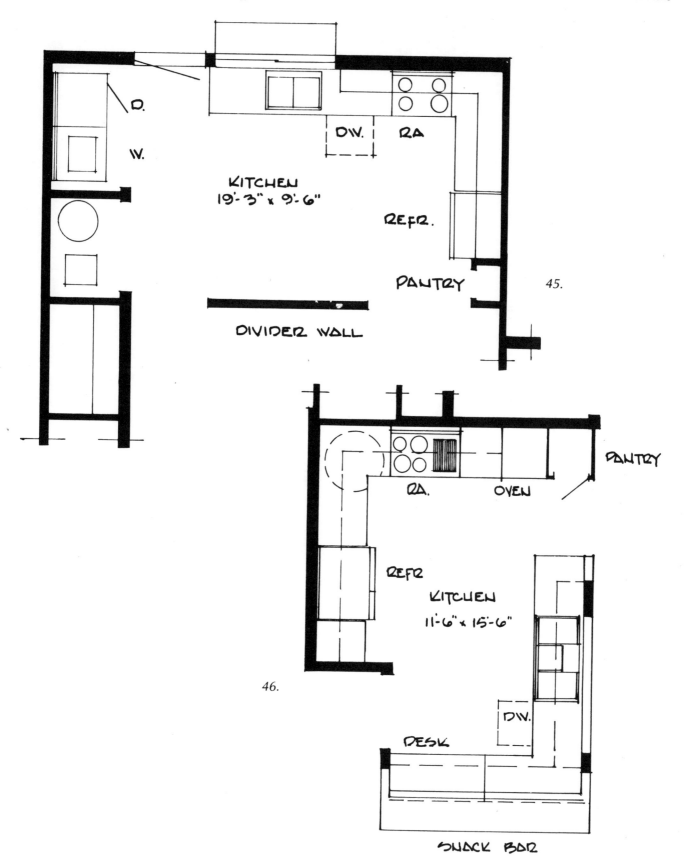

D.

W.

KITCHEN
19'-3" x 9'-6"

DW.

RA

REFR.

PANTRY

45.

DIVIDER WALL

PANTRY

RA.

OVEN

REFR

KITCHEN
11'-6" x 15'-6"

46.

DW.

DESK

SNACK BAR

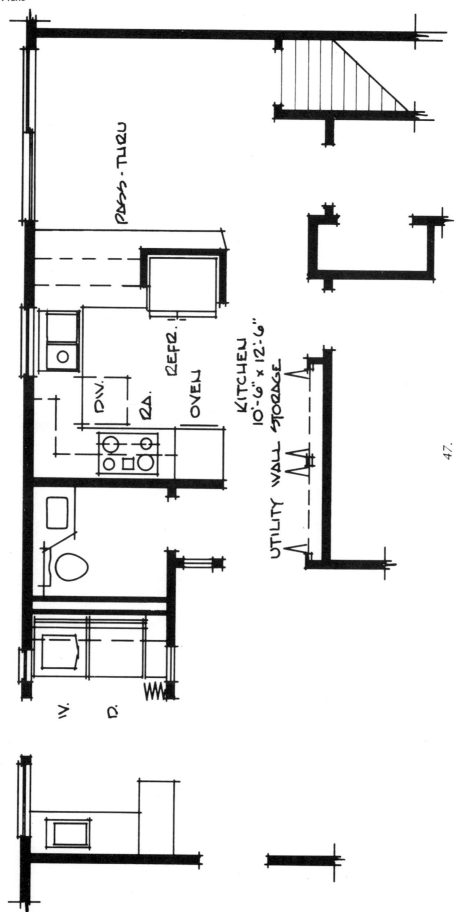

PASS-TRU

REFR.

DW.

RA.

OVEN

KITCHEN
10'-6" x 12'-6"

UTILITY WALL STORAGE

W.

D.

47.

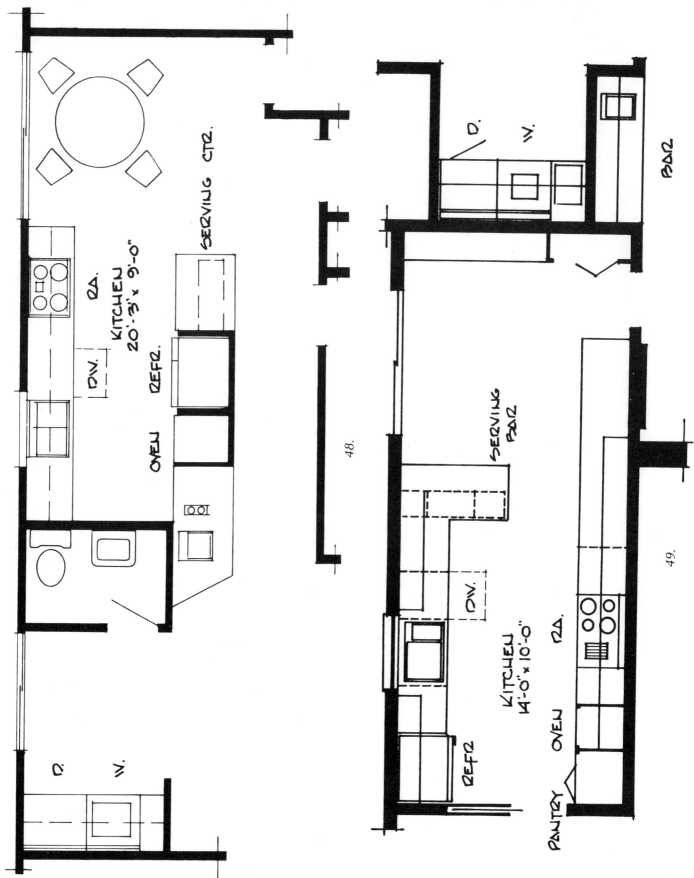

KITCHEN 20'-3" x 9'-0"

SERVING CTR.

OVEN

REFR.

DW.

RA.

D.

W.

48.

SERVING BAR

KITCHEN 14'-0" x 10'-0"

DW.

REFR.

D.

W.

BAR

49.

KITCHEN

PANTRY

OVEN

RA.

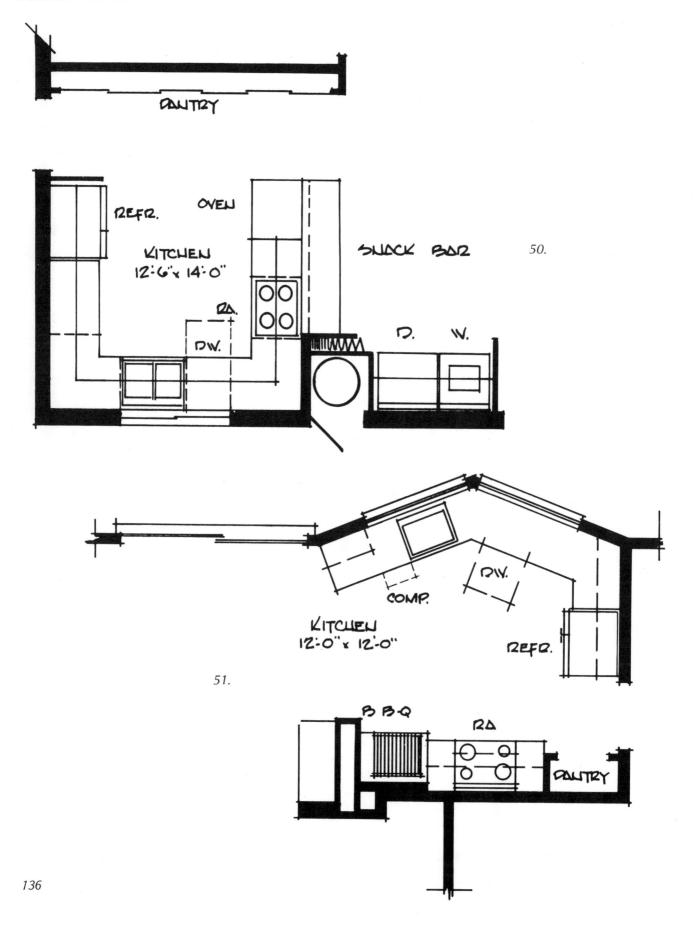

PANTRY

REFR.

OVEN

KITCHEN
12'-6" x 14'-0"

SNACK BAR

50.

RA.

DW.

D.   W.

COMP.

DW.

KITCHEN
12'-0" x 12'-0"

REFR.

51.

BBQ

RA

PANTRY

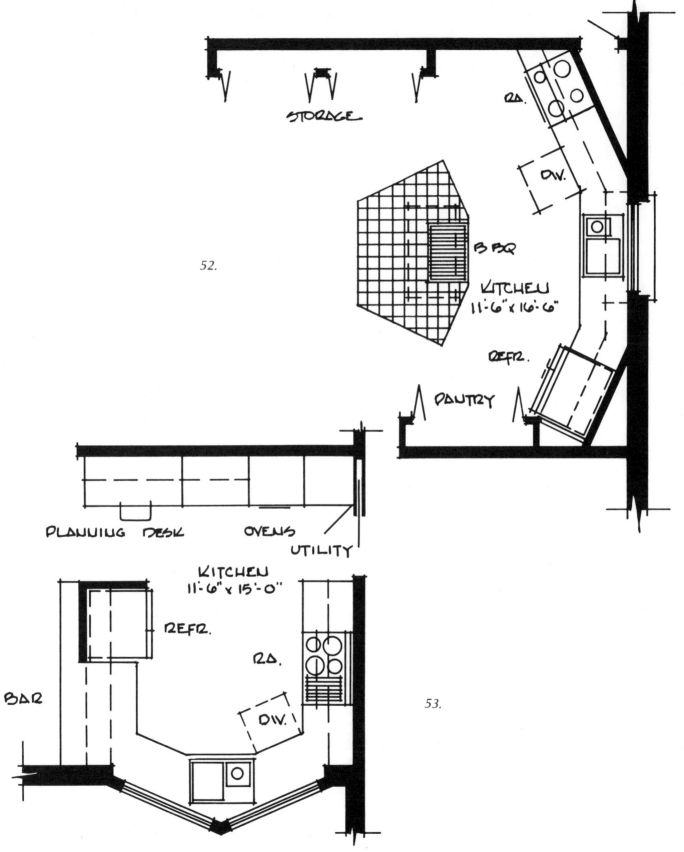

STORAGE

52.

BBQ

R.

DV.

KITCHEN
11'-6" x 16'-6"

REFR.

PANTRY

PLANNING DESK   OVENS

UTILITY

KITCHEN
11'-6" x 15'-0"

REFR.

R.

BAR

DV.

53.

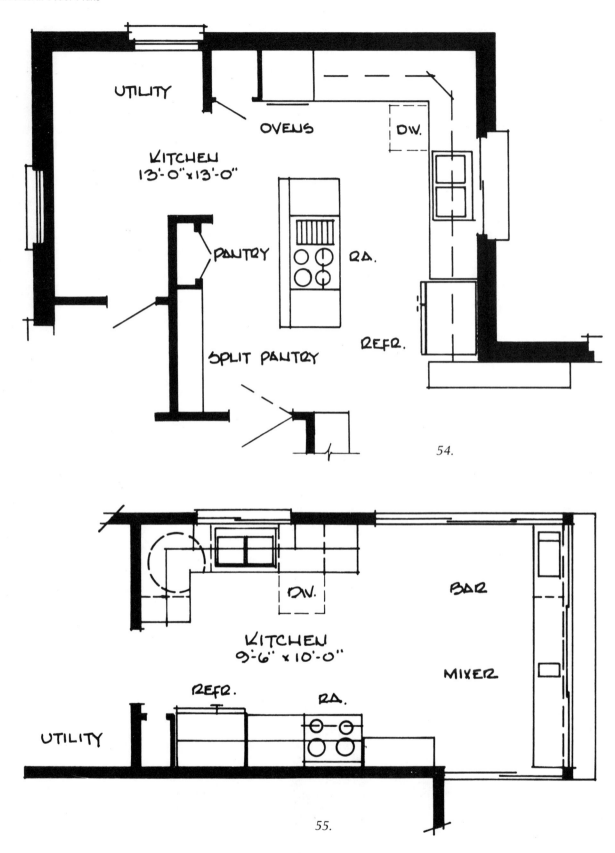

UTILITY

OVENS

KITCHEN
13'-0" x 13'-0"

DW.

PANTRY

RA.

SPLIT PANTRY

REFR.

54.

DW.

KITCHEN
9'-6" x 10'-0"

BAR

MIXER

REFR.

RA.

UTILITY

55.

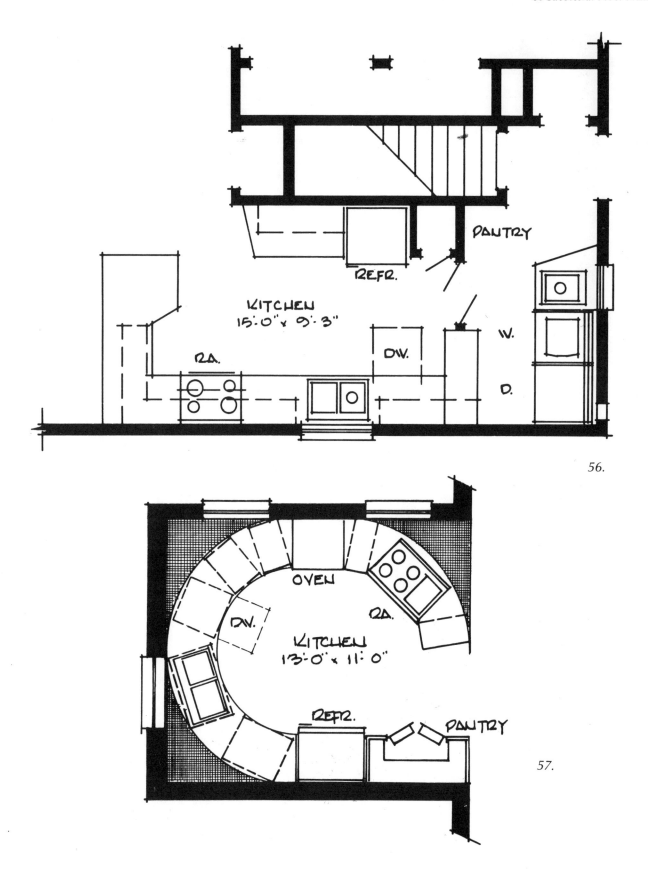

KITCHEN
15'·0" x 9'·3"

PANTRY

REFR.

RA.

DW.

W.

D.

56.

OVEN

DW.

RA.

KITCHEN
13'·0" x 11'·0"

REFR.

PANTRY

57.

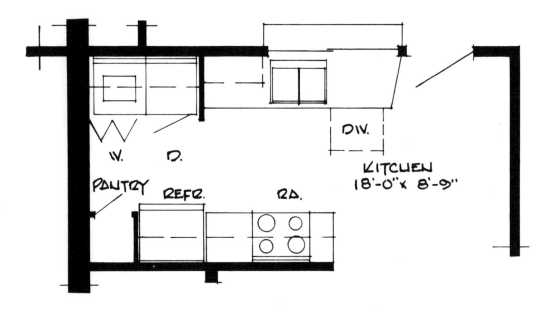

58.

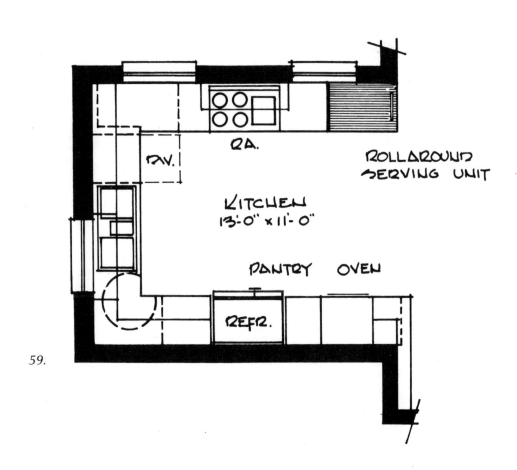

59.

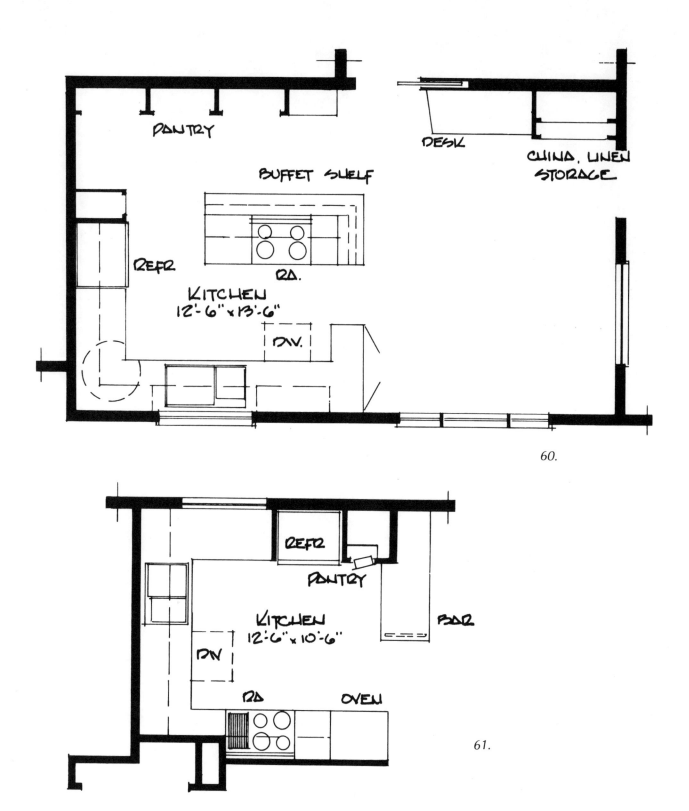

PANTRY

DESK

CHINA, LINEN STORAGE

BUFFET SHELF

REFR

RA.

KITCHEN
12'-6" x 13'-6"

DV.

60.

REFR

PANTRY

KITCHEN
12'-6" x 10'-6"

BAR

DV

RA

OVEN

61.

Quaker Maid's Clarion cabinets are used in this spacious kitchen which includes even a fireplace. Notice the large wood-framed ventilating hood which serves cooking island that has both a cooktop and a barbecue grill.

A built-in Sub-Zero refrigerator was used in this kitchen, and decorator panels matching the cabinets were used on both refrigerator and KitchenAid dishwasher to integrate the design.

Both countertop and work center extension feature tile for easy cleaning in this design by Kitchens Unlimited.

Yes, there are round kitchens. This unusual one has solid maple countertops and a space-saving drop-in range. Open shelving demands extra neatness from the housewife. Floor covering here is Armstrong's Carriage Park cushioned vinyl.

This is a real wrap-around kitchen, but the island cooking center keeps the work triangle tight and the eating counter in the foreground is great for entertaining. Cabinets are Kemper's Cortina, an oak line.

U-shaped kitchen designed by Howard Sersen of Reynolds Enterprises, River Grove, Ill., has wood beams to frame the chandelier. Countertop is angled at corner to avoid constricting the entrance, and corners are radiused to prevent hip bruises.

House & Garden magazine's 1972 "Super Family Room Kitchen" has a complete wall of equipment that disappears behind folding doors. The wall includes double wall oven, dishwasher, sink and refrigerator (all showing) plus incinerator, heater and laundry.

9

Lighting in the Kitchen

As a last resort, one can go to the statistics of the National Safety Council to underscore the need for good lighting in the kitchen. According to the NSC the kitchen is the most dangerous room in the home, accounting for 1,150,000 accidents per year, 26 percent of all falls and burns in the home, and 12 percent of all home fatalities.

All of these accidents are chiefly the results of poor illumination, according to the council.

But who needs last resorts? Lighting has a lot more going for it than the threat of accident.

It's useful, enabling us to see quickly and easily.

It can contribute to the beauty and individuality of the kitchen and the entire home. It even can be the salient feature of overall decor, if one wants to use it that creatively.

Unfortunately, the single ceiling fixture in the kitchen still is too much with us. It dates back to past decades when putting more light in the kitchen could be accomplished only by putting in a bigger bulb and hoping the fuse wouldn't blow.

It still probably is the most common way to light a kitchen, although modified now by a somewhat more modern fixture with three or four smaller bulbs and a much more efficient diffusing shield, or shade.

This is adequate, if bright enough, but adequacy does not add the charm that sells homes or makes an efficient kitchen.

This chapter will tell specifically how much light to use and where to put it, but first, the elementary facts of light.

In the planning stage and in choosing products, there are three basic terms that need definition.

The *candela* is the unit of luminous intensity of a light source in a specific direction. While its precise definition may be more than anyone really wants to know, for those interested it is 1/60 of the intensity of a square centimeter of a black body radiator operated at the freezing point of platinum, which is 2047 degrees Kelvin.

A *lumen* is the unit for measuring the light-producing power of a light source, and lamps are usually rated by their total lumen output. A lumen is the rate at which light falls in a one-square-foot area surface from a source which has an intensity of one candela. The number of lumens per watt indicates the efficiency of the light source.

A *footlambert* is a unit for measuring the brightness of light emitted or reflected from a surface directly into the eye at the rate of one lumen per square foot of area as viewed from any direction.

Light in the kitchen, as in other rooms of the house, usually is expressed in terms of watts. This is sufficient only when related to distance from light source to use area, transmittance through whatever shades are used, reflectance from all kitchen surfaces (which can make a tremendous difference in lighting efficiency) and absorptance, which is the amount of light lost by being absorbed by dark surfaces.

All of those factors can be calculated but, practically speaking, common sense can be relied on to make sure there is enough light — if it is educated common sense. The common sense of an architect will be much more reliable than the common sense of a home owner who seldom appreciates such technicalities as absorption or reflection factors.

The ultimate proof of lighting efficiency is measurement of the lumens in the various areas of the kitchen. They can be measured by using a General Electric light meter available from any photographic store or from the GE Large Lamp Department, Nela Park, Cleveland. (There are many brands of light meters, but many of them do not read in lumens, hence cannot be used for this purpose.)

Nela Park, incidentally, is a virtual university of lighting knowledge and techniques. Short courses are available there and many booklets are available, notably *Residential Structural Lighting* and *Light Measurement and Control.*

There are three sources of light to be considered in kitchen design:

1. *Natural daylight,* available through
   a. Windows, bright and cheerful in the morning with east exposure, miserable in late afternoon if exposure is west. No factor at night.
   b. Skylights, available in transparent or translucent plastics and a great sales point.
2. *Incandescent light,* from bulbs available in various shapes and sizes ranging from small night lights up to 300 watts. This light is produced by heating any material, usually metal, to a temperature at which it glows. Usually bulbs have a tungsten filament in a vacuum or mixture of argon and nitrogen.
   a. Bulbs can be clear or frosted, or colored to give a warmer light.
   b. Special types have reflector surfaces so they can be directed upward for indirect lighting, or downward for spot or flood-lighting, broad or narrow beam.
3. *Fluorescent light,* glass coated on the inside with fluorescent powder, filled with vaporized mercury and argon and sealed with two cathodes. Electric current activates the gas which produces invisible ultraviolet rays which causes the powder coating to fluoresce, producing visible light.
   a. All bulbs are tubular, but they might be straight or circular.
   b. Straight tubes vary generally from 9 to 60

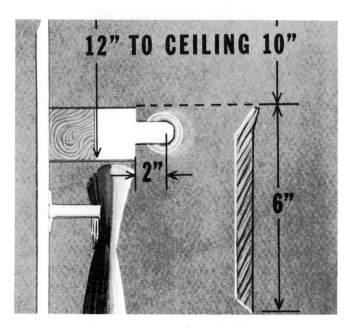

Structural lighting offers good solutions for the kitchen as well as for other rooms in the house. This drawing shows recommendations for a valance lighting installation. Faceboards should be not less than 6", not more than 10". Inside should always be painted flat white.

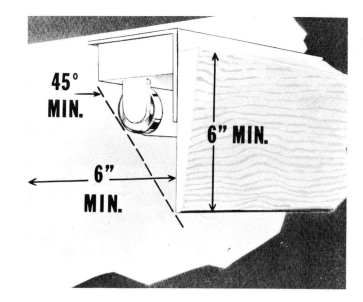

In cornice construction, there should be 2" to 3" between center of fluorescent tube and surface to be lighted. Faceboard should be painted flat white on inside, and channel should be as close to faceboard as possible.

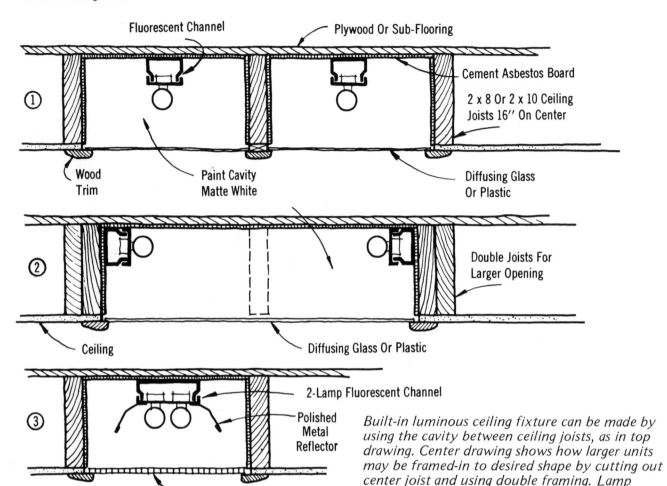

① Fluorescent Channel — Plywood Or Sub-Flooring — Cement Asbestos Board — 2 x 8 Or 2 x 10 Ceiling Joists 16″ On Center — Diffusing Glass Or Plastic — Wood Trim — Paint Cavity Matte White

② Double Joists For Larger Opening — Ceiling — Diffusing Glass Or Plastic

③ 2-Lamp Fluorescent Channel — Polished Metal Reflector — Louvers

Built-in luminous ceiling fixture can be made by using the cavity between ceiling joists, as in top drawing. Center drawing shows how larger units may be framed-in to desired shape by cutting out center joist and using double framing. Lamp arrangement shown is for decorative, non-uniform effect. Where more light is desired, two lamps with reflectors can be used, using louver as bottom shield instead of diffusing plastic.

inches and 6 to 100 watts. Length of the tube is a factor in the wattage.

c. Color choices are all shades of white including Daylight, which emphasizes blues and greens; White, emphasizing yellows and yellow greens; Standard Cool White and Standard Warm White, lacking in reds; Deluxe Cool White and Deluxe Warm White, with some reds; Soft White, good for pinks and tans.

d. Deluxe Warm White is generally most satisfactory.

e. A newer option is the fluorescent "grow-light" tube commonly sold to help plants grow. Actually, any light helps plants grow, but the color balance particularly of

the Duro-Test Optima is excellent for kitchens with a lot of reds or other warm colors.

Incandescent and fluorescent bulbs both have their advantages, and that means it is a good idea to use a mixture of both in the kitchen.

Advantages of incandescence are:

1) Fixtures and bulbs are less costly.
2) Light is warmer and generally more acceptable because we are accustomed to it.
3) Textures and forms usually are more attractive because the light comes from a relatively small source.
4) The light is instant-on.
5) There is no flicker or hum, as is often the

case with fluorescence, and less chance of interference with radio or television.

Advantages for fluorescent tubes include:

1) Much more efficient light production, about 250 percent more than incandescence for the current used.
2) Bulbs last about seven times longer than incandescent bulbs.
3) Large light source produces much less glare and spreads the light more.
4) Almost no heat is produced, whereas incandescent bulbs are a definite heat factor.

In planning for lighting, bulbs and tubes can be mixed. For example, the heat and glare factors are insignificant if an incandescent ceiling fixture is used for general lighting, and here the instant-on factor would be valuable. So the planner might want this pleasant general illumination.

But the planner also must have sufficient glareless light where it is needed for close work, and good illumination at danger points, and there must be an esthetic consideration — the lighting should add to the beauty of the kitchen.

If the cabinets in the kitchen are dark the quantity of light must be increased, since dark surfaces absorb a lot of light. Dark flooring also calls for more light.

A dim light level tends to be relaxing and restful.

A bright light level tends to be stimulating and makes people feel more energetic.

Lights at eye-level are not desirable, usually, and must be well shielded so they do not shine directly into the eyes. Lights at levels high in the room tend to seem formal, and lights below eye-level seem friendly and attractive. But here again, they should not shine directly into the eyes.

Warm light is flattering to people and good for warm color schemes in the kitchen, but it deadens the blue end of the spectrum. Cool light is unflattering to people, but it adds to a sense of spaciousness. A favorable combination of these qualities would use warm light for general illumination and cool light for more specific lighting, but probably the best over-all solution, in the absence of an expert to develop special lighting effects, is to combine warm incandescence with warm fluorescent tubes.

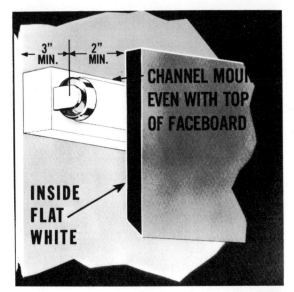

Wall brackets are most useful in structural lighting. The high wall bracket is really a valance without a window. Bracket must be high so light will spread over ceiling.

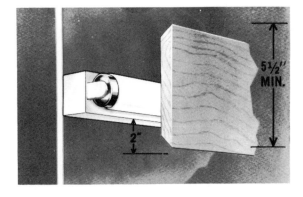

Low wall brackets are good for local or task lighting. Lamp should not be lower than 2" above bottom of shield. These are not used at more than 65" from floor.

All lighting experts and all kitchen experts and all home economists (and all lighting salesmen) will recommend two types of lighting in any kitchen:

1) General illumination, such as might be provided by the single ceiling fixture, an illuminated ceiling or perimeter soffit fixtures.
2) Task lighting, which puts light from separate sources directly onto specific work areas.

For general lighting, the American Home Lighting Institute recommends one fixture for every 50 square feet of area.

Each fixture should contain from 175 to 200 watts if incandescent, with a minimum 14-inch diameter for the fixture, or 60 to 80 watts if fluorescent; or, if the floor area of the kitchen is no more than 50 square feet, one suspended luminous-ceiling fixture measuring 24 square feet and with at least 360 watts incandescence.

For a fluorescent luminous ceiling in this application, the minimum depth from louvers to tube centers is 8 inches. A 40-watt tube is needed for every 12 square feet of room area. With incandescent bulbs, a 60-watt bulb is needed for every square foot of panel.

This applies, of course, for a normal, 8-foot ceiling. Light loses its effectiveness inversely with the square of the distance, and a 10-foot ceiling would call for more light. The visual criterion is that the general illumination should give adequate vision into drawers and cabinets, and there should be no difficulty reading labels.

Task lighting is needed in all food preparation areas along the countertop, over the range, over the sink, and at any other place where specific tasks are performed.

For countertop work surfaces, a fluorescent tube mounted at the bottom front of the overhanging wall cabinet will be about 18 inches above the counter, normally, and this calls for one 20-watt tube for every three feet of counter.

To break this down to a practical situation, this means a 20-watt tube for from 24 to 36 inches of counter; a 30-watt tube for from 36 to 48 inches of counter, and a 40-watt tube for from 48 to 60 inches of counter.

This wattage is good for up to 22 inches above the counter, a height that is unfortunately high for wall cabinets, but it is not uncommon in cost-cutting kitchens.

A 2-socket incandescent bracket with 60 watts in each socket is the equivalent for each three feet of counter, but the fluorescent tube adapts so easily to this application that there is little reason to make the job harder with incandescence. Overhang of the wall cabinet's face frame often provides all the shielding necessary for a fluorescent tube.

If there is no wall cabinet, the tube will have to be shielded fully so it does not shine in the eyes. In this case it will be wall-mounted with the tube toward the front. When a standard channel fixture is mounted at the bottom front of a wall cabinet, the tube goes toward the rear. In this case shielding will not be needed even if there is no face frame overhang, as long as the wall cabinet is at standard height — 51 inches from the floor.

Task lighting over the sink may come from the ceiling or the soffit, or it may be wall-mounted.

From ceiling or soffit, a situation where normally there is a window flanked by cabinets, there can be:

1) One recessed fixture with three 75-watt incandescent bulbs in a box at least 24 inches long, or two 40-watt or three 30-watt fluorescent tubes, or
2) Two recessed fixtures with inner reflectors with a 100-watt incandescent bulb in each, centered 18 inches apart, or
3) Two, or preferably three, bullets which might be recessed, pendant or surface-mounted, each with a 75-watt flood bulb.

All of these might or might not be shielded by a face frame connecting the flanking wall cabinets.

The same requirements apply to a cooktop or range in this location. But a range is usually mounted under a plain wall, with a hood 24 inches above and a cabinet above the hood. The hood should have one or two incandescent sockets or tubes.

If there is no hood there should be a wall bracket mounted from 14 to 22 inches above the range (or sink) allowing some upward light. Minimum is one 30-watt fluorescent tube or multiple-socket incandescent in a box at least 18 inches long

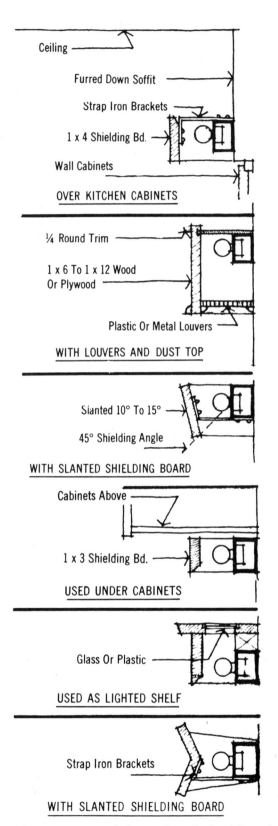

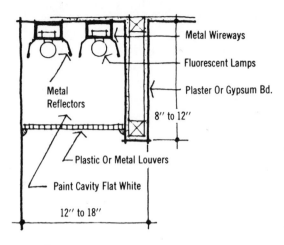

When soffit over work area must provide a high level of light directly below, polished reflectors can double light output when used with open louvers. Only two rows of lamps are needed when polished metal reflectors are used.

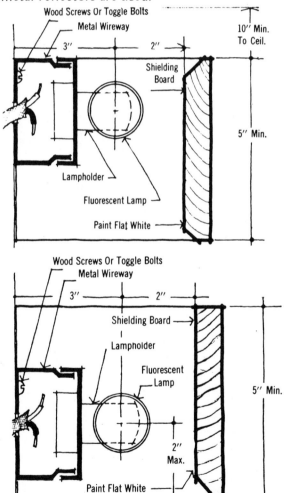

Detail of high and low type wall brackets.

Here are some of the options in building the light on the job in the kitchen, for over the cabinets, shelving or under the wall cabinets.

with 60 or 75 watts in each socket.

A dining area in the kitchen area (not a brunch counter) requires separate illumination, even though it will benefit from the lighting in the kitchen.

Incandescence is favored here. It makes food look better and it is more flattering to the people and the colors of dishes and clothing.

It requires at least 150 watts in a fixture that directs light both upward and downward. A close-to-ceiling pendant fixture, or other suspended fixture, should be at least 17 inches in diameter, single or multiple sockets.

If fluorescence is used, a wall bracket would require one 36-inch 30-watt Deluxe Warm White tube, and light should be directed both upward and

downward.

A brunch area in the kitchen that uses a countertop can use the same task lighting that has been installed for food preparation, but if any light is added, it should be consistent in design with the kitchen lighting. A higher intensity is called for here, as compared with the dining area, because brighter light makes people feel more energetic, as they would want to feel at breakfast or lunch time.

In this chapter there have been various references to the effect of light on color. It should be remembered that light and color are so interrelated that there really is no such thing as a light that shows color "as it really is." Color is a function of light. For more on this, see Chapter 8, which discusses the use of color in the kitchen.

Luminous ceiling gives daylight effect to this kitchen. Added lighting recessed under each wall cabinet and over sink give continuous task lighting along counters. All is deluxe warm fluorescent, by Westinghouse.

Location	Use	Cavity Dimensions				Deluxe Warm White Lamps	Parabolic Aluminum Reflectors	Material for Bottom Closure
		Depth	Width	Length	Finish			
Kitchen	Over sink or work center	8 to 12 in.	12 in.	38 in. min	Flat white	Two rows to fill length. Two 30-watt minimum.	Yes	Louvers
Bath or Dressing Room	Over large mirror	8 in.	14 to 18 in.	Length of mirror	Flat white	Two rows to fill length. Two 40-watt minimum.	No	White diffusing glass or plastic
		8 in.	18 to 24 in.	Length of mirror	Flat white	Three rows to fill length. Three 40-w. minimum.	No	White diffusing glass or plastic
								Lightly etched material acceptable
Living Area	Over piano, desk, sofa, or other seeing area	10 in.	Fit space Available 12 in. min	Fit Space Available 50 in. min	Flat white except matte black painted back wall surface	Two rows to fill length. Two 40-watt minimum.	Yes	Lightly figured or etched glass or plastic

Soffit construction data, as recommended by Nela Park.

Lighting fixture manufacturers make "false" luminous panel lights also, as well as fixtures that recess. Recessed squares are by Progress Lighting. Progress, Lightolier and NuTone are among those who make the types that attach below the celing.

153

Night-time view of kitchen from patio shows general illumination from recessed incandescent down lights in ceiling, including unit directed to art on left wall. There also is a small fixture at desk in background. Westinghouse photo.

10
Creative Color and How to Use It

A New York tool manufacturer, bothered by production and quality-control problems, decided to coordinate colors of all machinery and walls. Production jumped 15 percent, rejected parts were reduced by 40 percent and absenteeism was reduced by 60 percent.

Firebrand football coach Knute Rockne had his team's dressing room walls painted bright red so the players would be stimulated through the halftime break. But he had the dressing room of the visiting team painted a restful blue so those players would lose their edge.

You can win a bet with your bartender by betting that a green $5 bill actually is red. Actually, it is every color except green because it absorbs all other colors and reflects, or rejects, green. So it isn't green. But try this only on a bartender who will listen to reason.

Color is possibly the most-used and least-understood phenomenon of both our physical and psychological worlds. It can be defined in terms of pigments and dyes, but the definition will fall short because it ignores both sensation and light. Some theorists insist it really is a sensation relating very personally to the viewer.

Anyone who buys a bright red car, parks it in daytime and then tries to find it later under a mercury street light will attest to the fact that color is very much a function of light source.

The consumer may become confused by the vagaries of light and color. A homeowner may visit a kitchen showroom and select cabinets for their warm, rich, reddish woodtones. When they are installed in his home, however, they may appear flat and gray. But he got the right cabinets. The difference in this case was that the showroom was lit by incandescent bulbs and his kitchen was lit by fluorescence.

Light has its peculiarities. We call it white light, but when it is directed through an optical prism we find it contains all colors, splitting up into a spectrum ranging from infrared to ultraviolet. This is white light, and with all those colors in it, light itself is invisible. Yet without it, everything else is invisible.

The full spectrum contains more radiant energy both above and below the visible spectrum. Above ultraviolet, progressively, are X-rays, gamma rays, and cosmic rays. Below infrared are microwaves (used for cooking in microwave ovens, and used in radar), television, radio, and electric power.

All of these have repeating wave patterns traveling in straight paths, in all directions from their source. All travel at 186,000 miles per second. All are identified by their particular ranges of frequencies, or number of wave cycles per second. The shortest wavelength known is that of the cosmic ray, one thousand-millionth of a second, or one twenty-five millionth of an inch. An electric power wave, at the other end of the spectrum, has an average wavelength of 3100 miles.

The visible spectrum is but a small part of this broad band, from 15 to 30 millionths of an inch. Wavelengths longer or shorter than this do not stimulate the receptors of the eye and so cannot be seen. Physically, the only difference between ultraviolet and infrared, or between blue and green and yellow and red, is progressively longer wavelengths.

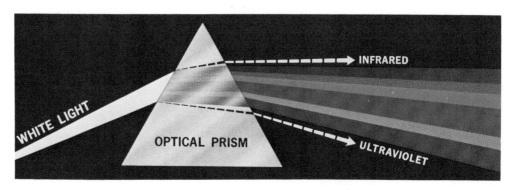

We call it white light, but it contains all colors. We discover that by bending a ray of light through a prism. This is the visible spectrum.

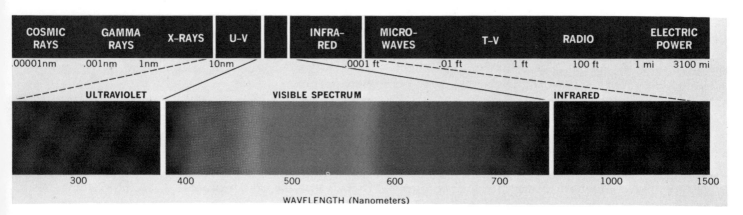

The visible spectrum is only a small part of the total spectrum of radiant energy, as indicated here. It ranges from a cosmic ray, one 25 millionth of an inch, to electric rays with wave lengths 3100 miles long.

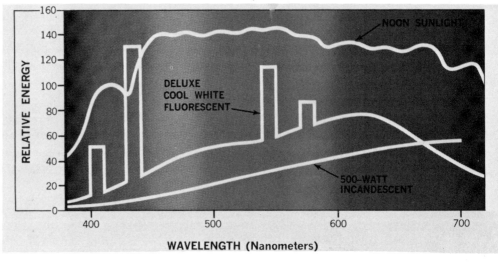

(From "Light and Color," publication of the Large Lamp Dept., General Electric)

This drawing shows the relative color rendering of different light sources. Incandescent lamps, the bottom line, have higher relative energy in the red end of the spectrum, which is to the right. Fluorescent lamps drop off in the red end, but are high in the blue area of the spectrum to the left.

156

Without light there would be no colors, since colors are simply other ways to describe different mixtures of wavelengths of light.

How then can colors be physical properties of objects?

An apple is always red or a head of lettuce is always green because of "color constancy," which means they always reflect or transmit light waves only in a particular narrow color range while absorbing all others. They are selective in the waves they reflect and this selectivity remains the same.

When we look at a red apple, however, we look at it and can see it only because light is present from whatever light source. That light might be white light, which contains all colors. The apple absorbs all the blues and greens and reflects only red and it looks as we think it should look. If we put a green filter over the white light it will absorb all colors other than its own color, transmitting only green. The apple then will appear much darker and virtually colorless because there is very little red energy to be reflected in the green light.

That is, what happened to the consumer we mentioned earlier, whose red car turned brown and whose kitchen cabinets turned gray.

It becomes obvious, then, that all this talk of wavelengths is not quite enough. There also is the matter of the human eye — plus the element of human interpretation.

A person who is totally color blind cannot distinguish between the various wavelengths of light. They all look gray to him, but this does not change the facts of those wavelengths. If one person sees a red apple and the other person sees the same apple as gray, it is only the *concept* that is different. Now we are out of the realm of physical laws and in the realm of personal concepts.

From there it is an easy step to *impressions*, but they are different for light and for pigments.

The primary colors of light are red, green, and blue. They are called additive primaries because they can be added to produce the secondary colors, magenta (red plus blue), cyan (green plus blue), and yellow (red plus green). A secondary color of light, mixed with its opposite primary, will give white light.

Primary colors in pigments are magenta, cyan, and yellow. These are subtractive primaries because in pigments a primary color is defined as one that subtracts, or absorbs a primary color of light and reflects the other two.

To get familiar with all the terms:

1) Hue is the name of the color.
2) The lightness or darkness of a color is its value.
   a. Adding black to a color gives a shade.
   b. Adding white to a color gives a tint.
   c. Adding gray gives a tone.
3) A color's purity or strength is called its intensity.

Complementary hues are those directly *opposite* each other on the color wheel. Analogous hues are those *next* to each other. *(For typical color wheel, see page 24.)*

To mix complementary hues is to neutralize. If you physically mixed the pigments you would end up with a neutral gray, but putting them next to each other adds contrast — extreme contrast.

Extreme contrast is great, if not overdone. If the entire color scheme of a room is based solely on contrast, the result is disastrous.

There are as many color theories as there are color theorists.

From this point on we will be thoroughly practical and use the terms as they probably will appear on the color wheel that might be picked up from any paint supplier. If a retail paint store does not have one, the retailer can order it from any major manufacturer.

To blend colors properly in a kitchen, a color wheel should be used.

The color wheel will show three primary colors, red, blue and yellow. Secondary colors will show as the blending of any two primary colors. Between red and blue there will be purple. Between blue and yellow will be green. Between yellow and red will be orange. All of these are secondary colors.

If any chosen color is mixed in with its complementary color (the color directly across from it in the color wheel) the mixture results in a neutral gray. The sum of all colors, remember, is gray. If red is the chosen color the complement must be the sum of the other colors to make up a gray so, going directly across the color wheel, that would be the point directly between yellow and blue, which would be green. So green, containing both yellow and blue, is the complement of red.

The human eye always strives for natural balance. The eyes like colors which, if mixed, would add up to a gray.

A kitchen that is all red might look exciting at first to a homeowner, but it will wear on the nerves and, sooner or later, need to be changed. One that contains all elements of all three primaries, with one dominating and the other highlighting, will be pleasing for a long time.

In a kitchen the elements to consider for color are the cabinets, the appliances, the countertops, the ceiling, the walls, and the floor. Beyond that, accessories can be color highlights.

The procedure is:

1) Establish the dominating color.
2) Decide where it will go.
3) Using the color wheel, establish the complementary colors.
4) Decide where they will go.

For the dominating color — and by dominating, here, we mean the one that will be most generally used in the kitchen — you might decide on the popular avocado, which is a green. The color wheel shows red directly across, so some red will have to be used in the kitchen. There might be avocado cabinets, and the green could be picked up in a lighter tint in the soffit and on the ceiling. There could be a dramatic red countertop, or even red appliances, or the red might be only a curtain at the window. Red would have to be there somewhere.

You might choose a blend of greens and yellows for cabinets, countertop, appliances, walls, and ceiling. Directly across the wheel from green and yellow is red-purple, and even a simple dish display on a wall in this tertiary color would suffice. But it must be there, however small.

Here are some other points to remember:

1) You cannot get appliance and cabinet colors to match exactly. So use complementary colors, or contrasting shades of the same color.
2) Usually, the fewer colors used the better, and keep window and door trim the same color as the walls.
3) Color intensifies in a north room or in a small room, so use tints except for accents.
4) North light is cold. If the room has a north window it is best to use colors from the warm side of the wheel with the cold colors for accents.
5) A strong color on the ceiling tends to make the ceiling "come down" oppressively. Use very light colors on the ceiling or keep it neutral gray or white.
6) It usually is better to keep darker colors lower in the kitchen than the countertop.
7) Remember the lighting. Incandescence can brighten warm colors, such as yellow. Blue shaded toward green can appear green when the lights are on.
8) An *expensive* dish or drape can furnish a ready-made color scheme. Such expensive items are not color-keyed by cheap labor. They are designed by the best color brains in the business.
9) Warm hues are conspicuous, cheerful, stimulating. They appear to come toward you, to pull things together, to make objects look larger.
10) Cool hues are more restful, separate things, and make objects look smaller. They can be cold and depressing.
(There is a physiological explanation for some of that. Red rays register behind the eye's retina, and the eye pulls them forward simply by pulling them into focus. Cool rays register in front of the retina and are pushed back in focusing.)
11) While warm hues *increase* the apparent size of things within a room, when these hues are used as wall colors they *decrease* the apparent size of the room. The same is true of high intensities. Sharp contrast brings objects forward.
12) Be sure colors are selected under the same lighting conditions as will exist in the kitchen. All colors, even white and black, will look different under fluorescence and under incandescence.
13) If there is a lot of natural light in the kitchen, dark colors can be used more effectively. If the kitchen must depend on artificial light, lighter colors are usually more satisfactory.

11
Floors, Walls and Ceilings

Floorcovering is one of the most important parts of the kitchen because it is one of the most readily noticeable design elements. It affects color scheme. It affects lighting. It can help make the room seem larger or smaller, warmer or colder.

The first choice that must be made is between carpeting and resilient floorcovering.

The resilients dominate by far. As a category there are no bad ones, although some are better than others. They range from cheap to expensive, and the really good ones incorporate softness without sacrificing durability.

Carpeting is used more in remodeled kitchens, although still far outdistanced by resilients. It puts a real luxury look and feel into a kitchen and, despite its critics, it is very practical. It does, however, arouse considerable sales resistance among people who have never tried it.

Here are the flooring choices, with their good and bad points.

1. *Asphalt Tile* — low in cost and resistant to alkali stains. This material is fairly easy to maintain and it can be installed directly over concrete base below or above grade.
   However, it is only fair in resiliency and, being harder, is not as quiet as other materials. Lighter colors are much higher in price.
2. *Asbestos Vinyl Tile* — an improvement over asbestos tile, blending asbestos and vinyl for clearer, cleaner colors and more resiliency. It can be laid on, above or below grade. It is somewhat more expensive than asphalt tile. It is durable and stain resistant.

3. *Vinyl* — in tiles or sheets, plain or cushioned. In tiles, this is luxury material with excellent colors and patterns. In sheet form it is moderately priced. It is very durable and has superior resistance to stains and can be laid on, above or below grade. Tiles are less expensive, and any vinyl must be laid over very smooth base. It scratches fairly easily.
4. *Others* include rubber tile, very quiet and very resilient with good resistance to grease and alkalis; vinyl cork tile, very expensive, but worth it; vinyl bonded ceramic tile, a new, very expensive product which overcomes many objections of ceramic tile because the little 1-inch tiles are embedded in vinyl, making it softer, quieter and more acceptable to the home buyer.
   For an ultra-luxury look, a builder might want to use ceramic tile or experiment with the genuine wood veneers embedded in clear plastic.

And then there is carpeting. The advent of man-made fibers such as nylon made it a suitable material for kitchen installation, and residential kitchen installation are known that date back to 1955.

Now there are several such chemical fibers, and their comparative characteristics can be seen in the accompanying chart.

The important point to recognize is that kitchen carpet is not the same as indoor-outdoor carpet, although salesmen often tend to confuse this issue.

Indoor-outdoor carpet is a good, practical material for its application because water passes

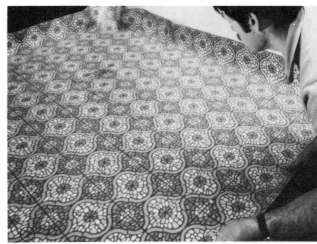

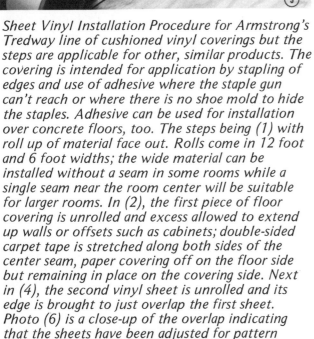

Sheet Vinyl Installation Procedure for Armstrong's Tredway line of cushioned vinyl coverings but the steps are applicable for other, similar products. The covering is intended for application by stapling of edges and use of adhesive where the staple gun can't reach or where there is no shoe mold to hide the staples. Adhesive can be used for installation over concrete floors, too. The steps being (1) with roll up of material face out. Rolls come in 12 foot and 6 foot widths; the wide material can be installed without a seam in some rooms while a single seam near the room center will be suitable for larger rooms. In (2), the first piece of floor covering is unrolled and excess allowed to extend up walls or offsets such as cabinets; double-sided carpet tape is stretched along both sides of the center seam, paper covering off on the floor side but remaining in place on the covering side. Next in (4), the second vinyl sheet is unrolled and its edge is brought to just overlap the first sheet. Photo (6) is a close-up of the overlap indicating that the sheets have been adjusted for pattern match. A utility knife is used to cut out a U-shaped section from the excess extending up the wall or cabinet at both seam ends so that the seam area will lie flat on the underlayment. And then in (7), the knife with the help of a steel straightedge is used to cut through both vinyl sheets to produce a perfectly butted seam. Photo (8) indicates lifting of sheet edges to pull out top paper covering from the carpet tape and pull away the trimmed off portion of the under vinyl sheet. In (9), seam sealing cement or adhesive is being applied. The installation is completed by trimming at borders and fitting around cabinet corners. Shown here in (10) is an upward knife cut of the floor covering at an inside corner in order to permit covering to be fitted tightly down. In photo (11), an outside cabinet corner is to be trimmed and the corner cut is started at the floor line. A steel straightedge (12) is used for cutting along wall or cabinet and the floor covering sheet is turned back (13) to allow application of adhesive or cement. Finally a manual staple gun is used with 3/8 to 9/16 inch long staples spaces at about 3-inch intervals. Edge and staples are then covered with a base shoe molding strip.

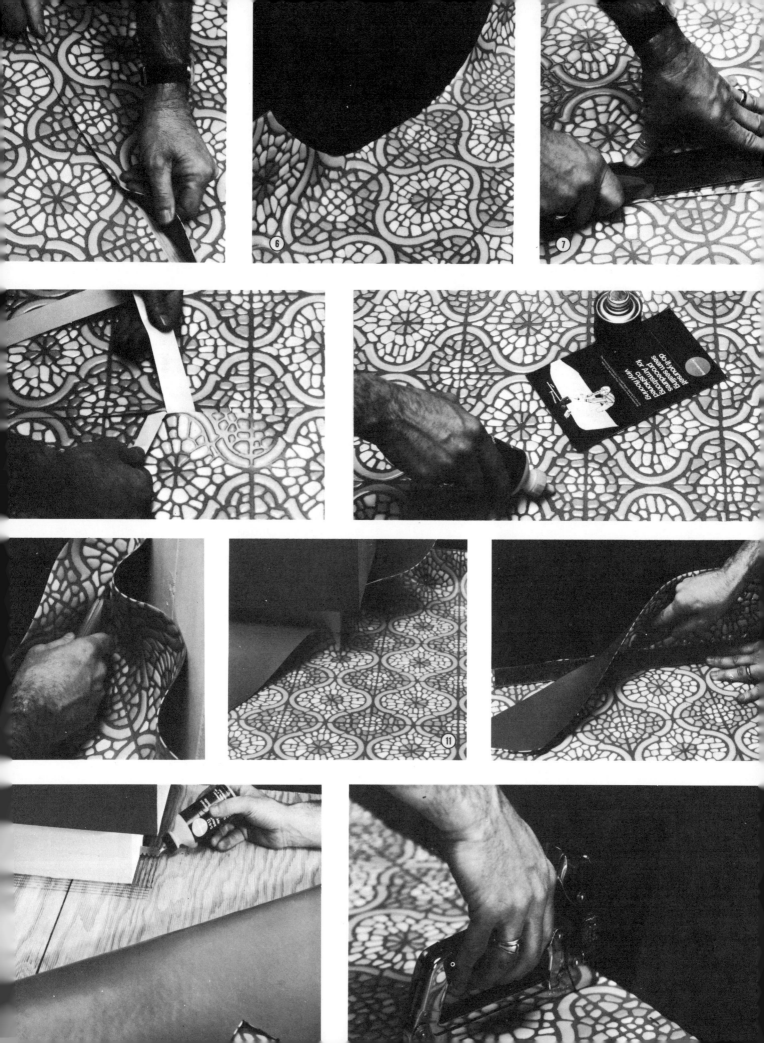

through it. It can be washed with a hose. This is great for a patio, but hardly practical in a kitchen.

Kitchen carpet, on the other hand, consists of a carpet surface separated from its sponge or foam backing by a water-proof bonding membrane. Water can not pass through it to the floor underlayment below. This means any spill — milk, eggs, or grease — can be washed up almost as easily as from resilient floorcovering. In the event of more serious damage, it can be patched easily.

Manufacturers recommend that a mastic be used to hold it tight to the floor. This author laid it loose, wall to wall and coved up into the kick-space of the cabinets, with 2-sided Scotch tape to hold it down at the two doorways, where it served for six years in a New York City apartment. It was then lifted and moved to a new suburban home, cut and

patched to fit the new kitchen, with 2-sided tape used again to hold down all cut edges. The patchwork is absolutely undetectable, and it has served in the new home for three years and still looks like new. This is a good material.

Few things are more luxurious on a lazy Sunday morning.

Any flooring material must be chosen with design and color in mind. A small kitchen demands small patterns. A large kitchen can take bold motifs and large patterns. Stripes can add length or width to a room, adding the dimension in the direction of their axis.

Light colors are nearly always preferred for kitchen floors, unless a skilled decorator specifies otherwise for dramatic effect.

Steps in Laying Floor Tiles are just about the same whether all-vinyl or vinyl-asbestos tiles are being used. Cutting of all-vinyl tiles is easy with a scissors while the vinyl asbestos type tiles may better be cut with scoring tools or a tile cutter. Layout of starting center lines is important to get good tile alignment and photo (1) indicates careful measurement to obtain proper perpendicular center lines. In (2), tile units are temporarily laid out to check border widths and thus verify suitable position for center lines. Once the lines are established and marked on the underlayment, adhesive is spread (3) with a brush or notched adhesive trowel, keeping within one quarter of the room. A short wait may be needed (4) until the surface of the adhesive feels tacky to the touch rather than wet.

Tile units are started at the juncture of the center lines, and work of laying unit by unit proceeds toward the outer edges (5). When all field tiles have been laid, carefully butting each new tile to the adjoining tiles, it's time to work on the border tiles. First, in (6), the full tile piece to be cut for border installation is held on top of last full tile for marking. A line drawn across edge marks allows accurate cutting (7) and then in (8), the cut border piece is slipped into place first butting it to the last previous tile. For many resilient floor covering installations, vinyl cove base is an appropriate trim that lends a hand in floor maintenance by keeping floor corners clean. In (9), cove base is being applied and (10), the final step: rolling the tiles in both directions using a heavy steel floor roller.

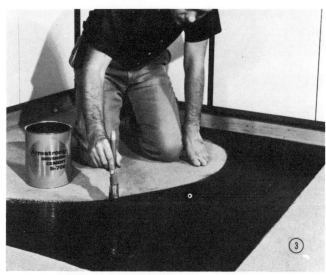

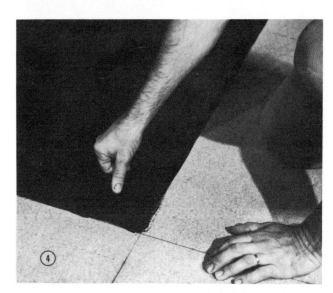

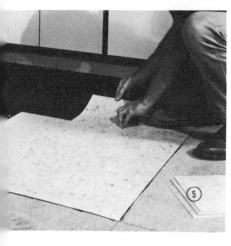

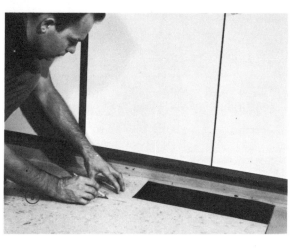

Carpeting made with synthetic fibers is the growing thing in the kitchen, although it may never approach resilient flooring. This chart shows some of the comparative qualities of the various synthetic fibers.

Comparison chart of carpet fiber characteristics

Performance characteristics	Acrylic	Polyester	Nylon	Poly-propylene	Wool
Wear life	high	high	extra high	extra high	high
texture retention	good	good to medium	exceptional	good	good
abrasion resistance	good	very good	exceptional	exceptional	good
soil resistance	high	medium	medium	high	high
stain resistance	high	medium	medium	exceptional	medium
wet cleanability	good	good	high	high	good
static buildup	little	only in low humidity	very much	very little	only in low humidity
moisture absorbency	little	little	some	lowest	highest
mildew	resists	resists	resists	resists	subject to mildew
moth protection	no effect	no effect	no effect	no effect	needs treatment
non-allergenic	completely	completely	completely	completely	minor

Appearance characteristics

Appearance	warm, soft, luxurious	soft, luxurious	dull to lustrous	subdued luster	soft, warm, luxurious
Dyeability	good	good, but brilliance limits	good	medium	good
Crush resistance	medium	medium	good	low	medium
Resilience	high	medium	high	medium	high
Fade resistance	good	good	medium	good	medium

Economy characteristics

Price range	medium	medium	low-medium	low-medium	high
Carpet yield per lb. fiber	medium	medium	high	highest	lowest

Walls

In the common concept, the walls of any kitchen are nearly covered with the cabinets and appliances, so what is there to do with them except paint them?

That is one easy solution, but visit any good kitchen showroom for some surprising answers to what is possible and much more commendable.

A kitchen is a special place. Things happen there that don't happen anywhere else in the home, things such as food preparation and cooking and cleanup. There are differences in heat, humidity, and in the characteristics of the air. In addition, it is a separate enclave with its own design that usually is quite independent of the design characteristics of the rest of the house.

Here are some of the options.

1) Plastic brick or stone, a lifetime material that simulates the original very precisely, but is light-weight and easily cleaned. It can be used on a wall or a section of one wall, but if more than that is used it tends to dominate the room. It is good for the sides of islands or peninsulas.

2) Plastic laminate, the same as on the countertop, often is extended all the way from the countertop to the bottoms of the wall cabinets. This is an excellent treatment and is unbeatable for cleanability and neat appearance. It is not advisable behind a cooktop, however, because it can be darkened by the heat. It can be used on other walls and above the wall cabinets.

3) Panels of copper, stainless steel, porcelain enameled steel, or aluminum can be used behind a cooktop, in either sheet or tile form, for good protection and a very decorative effect.

4) Ordinary wall coverings can be decorative and effective, but they must not be of poor quality. A vinyl-coated wallpaper must be high quality to hold up under the necessary washing. A vinyl-coated fabric would be much better. When any of these are used, use large patterns only for large areas and small patterns for small areas. Light colors go best in small areas, and darker colors should be used only in large areas with good natural lighting.

5) Paint is the most common material for kitchen walls. A semigloss is best because enamels with their high gloss characteristics result in too much glare, and flat finishes are difficult to wash.

6) Vinyl-surfaced wall paneling can be very effective, especially in the light woodgrains. Darker woodgrains often are used to achieve separation of a dining area in or adjacent to the kitchen.

7) Ceramic tile is a beautiful and luxurious material for backsplash areas or for entire walls, although high first-cost and high installation costs usually have ruled it out among builders of speculative homes.

In Mexico, where both tile and labor are inexpensive, this bright and colorful material is used often for entire walls, floors and even ceilings. The effect is love at first sight, although the color combinations that we applaud in Mexico are usually too uninhibited for our homes in the United States.

It is well worth considering, though, for a spectacular model home or a distinctive option.

8) Kitchen carpeting is used effectively as a wall material by many kitchen specialists. They seldom use it all the way to the ceiling (although they might if it is a large room), but they often will cove it up to the window line or up the walls of an island or peninsula. This can be done easily and inexpensively with simple flooring adhesives.

9) Previously, we mentioned a unique cultured marble called "Corian" for countertops. This material also comes in 1/4-inch thickness for walls and it is superb for cleanability and luxurious appearance. This author, in a recent remodeling of his own kitchen, used 3/4-inch Corian on the countertops, grooved 1/4-inch around where it met the walls and recessed the 1/4-inch sheet into the grooves, so the walls are Corian-covered from counter to ceiling. Other cast marbles also can be used for this wall application and offer a much wider range of colors and patterns. Most cast marble manufacturers offer a 1/4-inch sheet for walls.

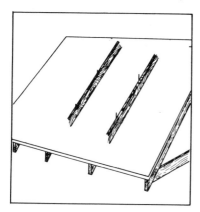

1. *Allow yourself 2 to 4 hours of clear weather for the job. To install Skymaster low-profile skylight, which fits cleanly in with shingles and has no curb, drive 3-in. nail up through the roof at the four corners marking the location of your skylight. Be sure there are no electrical wires, pipes or ducts in the way.*

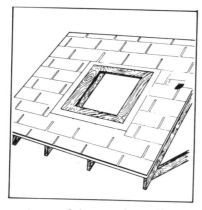

2. *Go up on the roof, locate the nails protruding through, and remove roofing material back about 12 in. around the area. Cut hole through the roof decking.*

3. *Frame the opening, top and bottom. Rafters will form the sides of the framing. If you are using a bigger skylight and rafter runs through the opening, cut the rafter back to make room for the new framing.*

Ceilings

Kitchen ceilings, like kitchen walls, usually are painted. Paint always is adequate. It should be light colored semigloss.

The best surfacing for a kitchen ceiling is acoustical tile or sheet. It can absorb up to 70 percent of the noise striking it, according to research by Armstrong Cork, and it also helps prevent kitchen noise from invading quiet areas above the kitchen.

Acoustical ceiling systems have matching lighting fixtures for clean-looking recessed installation.

The problem with acoustical tile is to get the border tiles on opposite sides of the room the same size, and as large as possible. The easy (cheap) way is simply to start at one end with full tiles and then to cut them off to the required size when the other end of the room is reached.

Armstrong Cork's formula for finding the right size for border tile is a simple one:

To find the size of the border tile for the *long* wall, using 12" x 12" tile:

1) Measure one of the *short* walls of the room.
2) If this is not an exact number of feet, add 12 inches to the inches left over.
3) Divide the total number of inches (ignoring the feet) by two.

For example, if the short wall measures 10'8", there are 8" left over. Following step 2, add 12 inches to the leftover 8" which gives you 20". Divide this by two and you get 10", the size of the border tile along the two long walls of the room.

Border tiles for the short walls can be figured with the same procedure, this time measuring the long walls.

When using 16" x 16" tile, convert the room measurement into inches. Divide this measurement by 16. Treat the extra inches the same way as with 12" tile, except that in step 3 add 16" instead of 12" and then divide by two.

Before installing acoustical tile, steps must be taken to be sure it goes up straight. Here is how to do it.

First, snap a chalk line the length of the second furring strip, down the center, along the long wall.

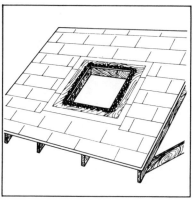

4. Apply rooting mastic around the opening about 1/4 in. thick, covering all exposed wood and felt. Use a black roofing mastic such as GAF, John-Manville, Bird & Son, or similar.

5. Position skylight over the opening. Drill small holes for the nails. Nail each corner down in line with the rafter, with 6d or 8d nail. Use 3/4-in. rust-proof roofing nails around the flange, about 3 in. apart.

6. Apply mastic over the edge of skylight right up to the bubble. Cut strips of roofing felt wide enough to go from the bubble to overlap the felt on the deck. Apply more mastic over these strips at the top and apply the top strip of felt. Don't put a strip on the bottom.

7. Apply mastic over the felt strips and replace shingles. After shingels are in place, apply mastic across the bottom of the skylight, as shown in small drawing at lower left.

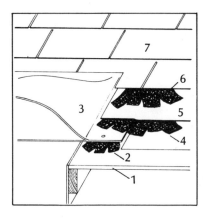

8. This drawing shows the sequence of materials: 1, roof deck; 2, mastic; 3, skylight; 4, mastic; 5, roofing felt; 6, mastic; 7, shingles.

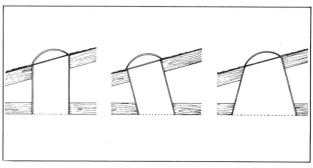

9. If you want to make a light shaft you can angle it to direct the sunlight. Straight down is best, but if there is some obstruction you can avoid it by angling the shaft. You also might want to make the bottom the shaft bigger to distribute the light over a broader area. You can use 1/4-in. plywood or hardboard for the shaft, paint the inside white, leave the bottom open or cut a plastic diffuser to cover it.

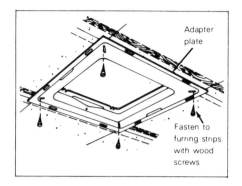

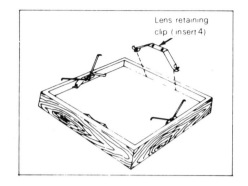

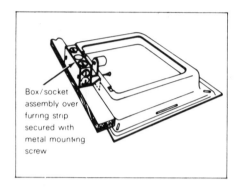

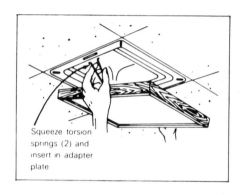

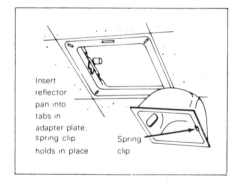

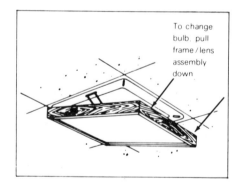

Ceiling systems using acoustical tile have lighting fixtures engineered to work with them. As an example, here is Armstrong system using its fixture, called Tilemate. In consecutive steps: (1) Adapter plate is installed; (2) Junction box is installed, according to directions; (3) Reflector pan comes next, fitting into tabs; (4) Glass lens then is installed in frame; (5) Frame/lens assembly then is attached to adapter plate; (6) For changing bulbs, assembly slides down and stops, allowing room for 100-watt bulb.

Using our previous example, this will be 10-1/2 inches from the wall because that is the width of our border tile (10" plus 1/2" for the stapling flange). The first furring strip, of course, went flush against the wall.

Second, establish a second reference line at right angles to the first chalk line. To do this we follow the same formula we used to determine how much walls were out of square. Referring to the accompanying drawing:

1) Locate point A on the reference line, using short border tile measurement.
2) From Point A measure in exactly 3 feet along the reference line and mark that point as Point B.
3) Starting with Point A, measure exactly 4 feet and mark a small arc on the sixth furring strip.
4) From Point B measure exactly 5 feet toward the first arc, marking the point of intersection as Point C.
5) Snap a chalk line through Points A and C across all furring strips. This second reference line will be precisely perpendicular to the first.

In all cases, the first furring strips should be placed flush against the wall, the second strips at the widths of the border tiles, and the remainder on centers corresponding with tile size.

There are other things that can be done with ceilings.

Kitchen carpeting can be used creatively, as can be seen in the "Successful Kitchens" illustrations elsewhere in this book.

Solid wood (or apparent solid wood) beams are often used in large kitchens, but the heir apparent to the wood beam is the polyurethane beam. It is totally realistic, looking exactly like wood, but it is so light that a housewife can lift it with one hand and apply it to the ceiling with adhesive.

There is the modern version of the familiar skylight, made now of clear plastic that lets in lots of daylight but eliminates some of the old leakage problems.

Armstrong's vinyl-coated Lyria Cushiontone acoustic panels have abstract pattern that conceals the acoustical perforations. This is a suspended ceiling.

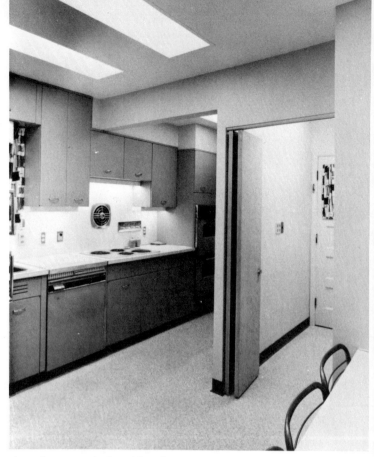

Another well-lighted kitchen has luminous ceiling panels for general light, fixtures under all wall cabinets.

But there are other interesting methods. This effect is gained with Armstrong's Marquee vaulted lighting system.

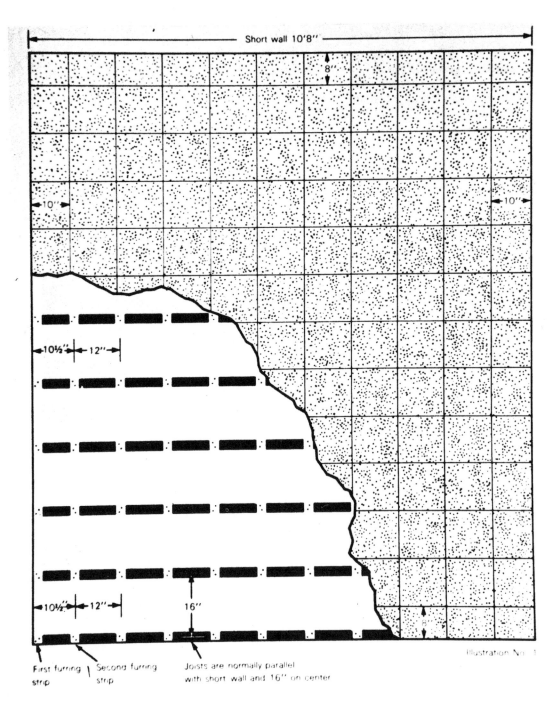

Short wall 10'8"

8"

10"

10"

10½" 12"

10½" 12"

16"

First furring strip

Second furring strip

Joists are normally parallel with short wall and 16" on center

Illustration No. 1

Acoustical tile is the best material for a kitchen ceiling because of noise in the kitchen, and this material can deaden 70 to 75 percent of the noise striking it. These two illustrations show how to make it work out right, as described in text.

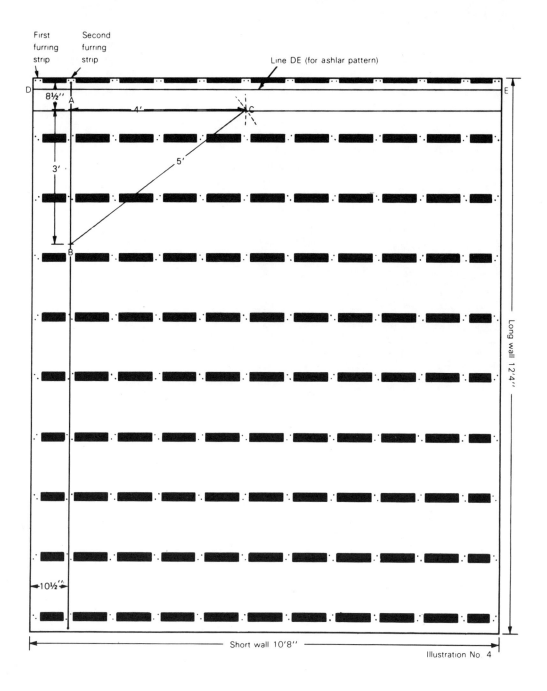

First furring strip
Second furring strip
Line DE (for ashlar pattern)
D
8½''
A
4'
C
3'
5'
B
10½''
Long wall 12'4''
Short wall 10'8''
Illustration No. 4
E

In this kitchen (by Kitchen Concepts, Ft. Lauderdale, Fla.), desk area is covered by cabinetry, drape and shingled soffit above. Imitation brick is used for oven wall. Built-in Sub-Zero refrigerator occupies other wall.

Don't be afraid to aim for a great kitchen. You might not have space for this one (above), but it can be scaled down. These are stock cabinets, Heirloom by IXL, and they are not cheap but they are far from the most expensive. They come in modular sizes so they can be fitted into any room. Check the chapter on kitchens first, so you know how to plan this in.

Wide countertop also serves as bar counter adjoining dining area. White cabinet surfaces add to feeling of space in what is actually a small kitchen.

This wall tile is the Florence series by H & R Johnson. It makes a durable, easy-to-clean, and very decorative wall.

Corridor kitchen is decorated by graphics to make it an eye-catcher despite small size. (design by General Electric).

New and very popular is this Chefblok style of cabinetry by Long-Bell. Note the pantry unit and wall of cabinets for plentiful storage, and 2-way access to cabinets in island.

12

Noise Control and
How to Achieve It

A University of Wisconsin psychiatrist, Dr. J. C. Westman, has reported that "the average kitchen is like a boiler room." He blames the growing cacophony for deterioration in marriage and family life.

The effects of noise, both in the home and at work, are being studied increasingly by government, industry, and consumer groups. Not too long ago a U.S. Department of Commerce panel on noise abatement produced a preponderance of evidence that noise—independent of loudness—can degrade the quality of our lives.

Manufacturers are really doing something about it. Some disposers come with rubber mounts and rubber hose sections, and therefore, are much more quiet than others. Members of the Home Ventilating Institute have not only quieted their products but put stickers on them with their sone ratings.

The builder or remodeler can do much more, and he should, not only for the good of his customers but also for his own protection. With the growing awareness of environmental noise, standards will come. That's for sure.

Here are some of the minimums.

1) Mount the dishwasher, garbage disposer, and other appliances on pads or springs to prevent vibrations from being transmitted through the floor and countertops.

2) Wrap the sides of the dishwasher with glass fiber insulating material to prevent transmission of sound to cabinets and counter tops.

3) Use sponge rubber isolation gaskets at the mouth of the disposer to prevent the sink bowl from amplifying the grinding noise.

4) Balance the refrigerator by adjusting the set screws on the front of the unit to eliminate annoying vibration. It is balanced properly when the door closes automatically from a half-open position.

5) Place sound-absorbing mountings on the exhaust fan, and make sure the fan is large enough to operate efficiently at low speeds.

6) Install a flexible pipe, similar to an automobile radiator hose, between the drain and the trap to keep vibrations from being transmitted to other plumbing and into the walls.

7) Install pneumatic anti-hammer devices in the water lines.

8) Place rubber bushings behind cabinet doors to eliminate banging.

9) Check the drawer slides, and if they are noisy demand something better. Quiet ones are available.

10) Install an acoustical ceiling to help stifle reflected noises.

The accompanying drawings are by courtesy of Owens-Corning Fiberglas Corp.

TABLE
Home Task Area Product Generated Noise Levels*

Column headers (dBA scale), with descriptive categories:

- maintains auditory attention and stimulates eye movement for localization
- threshold of annoyance environment - (50 to 90dB)
- airplane noises relatively unnoticed with background mus.
- activates autonomic nervous system***
- increase in peristalsis, saliva & gastric juice flow
- annoyance threshold**
- work efficiency reduced
- skin pales, pupils dilate, eyes close, adrenalin increases
- increased response and error averages over lower pressure levels
- perceptible ear discomfort human pain threshold
- "feeling" sensation noticeable in ear
- painful sensations

AREA	30	35	40	45	50	55	60	65	70	75	80	85	90	95	100	105	110	115	120	125	130	135	140
Kitchen																							

PRODUCTS*

Product	Approx. noise range (dBA)
Range vent fan	30 – 82
Garbage disposal	30 – 80
Dishwasher	30 – 70
Electric mixer	30 – 82
Blender	30 – 90
Refrigerator	50 – 90
Wall exhaust fan	30 – 90
12" portable fan	30 – 70
Knife sharpener	30 – 80

*Recorded at operator's or housewife's normal ear distance (dBA scale)
**Intermittent sounds
***Also occurs with loud or unexpected noises

Koss Electronics asked the Environmental Design department of the University of Wisconsin for deep research into "The Auditory Environment in the Home" and found the kitchen is a rough equivalent of a boiler factory. Tables I and II show everything except the refrigerator is above the annoyance threshold.

TABLE II
Home Task Area Product Generated Noise Levels*

Column headers (dBA scale), with descriptive categories:

- maintains auditory attention and stimulates eye movement for localization
- threshold of annoyance environment - (50 to 90dB)
- airplane noises relatively unnoticed with background mus.
- activates autonomic nervous system***
- increase in peristalsis, saliva & gastric juice flow
- annoyance threshold**
- work efficiency reduced
- skin pales, pupils dilate, eyes close, adrenalin increases
- increased response and error averages over lower pressure levels
- perceptible ear discomfort human pain threshold
- "feeling" sensation noticeable in ear
- painful sensations

AREA	30	35	40	45	50	55	60	65	70	75	80	85	90	95	100	105	110	115	120	125	130	135	140
Kitchen																							

PRODUCTS*

Product	Approx. noise range (dBA)
Coffee grinder	30 – 70
Elec. can opener	30 – 80
Pots and pans	30 – 70
Faucet	30 – 65
Drain (sink)	30 – 80
Range vent fan and dishwasher	30 – 82
Range vent fan and disposal	30 – 90

*Recorded at operator's or housewife's normal ear distance (dBA scale)
**Intermittent sounds
***Also occurs with loud or unexpected noises

177

WHAT TO DO ABOUT IT:

Ventilating systems can be improved greatly by following these recommendations.

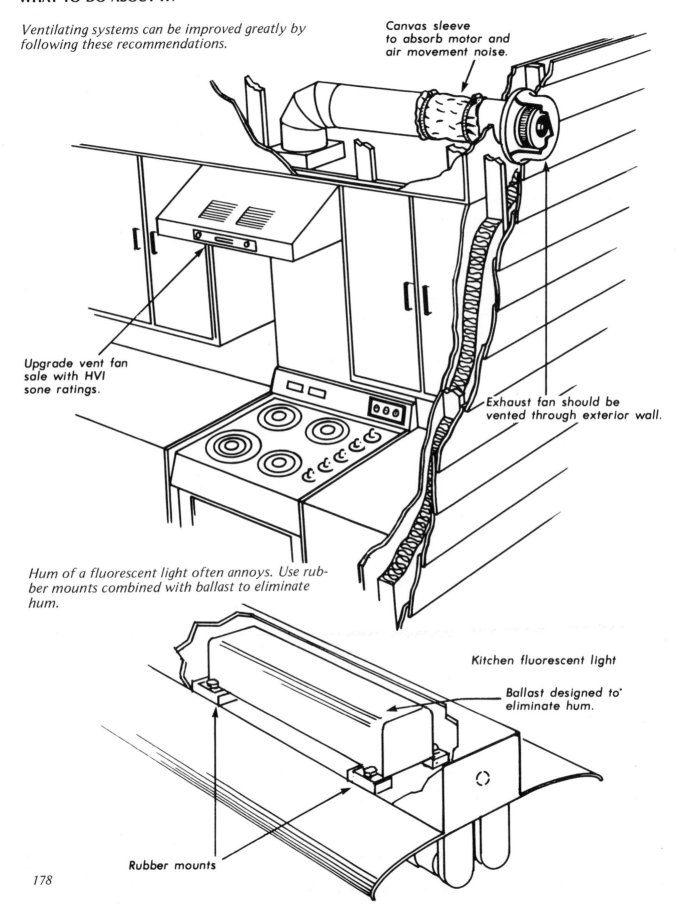

Canvas sleeve to absorb motor and air movement noise.

Upgrade vent fan sale with HVI sone ratings.

Exhaust fan should be vented through exterior wall.

Hum of a fluorescent light often annoys. Use rubber mounts combined with ballast to eliminate hum.

Kitchen fluorescent light

Ballast designed to eliminate hum.

Rubber mounts

Suspended ceilings with acoustical panels absorb up to 75% of the noise striking the surface.

Acoustical panels in ceiling, either suspended or applied direct, deaden all reflected noise.

Holes cut through common walls for plumbing and heating may leak noise. Seal them with a resilient material.

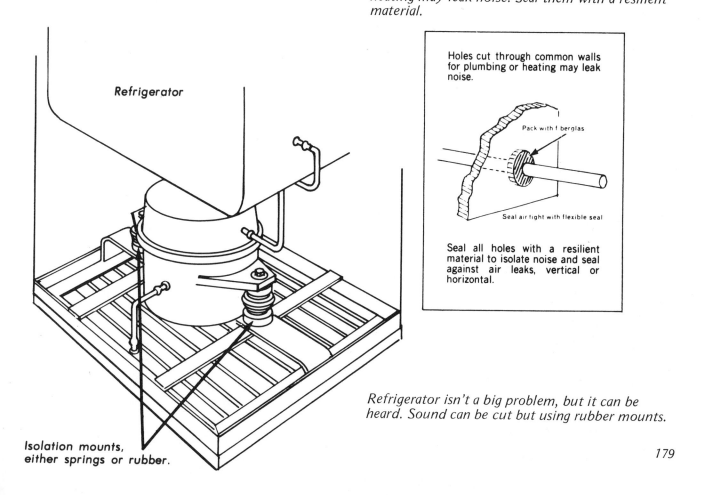

Refrigerator

Holes cut through common walls for plumbing or heating may leak noise.

Pack with f berglas

Seal air tight with flexible seal

Seal all holes with a resilient material to isolate noise and seal against air leaks, vertical or horizontal.

Refrigerator isn't a big problem, but it can be heard. Sound can be cut but using rubber mounts.

Isolation mounts, either springs or rubber.

179

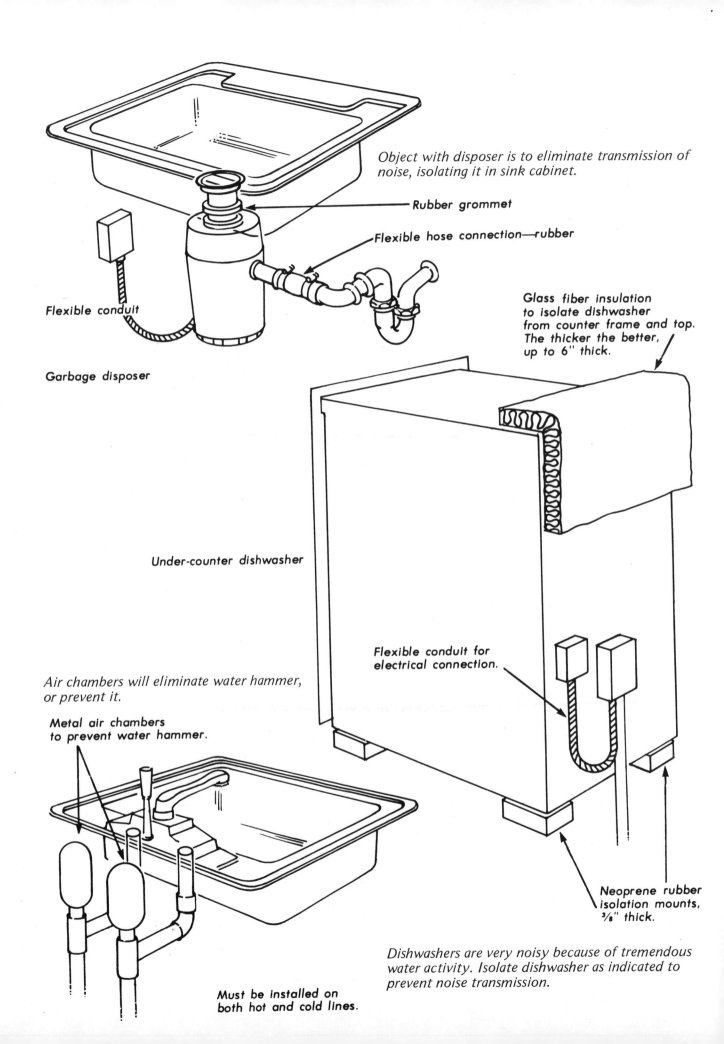

Object with disposer is to eliminate transmission of noise, isolating it in sink cabinet.

Rubber grommet

Flexible hose connection—rubber

Flexible conduit

Garbage disposer

Glass fiber insulation to isolate dishwasher from counter frame and top. The thicker the better, up to 6" thick.

Under-counter dishwasher

Flexible conduit for electrical connection.

Air chambers will eliminate water hammer, or prevent it.

Metal air chambers to prevent water hammer.

Neoprene rubber isolation mounts, ⅜" thick.

Must be installed on both hot and cold lines.

Dishwashers are very noisy because of tremendous water activity. Isolate dishwasher as indicated to prevent noise transmission.

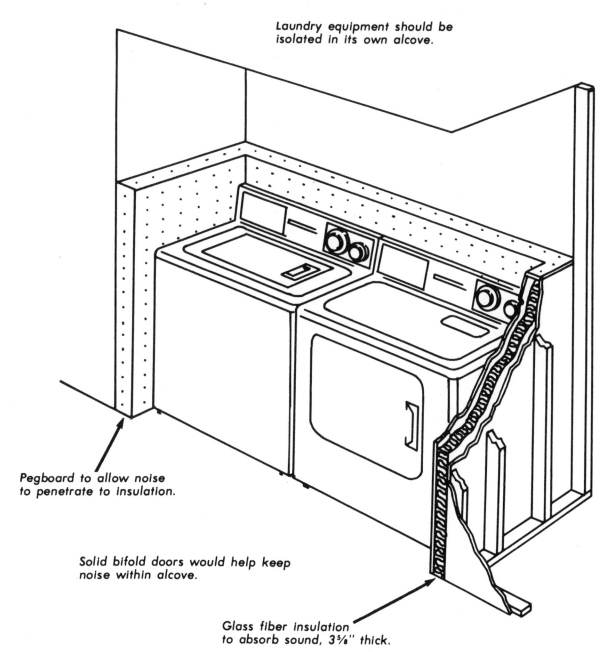

Laundry equipment should be
isolated in its own alcove.

Pegboard to allow noise
to penetrate to insulation.

Solid bifold doors would help keep
noise within alcove.

Glass fiber insulation
to absorb sound, 3⅝" thick.

Laundry equipment often is near kitchen. It should
be isolated in an alcove. There's no other way to
keep out the noise.

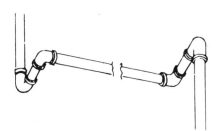

Long runs of hot water supply creak or snap as
they expand or contract. Differences up to 100
degrees can exist in piping, can cause expansion up
to 1/8 inch in 10 feet. To eliminate, use a swing
arm to allow movement and use collars of Fiberglas
insulation in straps.

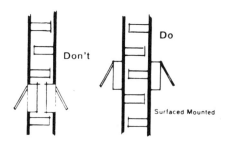

Don't

Do

Surfaced Mounted

Noise travels through walls when medicine cabinets
are mounted back to back. Put cabinets in separate
stud spaces, or surface-mount.

13
Kitchen Trends and Future Concepts

All things change.

And in the changing, will the kitchen of tomorrow become another part of the future shock of modern man?

We think not. There is a need for the kitchen as it exists today. And if it didn't exist, we would have to invent it.

But within the room that exists, there are big changes either here or just on the horizon.

For one thing, we used to laugh at the idea of computers for the home. Stop laughing. While we've been watching for them to appear on a distant horizon, they came in the back door.

What else but computers can you call the touch control now found on microwave cookers, on ranges, on washing machines and sewing machines?

This is an age when vest-pocket calculators selling for under $50 can outperform the 30-ton computers of 25 years ago, and it all is due to the development of solid-state technology and the microprocessor chip.

The only thing lacking is a memory-bank, which is easy to add; then comes consolidation of the controls, which is easy to do: the result is the home computer, which can let the cat out at 9 p.m. or call the police if a burglar breaks in, or tell the range to start cooking dinner at 5 p.m. Look for rapid developments in this field. It is limited only by the imagination.

There are other changing trends, with new and exciting products and materials fast becoming parts of the kitchen of a very near future. Here are some.

Cabinetry

More and more, they are spreading throughout the house. Nearly all cabinet manufacturers now are promoting built-in cabinet installations for every room in the home.

Polyurethane and polystyrene will increase in popularity for doors and drawer fronts. They have greater dimensional stability than wood, and can be printed and textured to be indistinguishable from wood in appearance. While wood will always be in demand, it is deteriorating in appearance as growth of trees is speeded up; the result is that wood character doesn't develop. The plastics offer greater design capability and greater production capability at less cost.

All-plastic cabinets are a possibility, built of reinforced glass fiber or polystyrene, not one by one but in assemblies which include the countertop and a molded-in sink. On this basis you might buy a 6-ft. kitchen assembly, or an 8-ft. assembly, or combinations to form L or U kitchens.

The trend right now is toward the European look, which is contemporary, simple, clean, with horizontal extruded pulls, and in solid colors with plastic-laminate finishes.

Ranges

The newest item right now is the magnetic induction system by Fasar. Fasar makes the parts and range manufacturers will be licensed for the

This "Homemaker's Command Post" by Westing-house includes closed circuit TV on all of the house. Telephone has 500 names and numbers stored in memory bank. She can unlock doors and windows by touching a button, or lock them, or a button will call firemen or police. It's in one of the Florida Westinghouse Electra homes.

Elkay conceptualizes this visionary sink of the future, its Cuisine 80. It combines all sink functions — food preparation, cooking and cleanup, plus closed-circuit TV, and, of course, a small computer.

finished products. Chambers is the first licensee.

This product cooks without heat, so the "burners" don't get hot except from the heat of the pans holding the food. The burner generates a magnetic field which causes heat to occur in the pan and, as in conventional cooktops, the pan heat cooks the food.

The principle was introduced by Westinghouse several years ago, but the Westinghouse unit was very bulky and retailed at $2,500. Fasar has benefited from solid-state technology, eliminated the bulk, and units have been selling in California for under $800.

This kind of unit affords a new freedom in design. The "works" can be under the countertop, but it can be wired to random burners placed anywhere in the counter, and since there is no heat these units can be ceramic tiles placed at random.

Other new developments in ranges are the combination microwave/conventional electric oven which gives the speed of microwave and the benefit of conventional baking or roasting in the same cavity, plus self-cleaning. These are here now in a few brands, and their numbers will increase.

Refrigeration

The big box is neat, efficient and pretty near failsafe, but it does not fit in with modern kitchen design. It can be great when built-in, but many kitchens are budgeted too low for built-in installation, and always will be.

A better system, known for years to technologists, is a central refrigeration plant with refrigeration piped or ducted to points of use. Thus there could be cool drawers and cool cabinets in different parts of the kitchen, den, bedrooms, or where desired. If the technology is known, can the product be far behind?

Microwave

Microwave cooking has been covered in the energy chapter and in the appliance chapter. But in talking of trends and the future, we can't ignore the tremendous leaps in computer technology in the controls. These units now think for themselves, and it is a fast-changing field. They come as close to a home computer as anything in the home. The microwave cooker is the cooker of the future.

It has survived the radiation scare (it is about as dangerous as sunlight) and now is within reach of anyone with a credit card. As more wives join the work force, the need for this fast-cooking appliance increases. When both husband and wife get home from work at 5:30 or 6, a regular, conventional family meal is easily possible through the wonders of microwave. This product will become really big.

Countertops

High-pressure plastic laminates are being challenged by petrochemical advances. Right now the only serious challenger is Corian (see Chapter 5), but there surely will be other developments in the field of synthetics.

But the high-pressure laminates have themselves been improved so much, and they offer such a wide range of colors, patterns and textures, that it will take revolutionary developments to dislodge them. They continue to be a very fine countertop material.

Fractional Kitchens

These are the bits of kitchens scattered through the house. There will be more of them. Compact refrigerators already are selling profusely for offices, and that engenders ideas.

At home they are popping up in bedrooms, dens, and recreation rooms. With them frequently goes a wet bar, which means bar sink with running water and cabinets, possibly even a microwave oven.

The industry makes unit kitchens, or compact kitchens, incorporating a small oven, sink, refrigerator, and one or two burners in as little as 19 inches of wall space. These usually are constructed of steel and are too commercial looking for a home. The fractional kitchens now showing up in homes are designed and made up for a particular place in the home.

Other Gadgetry

Built-in intercom systems are sophisticated and highly useful. They can be wired to as many rooms in the house as desired, and the deluxe ones include fire and burglar alarms and even phonographs.

Closed-circuit television can be a great thing for mother working in the kitchen. Covering the backyard play area it can be much more useful and convenient than the window in the kitchen, and it also can cover upstairs or downstairs play areas. The coming age of home videotaping has ramifications that can only be suggested.

The world is full of super-kitchen visions of the future, but it is not our purpose here to discuss them. We speak here of what exists, what is imminent, or what is both possible and logical. And so it isn't unrealistic to say this is the way it is going to be.

Is there a computer in our future? At $10,600 we doubt if this will show up in any HUD housing, but here it is, by Honeywell. In the price you get a 2-week course in programming for such things as menu-planning, home budgeting and income tax computation. Fiberglas components are made for Honeywell by Wehco Plastic, West Trenton, N.J.

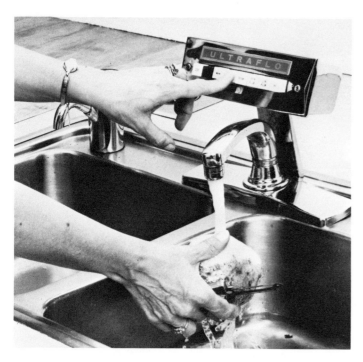

Pushbuttons can even control water in kitchen sink with this faucet by Ultraflow. The idea has been around for ten years, but now it is greatly improved and refined and perhaps its time has come. Pushbuttons operate low-voltage solenoid valves installed near water heater.

Cabinet look of the immediate future is the European look, as shown here by Poggenpohl, one of several German manufacturers now marketing in the U.S. The look is clean, contemporary, without face frames.

Touch controls on Frigidaire cooktop are representative of new microprocessor chip controls now used widely in microwave cookers and other appliances. These aren't pushbuttons. You simply touch the spot for different burners and time-temperature settings.

APPENDICES

1. ANSI A161.1/1973, Minimum Construction &
   Performance Standards for Kitchen Cabinets.

2. Minimum Light for Living Standards of American
   Home Lighting Institute.

3. Performance Standards for Fabricated High
   Pressure Decorative Laminate Countertops, 1977

4. Members, Council of Certified Kitchen Designers.

5. Addresses of Firms Mentioned in Text and Photo
   Captions.

6. Members, National Kitchen Cabinet Assn.

Construction
And Installation

General: 1. All materials shall be of sufficient gauge or thickness to insure rigidity in compliance with the performance standards, herein established. All lumber and plywood parts shall be kiln dried to a moisture content of 12 percent or less at time of fabrication. All surfaces of metal cabinets shall be rust resistant, clad or treated to insure against harmful corrosion, and all accessible edges and surfaces shall be free from sharp edges, corners, weld burrs, or metal shearing slivers.

2. Both wall and base cabinet assemblies shall consist of individual units joined into continuous sections. All units shall be fully enclosed with backs, bottoms, panels, and tops on wall cabinets. Exceptions: (a) vanity bases — backs not required; (b) vanity drawer bases, vanity bowl bases, vanity bowl fronts, oven cabinets, refrigerator cabinets, sink fronts and sink bases — bottoms and backs not required; (c) kitchen drawer bases—bottoms not required.

3. Fastenings shall be accomplished to permit removal and replacement of built in units, such as dishwasher, counter top range, oven, etc., without affecting the remainder of the installation. Cabinets containing water heaters or other equipment shall be provided with access panels for servicing or replacement of equipment.

4. Face frames, if used, shall be of necessary thickness to provide rigid construction. Face frames shall be glued, stapled, doweled, screwed, nailed, or welded to end panels.

5. Corner or lineal bracing shall be provided at points where necessary to insure rigidity and proper joining of various components, i.e., wall backs and bottoms.

6. All fixed shelves shall be recessed into grooves in the ends or in the fronts and backs or supported by cleats or weldments and must comply with Tests S-1 and S-2.

7. Intermediate shelves, both fixed and adjustable, shall be supported on ends and comply with Test No. S-1 and S-2.

8. Base cabinets designed to rest directly on the floor shall provide for a toe space at least 2 inches deep and 3 inches high.

9. Drawers of wood, metal, plastic, or any new type of construction shall comply with Tests No. S-1 and S-2. All drawer guides shall comply with Test S-6.

10. All exposed (EXPOSED PART OF CABINET IS ANY PART THAT CAN BE SEEN IN NORMAL USAGE AFTER INSTALLATION) construction joints shall be fitted in a workmanlike manner as per drawings 1 through 4. All exterior exposed parts of cabinet (except toe rails and parts normally covered after installation) shall have nails set and holes filled. Welds on metal cabinets shall be buffed smooth.

11. Swinging doors will have a device sufficient to hold doors closed.

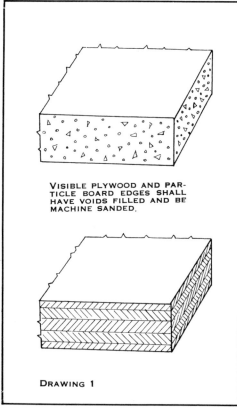

VISIBLE PLYWOOD AND PARTICLE BOARD EDGES SHALL HAVE VOIDS FILLED AND BE MACHINE SANDED.

DRAWING 1

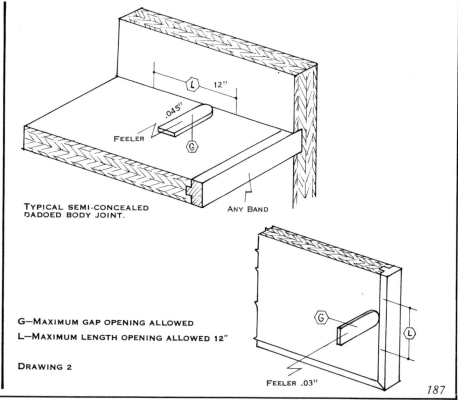

TYPICAL SEMI-CONCEALED DADOED BODY JOINT.

FEELER

.045"

12"

ANY BAND

G—MAXIMUM GAP OPENING ALLOWED
L—MAXIMUM LENGTH OPENING ALLOWED 12"

DRAWING 2

FEELER .03"

12. Improper application of the various finishing coats, such as runs, orange peel, fatty edges, blushing, etc., shall not be acceptable on exterior of cabinet.

13. Finish shall be clean and touch-up colors and/or burn-in repairs shall blend with the surrounding areas of finished surface. The finish will be free of any printing and/or pad marks.

14. Miscellaneous hardware such as drawer slides, shelf standards, brackets, rotating shelf hardware, etc., will support the design loads and operational functions described in this standard. It will be free from scratches and other damages. Paint or other cabinet finish not intended as a finish for the hardware will be removed.

15. Cabinet units will be installed level, plumb and true to line. They shall be fastened to suitable grounds as per fabricator's or manufacturer's instructions. When instructions are for other than normal mounting (such as ceiling hung units in island type installations), the cabinets will be tested in this installed position.

16. Use closer, filler strips and finish moldings as necessary for sanitary and appearance purposes.

17. The elastic limit of any material used in the cabinet system will not be exceeded when calculated by sound engineering practice for the anticipated design loads.

Base Cabinet Construction. In addition to general construction specifications, base cabinets shall have bottoms of sufficient gauge or thickness to support intended loads. To prevent excessive deflection or distortion, bottoms may be reinforced with spreader supports or support blocks adequately fastened to the cabinet shell. These bottoms must comply with Tests No. S-1 and S-2.

Wall Cabinet Construction. Wall cabinets shall be sufficiently rigid to withstand the full weight of the loaded cabinet in accordance with Tests S-1A, S-1B, and S-2 without racking or pulling loose in any joint.

Door Construction. In addition to general construction specifications, doors shall be in alignment with cabinet and adjacent doors when installed. Doors shall latch without excessive binding or looseness and shall comply with Finish Specifications.

Edges of plastic, plywood or veneer faced doors with exposed particle board core shall be capped or filled and painted to provide a finish complying with Finish Specifications.

Doors shall be of balanced or distortion resistance construction. Wood hollow core doors shall have: (1) Minimum of one piece of filler strip for each six inches of width or length in hollow portion; (2) Filled with paper honeycomb or equal.

All doors shall conform to Tests S-3, S-4, and S-5.

Oven and Utility Cabinet Construction. In addition to general construction specifications, minimum construction to be the same as for base and wall cabinets.

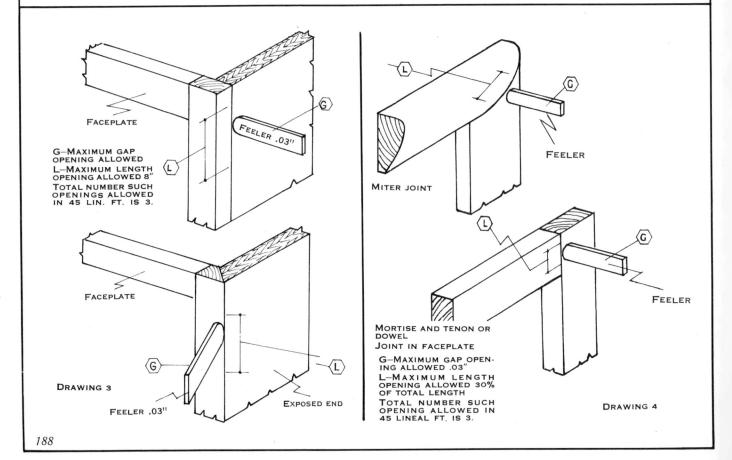

FACEPLATE

G—MAXIMUM GAP OPENING ALLOWED
L—MAXIMUM LENGTH OPENING ALLOWED 8"
TOTAL NUMBER SUCH OPENINGS ALLOWED IN 45 LIN. FT. IS 3.

FEELER .03"

FACEPLATE

DRAWING 3

FEELER .03"

EXPOSED END

MITER JOINT

FEELER

MORTISE AND TENON OR DOWEL
JOINT IN FACEPLATE
G—MAXIMUM GAP OPENING ALLOWED .03"
L—MAXIMUM LENGTH OPENING ALLOWED 30% OF TOTAL LENGTH
TOTAL NUMBER SUCH OPENING ALLOWED IN 45 LINEAL FT. IS 3.

FEELER

DRAWING 4

Contents of Tests

I. Structural Tests for Cabinets. Structural tests are basically concerned with the structural integrity of the cabinet and its installation. Each of the following structural tests were specially designed to measure the ability of the cabinet to withstand probable loadings and operational aspects.

S-1 Static Loading Tests.

Test A — This test measures ability of cabinets to withstand above average weight which would normally be kept on cabinet shelves and in drawers.

Test B — This test is to assure cabinet will stay on wall.

S-2 Impact on Shelves Under Static Load. This test will indicate the structural integrity of dropping cans and other objects onto cabinet shelves and drawers.

S-3 Impact on Cabinet Fronts (Doors), Base Cabinets. The test is designed to measure the impact received on base cabinet doors from knee closing, children hitting door with tricycles and other toys, and other impacts usually received on base cabinet doors.

S-4 Hinge Permanent Set Test and Door Racking. This test is designed to measure the structural integrity of a door when a four to six year old child attempts to climb on the counter by standing on the base cabinet door, or an adult pulling on the wall cabinet door to elevate himself to the counter.

Structural Tests for Cabinets

S-1 Static Loading — Test A: Mount upper and lower cabinet as per manufacturer's (fabricator's) instructions. Room temperature (68° to 80°F) and humidity (35% to 70%).

B. Load all shelves — uniform distributed load — 15 pounds per square foot. Load all drawers — uniform distributed load — 10 pounds per square foot. Arrange loads to avoid bridging effect. Metal revolving shelves shall meet the BHMA Cabinet Hardware Standard.

C. Maintain loading for 14 days under room temperature (68° to 80°F) and humidity (35% to 70%).
The following shall be the minimum performance for this test:

1. Examine loaded cabinet at end of 14 day test. There shall be no visible sign of joint separation or failure in any part of cabinet or mounting system.

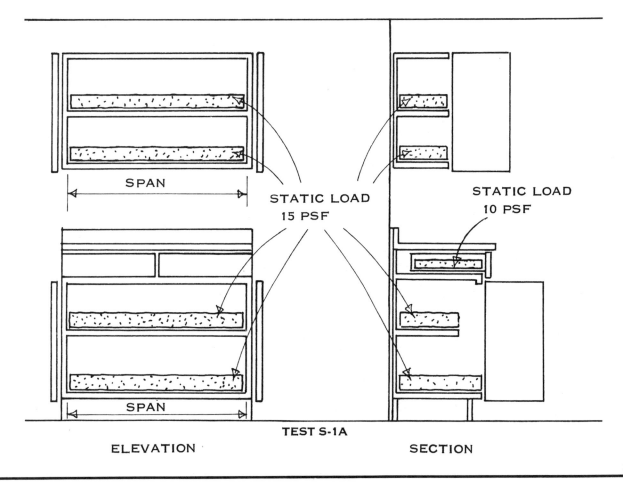

STATIC LOAD 15 PSF

STATIC LOAD 10 PSF

SPAN

SPAN

TEST S-1A

ELEVATION   SECTION

S-5 Operating Test for Door and Door Holding Device. This test designed to measure results of 10 years or more of normal opening and closing of doors.

S-6 Operating Test for Drawers. This test is designed to measure results of 10 years or more of normal opening and closing of drawers with above normal loads.

II. Exterior Wood Finish Specification. A cabinet door shall be used to evaluate the finishing tests. The door shall be representative of a normal production run. All tests shall be run on new surfaces after cabinet finish has aged 10 to 14 days.

The following tests were created to show the acceleration of kitchen conditions on pre-finished cabinets. Years of evaluation by paint manufacturers and wood fabricators of furniture, kitchen cabinets, TV, and other wood products, have determined through experience that finishes properly applied and performing under the following tests should last a minimum of five years or more.

F-1 Shrinkage and Heat Resistance
F-2 Hot/Cold Check Resistance
F-3 Chemical Resistance
F-4 Detergent and Water Resistance

III. Hardware Specifications and Standards. Cabinet hardware used on products complying with this standard shall comply with the Builders Hardware Manufacturers Association Cabinet Hardware Standard No. 201, October, 1968. (Write Builders Hardware Manufacturers Association, 60 East 42nd Street, New York, N. Y. 10017, for information on this standard.)

---

2. The loaded shelves shall not deflect more than $\frac{1}{16}''$ per lineal foot between supports, at the completion of the 14 day test. Maximum deflection will be $\frac{1}{4}''$ between supports.

3. The loaded drawers will be operable. Drawer bottoms will not be deflected to a positon where they interfere with drawer operation.

S-1 Static Loading — Test B: Wall cabinet installed to rigid test wall with screws furnished by the manufacturer or with #10 washerhead sheet metal screws as outlined below. Apply loading with hydraulic jack at a slow rate taking approximately four minutes to reach 500# loading. Cabinet passes if 500# loading can be reached. (See Illust.)

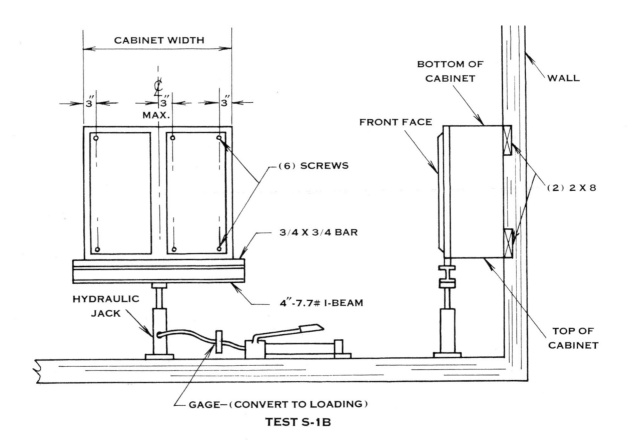

TEST S-1B

S-2 Impact on Shelves and Drawer Bottoms. **A.** Mount upper and lower cabinet as per manufacturer's (fabricator's) instructions. Room temperature (68°-80°F) and humidity (35% to 70%).

B. Drop a 3 pound weight from 4 inches above the shelf surface — see drawing.

C. Drop a 3 pound weight from 4 inches above the drawer bottom with drawer open ⅔ of the operating distance — see drawing.

The following shall be the minimum performance for this test:

1. The shelf shall not be damaged (except for superficial indentation where ball strikes) and will retain its original position.

2. The drawer shall not be damaged (except for superficial indentation where ball strikes) and will operate as before the test.

3. There shall be no visible sign of joint separation or failure in any part of the cabinet or mounting system.

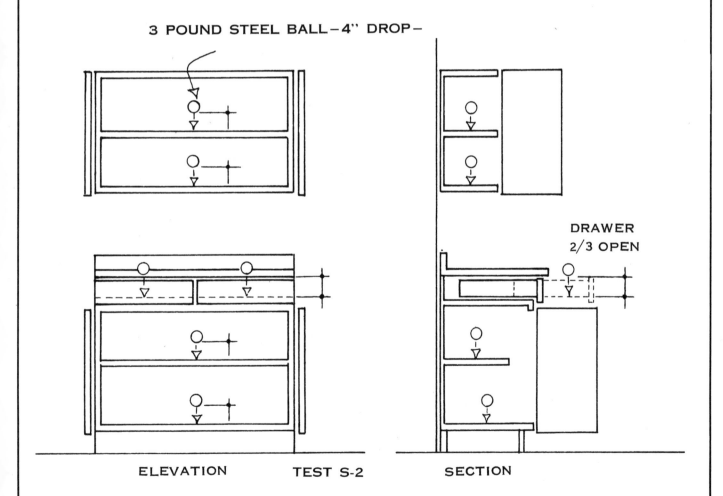

3 POUND STEEL BALL — 4" DROP —

DRAWER 2/3 OPEN

ELEVATION   TEST S-2   SECTION

TEST S-2

S-3 Impact on Cabinet Fronts (Doors) Base Cabinets. A. Mount lower cabinet as per manufacturer's (fabricator's) instructions. Room temperature (68° to 80°F) and humidity (35% to 70%).

B. Apply impact to center of cabinet door in accordance with test principle shown in drawing. Use 10 pound sandbag and 12 inch drop.

C. 45° open, Impact Test. This same test should be repeated with the door open at 45°.

The following shall be the minimum performance for this test:
1. After impact there will be no visible sign of damage to the cabinet door, hardware, or hardware connec-tions, after re-adjustment of hard-ware. Doors will operate as before the test.

2. There shall be no visible sign of joint separation or failure on any part of the cabinet or mounting system.

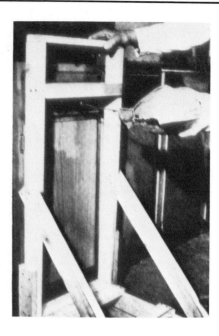

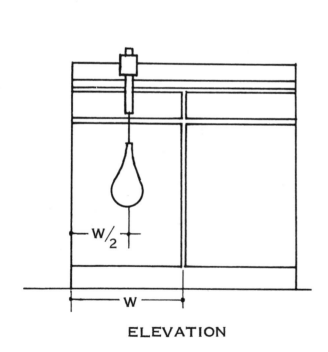

ELEVATION

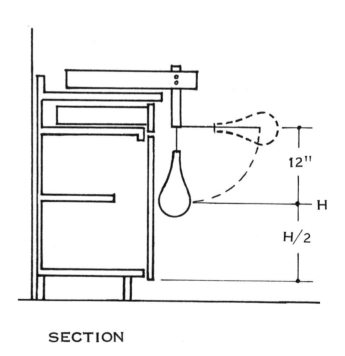

SECTION

TEST S-3

S-4 Door Racking and Hinge Set Test. **A.** Mount upper and lower cabinet per manufacturer's (fabricator's) instructions. Room temperature (68° to 80°F) and humidity (35% to 70%).

B. Record the shape of door with adjustable square or other device before application of weight.

C. With door in 90° open position, set measuring device at (M) and slowly apply weight, in accordance with test principle shown in drawing. Slowly operate through 10 cycles from 90° open position to 20° open and return to 90° open position.

Door must be so weighted for 10 minutes. Remove weight and test each door.

The following shall be the minimum performance for this test:

1. Measure the shape of the door after weight is removed. Door must retain its original shape and show no visible sign of damage. Door shall resist a minimum racking load of 45 pounds.

2. Measure the amount of set at point M. This will be called the hinge set, and shall not exceed .09 inches.

3. Hinges and hinge connections shall show no visible sign of damage.

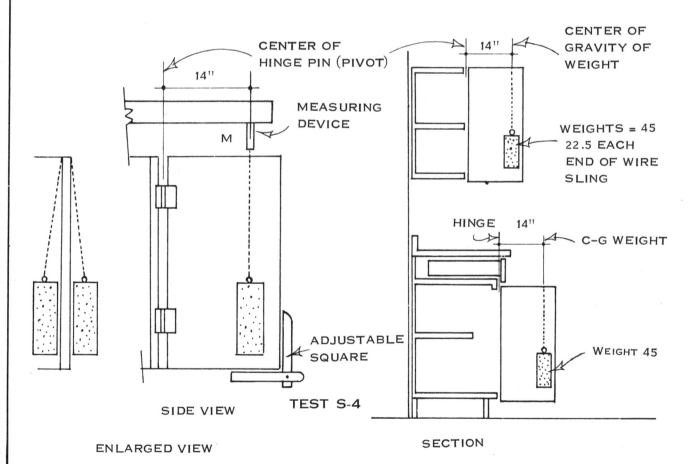

SIDE VIEW

TEST S-4

ENLARGED VIEW

SECTION

CENTER OF HINGE PIN (PIVOT)

MEASURING DEVICE

M

ADJUSTABLE SQUARE

14"

CENTER OF GRAVITY OF WEIGHT

WEIGHTS = 45
22.5 EACH
END OF WIRE SLING

HINGE   14"

C-G WEIGHT

WEIGHT 45

NOTE: FOR CABINET DOORS LESS THAN 15 INCHES WIDE. APPLY WEIGHT AT A POINT 1 INCH IN FROM OUTER EDGE.

S-5 Operating Test For Door and Door Holding Device. **A.** Mount upper and lower cabinet as per manufacturer's (fabricator's) instructions. Room temperature (68° to 80°F) and humidity (35% to 70%).

B. The door holding device (spring catch, magnetic catch, self-closing hinges, or other) will be part of this test.

C. Record the shape of the door with adjustable square or other device and record the door elevation (open 90°) at point M, before cycling. See drawing.

D. Attach cycling mechanism to door at normal operating position so that no additional loads are placed on hinges. One cycle shall consist of operation through 90° swing with full engagement and disengagement of holding device. Operate door through 25,000 cycles at a speed where excessive heat through friction is not developed.

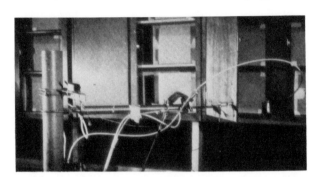

The following shall be the minimum performance for this test:

1. The door will be operable and the door holding device will be adequate to hold door in closed position.

2. The door shape will be the same as before the test recorded in part C.

3. The measurement at point M (sag) will not exceed .09 inches.

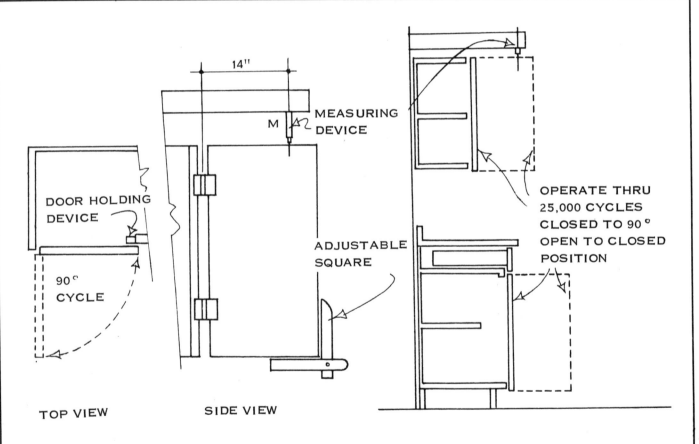

DOOR HOLDING DEVICE

90° CYCLE

14"

M — MEASURING DEVICE

ADJUSTABLE SQUARE

OPERATE THRU 25,000 CYCLES CLOSED TO 90° OPEN TO CLOSED POSITION

TOP VIEW   SIDE VIEW

ENLARGED VIEWS   TEST S-5   SECTION

NOTE: FOR CABINET DOORS LESS THAN 15 INCHES WIDE, POINT M SHALL BE 1 INCH FROM OUTER EDGE.

S-6 Operating Test For Drawers. A.
Mount a lower cabinet unit as per manufacturer's (fabricator's) instructions. Room temperature (68° to 80°F) and humidity (35% to 70%).

B. Load drawer — uniform distributed load — 10 pounds per square foot. See drawing.

C. Operate drawer through 25,000 cycles. One cycle shall consist of opening drawer ⅔ of travel distance and return to closed position. Attach cycling mechanism so that no additional loads are placed on drawer. Operate at a speed where excessive heat through friction is not developed.

The following shall be the minimum performance for this test:

1. Drawer will be operable at completion of test.

2. There shall be no failure in any part of drawer assembly or operating system.

3. Drawer bottoms will not be deflected to a position where they interfere with drawer operation.

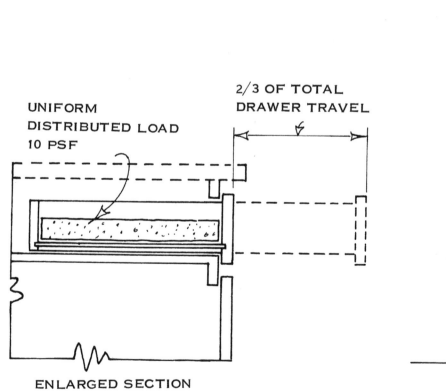

UNIFORM
DISTRIBUTED LOAD
10 PSF

2/3 OF TOTAL
DRAWER TRAVEL

ENLARGED SECTION

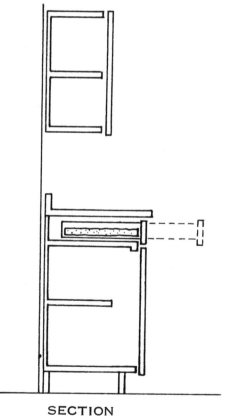

SECTION

TEST S-6

Finish Specifications

General. Unless otherwise specified herein, a cabinet door shall be used to evaluate the finishing tests. The door shall be representative of a normal production run. All tests shall be run on new surfaces after cabinet finish has aged 10 to 14 days. The following tests were created to show the acceleration of kitchen conditions on pre-finished cabinets. Years of evaluation by paint manufacturers and fabricators of furniture, kitchen cabinets, TV, and other household products, have determined through experience that finishes properly applied and performing under the following tests should last a minimum of five years or more.

Appearance. All exterior exposed surfaces (EXPOSED SURFACE OF CABINET IS ANY PART THAT CAN BE SEEN IN NORMAL USAGE AFTER INSTALLATION), including door and drawer front edges, shall be free of saw marks and other imperfections and shall be finished. Improper application of the various finishing coats on exterior of cabinet, i.e., runs, orange peel, fatty edges, blushing, etc., shall not be acceptable. Finish shall be clean and free of excessive dirt, dust, scratches, mats and residue. Touch-up colors and/or burn-in repairs shall be matched with the surrounding areas of the finished surfaces. The finish shall be free of any printing and/or pad marks which may be caused by padding.

All internal exposed surfaces shall be free of saw marks, poor workmanship, and shall with exception of drawers have a minimum of one coat of clear or pigmented finish.

Finish Tests for Cabinets

F-1 Shrinkage and Heat Resistance.

A. A cabinet door, without screw holes, or with all screw holes covered, shall be used for this test. Stabilize at room temperature (68° to 80°F) and humidity (35% to 70%).

B. Door, by visual examination will be free of finish defects.

C. Place the door in a hot box (120°F ± 5°F and 70% ± 5% humidity) for a 24 hour period.

The following shall be the minimum performance for this test:

1. By visual examination, the door finish will show no appreciable discoloration, evidence of blistering, film rupture, shrinkage checks or other film failure.

F-2 Hot/Cold Check Resistance.

A. A cabinet door (as described in Test F-1-A) shall be used for this test.

B. Door, by visual examination, shall be free of finish defects.

C. Cycle as follows: Place door in hot box (120°F ± 5°F and 70% ± 5% humidity) for one hour. Remove and allow to reach original room temperature and humidity conditions. Place in cold box (− 5°F) for one hour. Remove and allow door to reach original room temperature and humidity conditions. This will be one cycle.

The following shall be the minimum performance for this test:

1. After five cycles (see C), the door finish will show no appreciable discoloration, evidence of blistering, film rupture, shrinkage checks or other film failures.

F-3 Chemical Resistance.

A. Place 3 cc's of each of the following substances on the surface of the cabinet door tilted at an angle of 70 to 80° with the horizontal: Vinegar, Lemon, Orange and Grape juice, tomato catsup, coffee (prepared for drinking at 115° — one teaspoon of coffee per cup), olive oil, 100 proof alcohol.

B. Allow these substances to stand on the surface for a period of 24 hours under room temperature (68° to 80°F) and humidity (35% to 70%).

C. Mustard will be tested under similar conditions for one hour.

D. Sponge wash the surface with clear water and dry with a clean cloth.

E. In the event of any initial failure on F-3 Tests, the test laboratory will allow the door to sit for seven to ten days and re-examine for performance under these tests.

The following shall be the minimum performance for this test:

1. No excessive discoloration, stain or whitening shall result which will not disperse with ordinary polishing.

2. There will be no indication of film rupture or shrinkage.

F-4 Detergent and Water Resistance.

A. See drawing for suggested test equipment. Room temperature (68° to 80°F) and humidity (35% to to 70%).

B. Sponge; 1½″ thickness, Dupont cellulose #8A, or equal.

C. Detergent solution; 1% by weight, 1 ounce of Dreft to 1 gallon of water.

D. Level trough and fill with detergent solution to approximately ½ inch below top level of sponge.

E. Place the base cabinet door upright (top edge down) on the sponge as shown in drawing. Examine at 24 hours for delamination and finish failure.

The following shall be the minimum performance for this test:

1. After 24 hours there will be no delamination or finish failure.

2. The finish will show no appreciable discoloration, evidence of blistering, film rupture, shrinkage checks or other film failure.

F-5 Metal Cabinets Rust Resistance.

A. Finished end or section (approximately 5″ x 9″) thereof taken from regular production is to be tested.

B. Back of panel to be diagonally scratched from corner to corner with

razor blade to bare metal; 288 hours exposure at 100% relative humidity and 100°F ± 2°F; inspected each 24 hours for first 72 hours.

The following shall be the minimum performance for this test:

1. No blisters accepted after 288 hours.

2. Rust creepage from edges or scratches shall not exceed 1/16″ maximum.

(This test to be completed for metal cabinets only.)

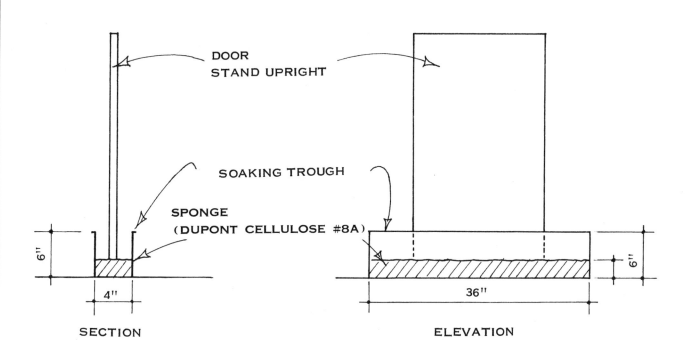

DOOR STAND UPRIGHT

SOAKING TROUGH

SPONGE (DUPONT CELLULOSE #8A)

6″   4″

SECTION

6″   36″

ELEVATION

TEST F-4

Appendix 2

Minimum Light for Living Standards of American Home Lighting Institute.

GUIDE to ADVANCED LIGHT for LIVING

Recommendations by the American Home Lighting Institute for fixture lighting installations which go beyond the MINIMUM Light for Living Standards.

Kitchen

1) For Local Work Surface—Counters
   a. Wall or cabinet-mounted (14 to 22 inches above counter) one 20-watt fluorescent or a two socket (60 watts each) incandescent bracket for every 3 ft. of counter. (See following 2 and 3, when no cabinets.)
2) For Local Sink or Range Surface—for ceiling or soffit location
   a. One recessed fixture containing three 75-watt incandescent in box at least 24 inches long, or two 40-watt or three 30-watt fluorescent tubes, OR . . .
   b. Two recessed fixtures with inner reflectors for 100-watt incandescent bulb each, centered 18 inches apart, OR . . .
   c. Minimum 2, preferably 3, "bullets" (recessed, surface or pendant) for 75-watt R-30 flood-lamps.
3) For Local Sink or Range Surface—wall mounting
   a. Wall bracket 14 to 22 inches above range, allowing some upward light; Minimum one 30-watt fluorescent, or multiple socket incandescent bracket (60 to 75 watts) approx. 18 inches long.
   b. When range hood is used, select one with one or two incandescent sockets.
4) For General Lighting—(in addition to local) use one fixture for approx. every 50 sq. ft. of area. May be surface mounted, recessed or pendant, depending on ceiling height, slope, construction,

placed for harmony with room shape, and contain each:
   a. 175 to 200 watts, incandescent (fixture minimum 14 inch diameter), 60 to 80 watts fluorescent, OR . . .
   b. One 24 sq. ft. suspended luminous ceiling-type fixture (minimum 360-watt incandescent) for rooms with finished floor area no greater than 50 sq. ft.

NOTE: When a luminous ceiling, or ceiling panels are desired, a minimum depth of 8 inches above plastic or louvers to tube centers is required. Use minimum of one 40-watt fluorescent tube for every 12 sq. ft. of room area, or 60-watt incandescent for every 4 sq. ft. of panel. In bathroom, add appropriate lighting at mirror.

MINIMUM LIGHT for LIVING STANDARDS

Recommended by AMERICAN HOME LIGHTING INSTITUTE

Kitchen Area

General Lighting: A minimum of one 12" diameter fixture to accommodate one 150-watt, two 75-watt, or three 60-watt bulbs

   . . . OR a minimum of two 40-watt, four 20-watt, or two circline fluorescent tubes
   . . . OR at least two 150-watt recessed fixtures,

Local Lighting: Above a sink, use recessed or surface-mounted fixture with 150 watts of incandescent or 80 watts of fluorescent.

Sink under cabinets, range, and work counter, use a minimum of one 20-watt fluorescent tube or two 40-watt incandescent bulbs for each 4' of counter.

Appendix 3

Performance Standards for
Fabricated High Pressure Decorative Laminate Countertops, 1977

PART 1 — COUNTERTOP BLANKS

1.1 SCOPE AND PURPOSE

1.1.1 Scope: This standard covers physical requirements and test methods for performance pertaining to structure and to resistance to water, impact, wear, scuff, boiling water, high temperature, light resistance, and other significant properties.

In addition, general requirements for materials and workmanship and finish of high pressure decorative laminate (HPDL) countertops (sink, vanity, work, etc.) are covered herein. Methods of tests are formulated which qualify the countertop for normal indoor use (residences, restaurants, public facilities, etc.).

1.1.2 Purpose: The purpose of the standard is to establish generally acceptable quality performance standards for high pressure decorative laminate (HPDL) countertops. Its purpose is also to serve as a guide for producers, distributors, architects, engineers, contractors, home builders, government agencies, code authorities, and users; to

1.1.3 TYPICAL COUNTERTOP CROSS SECTIONS

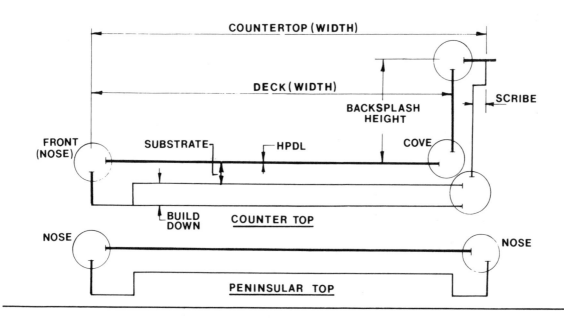

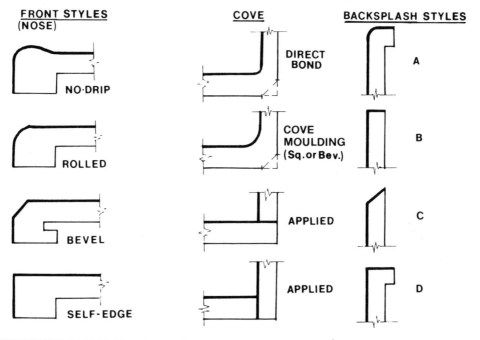

CONFIGURATIONS TO MANUFACTURERS SPECIFICATIONS

promote understanding regarding materials, manufacture, and installation; to form a basis for fair competition; and to provide a basis for identifying high pressure decorative laminate (HPDL) countertops that conform to this standard.

1.1.3 (Drawing-Left)

1.1.4 Glossary of Terms

Backsplash — A vertical member of the countertop connected to and rising above the back edge of the deck.

Backsplash height — dimension from the deck to the top of the backsplash.

Blisters — a raised area in the countertop surface caused by delamination of the HPDL within itself.

Bubble — a raised area in the countertop surface caused by a delamination between the HPDL and the substrate or within the substrate.

Build down strip — additional material applied to the underside of the deck to establish countertop thickness.

Chipped Areas — A void in the surface of the HPDL.

Countertop — a work surface.

Countertop (Bevel Edged Type) — A flat construction assembly with or without the backsplash.

Countertop (Postformed Type) — A three dimensional seamless countertop.

Countertop (Self Edged Type) — a flat construction assembly with or without the backsplash. The backsplash (if used) may be coved or applied types.

Countertop blank — a manufactured component countertop before customizing.

Countertop width (Depth) — dimension from the front edge of the countertop to the back edge of the backsplash including the scribe.

Countertop length — linear dimension of the countertop.

Countertop thickness — dimension from the deck to bottom of the build down strip.

Cove — junction of the deck and the backsplash.

Cove stick — support material at coved area.

Cracks — fractures in the HPDL surface.

Cutouts — openings cut through the countertop or the backsplash (for sink, range top, electrical fixtures, etc.).

Deck — work surface of the countertop.

Deck (width) — front edge of the countertop to the face of the backsplash.

Detergent solution — 1% dishwashing detergent (such as Lux or Joy) in water.

End cap — HPDL applied to finish an end of the countertop.

End splash — a vertical component similar to the backsplash at an end of the countertop.

Fingernail test — Place fingernail down at a 45° incline towards joint to be tested. Move fingernail across joint. There shall be no more than a slight catching or feeling of the joint by the fingernail.

High pressure decorative laminate (HPDL) — a decorative plastic sheet consisting of papers that have been laminated at pressures more than 500 pounds per square inch using thermosetting condensation resins as binders.

Joint (butt type) — machined ends of two countertop sections for assembly to each other.

Joint (mitre type) — matching machined ends of two sections of countertop cut at an angle to change direction of the countertop.

Joint assembled (butt and mitre types) — machined components drawn tight and assembled with water resistant material and mechanical fasteners as required.

Nose — Leading edge of typical countertop including side edges of peninsular top.

Riser — raised area at the front edge of the countertop which produces the no-drip feature.

Riser height — dimension measured from the top of the riser to the deck surface.

Rolled leading edge — curved front edge of the deck without riser.

Scribe — material at top rear edge of the backsplash to allow for fitting to the wall.

Scribe width (depth) — dimension from the back of the backsplash to the extreme edge of the scribe area.

Self edge — a strip of HPDL applied to an edge of the countertop.

Substrate — supporting material for the HPDL.

See 1.1.3 Typical Countertop Cross Sections

1.2 GENERAL REQUIREMENTS

1.2.1 Materials: The countertop shall be assembled using HPDL bonded by a suitable adhesive to a substrate material. The HPDL shall be manufactured in conformance to NEMA Standard LD3-1975 of the National Electrical Manufacturers Association, 155 East 44th Street, New York, New York 10017. The other raw materials shall be of such quality that the finished countertop will meet all the performance requirements established in this countertop standard.

1.2.2 Conditioning: Countertop units to be inspected and tested shall be conditioned for a minimum of 10 days at a temperature of 73°F ±4°F (23°±2°C) and a relative humidity of 50%±5% R. H.

1.2.3 Dimensional Tolerances: (As applied to the fabricators stated dimensions)

A. Height of riser strip: ± .010" (.254mm)
B. Deck (width) measured at 2" (50.8mm) above the deck: ± .032" (.813mm)
C. Height of the backsplash: ±.032" (.813mm)
D. Depth of the scribe (when used): minimum of .250" (6.35mm)
E. Deck warpage in length: .062" (1.57mm)/ft. (305mm)
F. Deck warpage in width (depth): .062" (1.57mm)/ft. (305mm)

1.3 APPEARANCE

1.3.1 Cleaning for Testing: The countertop unit shall be washed with the standard detergent solution, rinsed with clear water and dried.

1.3.2 Method of Inspection of the Countertop Surface:
The surface of the countertop unit shall be visually inspected for defects and blemishes in the plane of intended use from a distance of 60" (1524mm) to 84" (2134mm), and from a height of 30" (762mm) above the surface. The light source shall be diffused north daylight, or substantially equivalent artificial light giving 75 to 100 foot candles illumination intensity near the surface to be inspected.

1.3.3 Allowable Defects or Blemishes:

Defect or Blemish	Max. no. allowed Per Sq. Ft.
Cracks	None
Chipped Areas	None
Blisters	None
Bubbles	None

1.3.4 Delamination at the Glue Line:
None.

1.4 PHYSICAL CHARACTERISTICS OF THE HIGH PRESSURE DECORATIVE LAMINATE SHEET

1.4.1 Materials:
The countertop blank manufacturer shall purchase high pressure decorative laminate sheets made and tested in compliance with NEMA Standard LD3-1975 of the National Electrical Manufacturers Association, 155 East 44th Street, New York, New York 10017, with minimum performance properties as listed below and shall submit with the countertop test sample a copy of certification of compliance to the above standard from the manufacturer of the HPDL sheets.

In the absence of such certification, the countertop testing laboratory shall conduct the following NEMA tests.

1.4.2 NEMA LD 3-3.01 Wear Resistance.
Shall pass 400 cycles.

1.4.3 NEMA LD 3-3.02 Scuff Resistance.
Shall have no effect — no visible change of any kind.

1.4.4 NEMA LD 3-3.05 Boiling Water Resistance.
Shall have not more than a slight effect — a change in color or surface texture which is difficult to perceive.

1.4.5 NEMA LD 3-3.09 Stain Resistance.
Shall have no effect from reagents 1 thru 23. Shall have not more than moderate effect from reagents 24 thru 29.

1.4.6 NEMA LD 3-3.10 Light Resistance.
Shall have not more than a slight effect — a change in color or surface texture which is difficult to perceive.

1.4.7 NEMA LD 3-3.12 Cleanability.
Shall be cleaned with maximum of 25 strokes with no change in appearance.

1.5 IMPACT TESTS

1.5.1 Deck Surface: (See Drawing A)

Purpose: To test the durability of the deck surface with respect to impact hazards.

Test Procedure: A 1.50" (38.1 mm) diameter polished steel ball (ball bearing type) having no damaged or flattened areas on its surface shall be dropped 30" (762mm) on to the deck of a countertop secured by a clamping jig holding the test specimen flat on a solid horizontal bench. The ball shall be caught after the first bounce to prevent reimpaction.

The test shall be repeated at three locations on the unit. After 30 minutes, the contacted areas shall be examined.

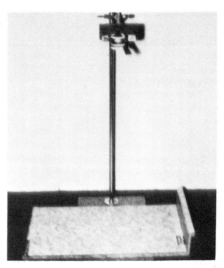

Impact Test 1.5.1: 30" Ball Drop of countertop deck

Minimum Performance: There shall be no cracking, chipping, or indentation of the surface of the HPDL.

1.5.2 Crown of Riser and Rolled Edge:
(See Drawings A and B) (1.5.2 applies only to rolled edge countertops).

Purpose: To test the durability of the crown of riser and the rolled edge with respect to impact hazards.

Test Procedures:

Crown of Riser (Drawing A, Test 1.5.2A): A 1.50" (38.1mm) diameter polished steel ball (ball bearing type) having no damaged or flattened areas on its surface shall be dropped 10" (254mm) through a rigid guide tube having an inside diameter of not less than 1.56" (39mm) on to the crown of the riser of a countertop secured by a clamping jig holding the test specimen flat on a solid horizontal bench. The ball shall be caught after the first bounce to prevent reimpaction.

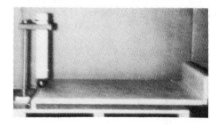

Impact Test 1.5.2A: 10" Ball Drop on outside radius of no-drip edge.

Rolled Edge (Drawing B, Test 1.5.2B): The countertop shall be supported in a rigid V-shaped frame resting on a solid horizontal bench so that the front of the deck shall

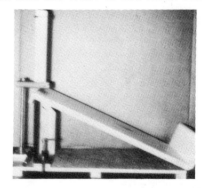

Impact Test 1.5.2B: 10" Ball Drop on rolled edge radius of countertop.

be 45° above the rear of the deck. A 1.50" (38.1mm) diameter polished steel ball (ball bearing type) having no damaged or flattened areas on its surface shall be dropped 10" (254mm) through a rigid guide tube having an inside diameter of not less than 1.56" (39mm) on to the rolled edge of the supported countertop. The ball shall be caught after the first bounce to prevent re-impaction.

The respective tests shall be repeated at three locations on the appropriate unit. After 30 minutes, the contacted areas shall be examined.

Minimum Performance: There shall be no cracking, chipping, or indentation of the surface of the HPDL.

IMPACT TESTS 1.5 and STATIC LOAD TESTS 1.7

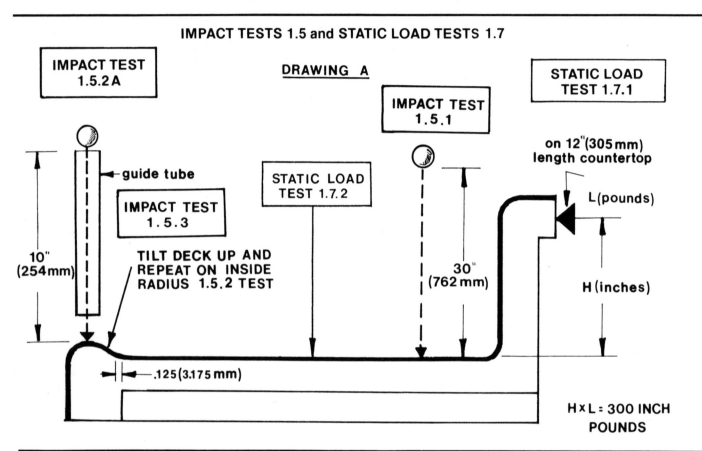

DRAWING A

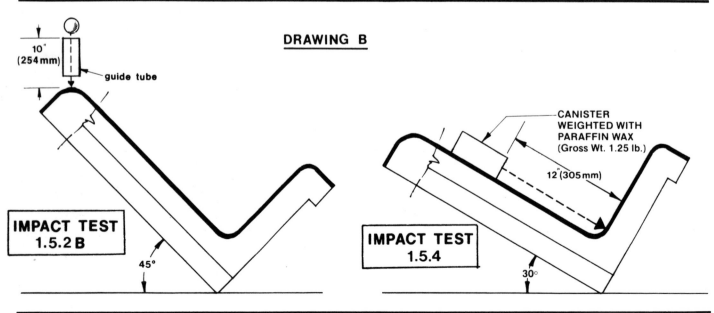

DRAWING B

1.5.3 Riser-Deck Junction (Valley where riser intercepts deck): (SEE DRAWING A) (1.5.3 does not apply to self edged countertops).

Purpose: To test the durability of the riser-deck junction with respect to impact hazards.

Impact Test 1.5.3: 10" Ball Drop on inside radius of no-drip edge.

Test Procedure: The countertop shall be supported in a rigid frame resting on a solid horizontal bench so that the rear of the deck shall be 22.5° above the front of the deck. A 1.50" (38.1mm) diameter polished steel ball (ball bearing type) having no damaged or flattened areas on its surface shall be dropped 10" (254mm) through a rigid guide tube having an inside diameter of not less than 1.56" (39mm) on to the inside radius where the riser joins the deck of the supported countertop. The ball shall be caught after the first bounce to prevent reimpaction.

The test shall be repeated at three locations on the unit.

After 30 minutes, the contacted areas shall be examined.

Minimum Performance: There shall be no cracking, chipping, or indentation of the surface of the HPDL.

1.5.4 Cove Test: (See Drawing B)

Purpose: To test the durability of the cove with respect to impact hazards.

Test-Procedure: The countertop shall be supported in a rigid V-shaped frame resting on a solid horizontal bench so that the front of the deck shall be 30° above the rear of the deck. A canister weighted with parrafin wax and having an approximate diameter of 5.0" (127mm) and a gross weight of 1.25 lbs. (.663kg) shall be placed on the HPDL deck 12.0" (304.8mm) from the backsplash. The canister shall

Impact Test 1.5.4: 1.25 lbs. Cove Test with 12" canister free-slide down a 30° plane.

be released and caught after the first bounce to prevent reimpaction.

The test shall be repeated at three locations on the unit.
After 30 minutes, the contacted areas shall be examined.

Minimum Performance: There shall be no cracking, chipping, or indentation of the surface of the HPDL.

1.6 HIGH TEMPERATURE RESISTANCE

Purpose: To test the durability of the surface of the countertop deck with respect to high temperature hazards.

Test Procedure: The test method in Section LD3-3.06 of the High Pressure Decorative Laminates' Standards, LD3-1975, of the National Electrical Manufacturers Association, 155 East 44th Street, New York, New York 10017, shall be used except that the test shall be run on the center of the countertop deck.

Minimum Performance: A slight effect shall be allowed — a change in color or surface texture which is difficult to perceive. There shall be no cracking, crazing, blistering, discoloring, whitening, or delamination.

1.7 STATIC LOAD

1.7.1 Backsplash: (See Drawing A)

Purpose: To test the durability of the bond between the countertop and the backsplash with respect to load hazards.

Test Procedure: A 300 inch-pound evenly distributed load shall be applied on a 12" (305mm) section

Static Load Test 1.7.1: Evenly distributed hydraulic loading to 300 in/lbs. along top edge of backsplash.

of the backsplash of a countertop secured by a clamping jig. The load shall be above and parallel to the deck on the back of the backsplash.

The load shall be held for 5 seconds and then released.

Minimum Performance: There shall be no visible evidence of the breaking of the adhesive bond. There shall be no cracking or chipping of the surface of the HPDL.

1.7.2 Deck: (See Drawing A)

Purpose: To test deflection of deck section with respect to load hazards.

Test Procedure: A 300 lb. (136 k.g.) static load shall be applied to the centre of a 12" (305mm) wide sample supported by 1" (25.4mm) high spacers under the deck to provide 20" (508mm) of space between. The load shall be perpendicular to the deck and be maintained during measurement.

Minimum Performance: Deflection shall not exceed 0.250" (6.35mm).

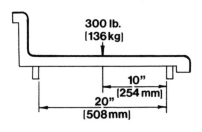

1.8 SELF EDGES

1.8.1 Assembly: Self edges shall be applied with a water resistant adhesive to the substrate and trimmed with no visible effect to the HPDL surface and with no surface projection over .005" (.127mm) as tested by the fingernail test.

1.8.2 Water Drip Test for Applied Self Edges
Purpose: To test the durability of the junction between the countertop and the self edge with respect to water hazards.

Test Procedure: A folded, clean cotton rag shall be wet in the detergent solution and placed over the junction between the applied self edge and the HPDL deck only.

Using the detergent solution, the rag shall be kept wet with a dripper for 24 hours.

After 24 hours, the test area shall be dried and examined.

Note: The water shall not contact the unprotected substrate.

Minimum Performance: There shall be no visible sign of delamination or swelling of the substrate adjacent to the junction.

1.9 APPLIED BACKSPLASH

1.9.1 Assembly: The backsplash and countertop shall be assembled with water resistant adhesive or mechanical fasteners or both.

1.9.2 Water Drip Test for Applied Backsplashes
Purpose: To test the durability of the junction between the backsplash and the countertop with respect to water hazards.

Test Procedure: A folded, clean cotton rag shall be wet in the detergent solution and placed over the junction between the backsplash and the countertop only.

Using the detergent solution, the rag shall be kept wet with a dripper for 24 hours.

After 24 hours, the test area shall be dried and examined.

Note: The water shall not contact the unprotected substrate.

Minimum Performance: There shall be no visible sign of delamination or swelling of the substrate adjacent to the junction.

PART II — CUSTOMIZED COUNTERTOPS

2.1 SCOPE AND PURPOSE

This standard covers the performance, appearance, and test methods for the additional work which must be done in order to make the certified countertop blank a complete assembly ready for installation.

2.2 UNASSEMBLED MITRE JOINTS

The length of all mitre cuts of countertop components for assembly shall be matching within .048" (1.12mm).
The edges shall be deburred.
There shall be no chipping of the surface of the HPDL.

2.3 ASSEMBLED (BUTT AND MITRE) JOINTS

2.3.1 Assembly: Butt and mitre joints shall be made with water resistant material and mechanical fasteners as required. The deck area joint shall have a maximum of a .005" (.127mm) gap. The fingernail test shall be used on deck area to test the smoothness of the joint. All other areas of the joint may have a maximum of .030" (.762mm) differential in surface alignment.

2.3.2 Water Drip Test for Butt and Mitre Joints.
Purpose: To test the durability of butt and mitre joints with respect to water hazards.

Test Procedure: A folded, clean cotton rag shall be wet in the detergent solution and placed over the joint at the deck area only.

Using the detergent solution, the rag shall be kept wet with a dripper for 24 hours.

After 24 hours, the test area shall be dried and examined.

Minimum Performance: There shall be no visible sign of delamination or swelling of the substrate adjacent to the joint.

2.4 APPLIED END CAP

2.4.1 Assembly: The end cap shall be applied with a water resistant adhesive to the substrate and trimmed with no visible effect to the HPDL surface and with no surface projection over .005" (.127mm) as tested by the fingernail test.

2.4.2 Water Drip Test for Applied End Caps
Purpose: To test the durability of the junction between the end cap and the HPDL deck with respect to water hazards.

Test Procedure: A folded, clean cotton rag shall be wet in the detergent solution and placed over the junction between the end cap and the HPDL deck only.

Using the detergent solution, the rag shall be kept wet with a dripper for 24 hours.

After 24 hours, the test area shall be dried and examined.

Minimum Performance: There shall be no visible sign of delamination or swelling of the substrate adjacent to the junction.

2.5 APPLIED END SPLASH

2.5.1 Assembly: The end splash shall be applied with water resistant material or mechanical fasteners or both (as required).

2.5.2 Water Drip Test for Applied End Splashes

Purpose: To test the durability of the junction between the end splash and the countertop with respect to water hazards.

Test Procedure: A folded, clean cotton rag shall be wet in the detergent solution and placed over the junction between the end splash and the countertop only.

Using the detergent solution, the rag shall be kept wet with a dripper for 24 hours.

After 24 hours, the test area shall be dried and examined.

Minimum Performance: There shall be no visible sign of delamination or swelling of the substrate adjacent to the junction.

2.6 CUTOUTS

Cutouts shall be machined to match the accomodating insert (sink, range top, etc.) as per appliance manufacturers' specifications +.125" (3.17mm) — 0". The corners of the cutouts shall be made with a minimum radius of .25" (6.35mm). All radius edges shall be made smooth.

There shall be no chipping of the HPDL that will not be covered by the appliance.

Appendix 4
Members, Council of Certified Kitchen Designers

ALABAMA

Birmingham
C. H. Seeds, CKD
Evans Kitchens & Baths
1914 Avenue E, Ensley
zip 35218

ARIZONA

Phoenix
A. M. Buck, CKD
Crowe Lumber & Construction Co.
1445 E. Indian School Road
zip 85014

CALIFORNIA

Burbank
C. W. Todd, CKD
Time Construction Company, Inc.
4111 West Olive Street
zip 91515

Downey
C. A. Olson, CKD
Downey Plumbing &
Heating Company
11829 South Downey Avenue
zip 90241

LaJolla
J. H. Baldwin, Jr., CKD
St. Charles of Southern Calif.
7426 Girard St.
zip 92037

Los Angeles
W. E. Peterson, CKD-ASID
St. Charles of Southern Calif.
3712 Barham Blvd., Apt. C114
zip 90068

Mountain View
T. J. Aylward, CKD
St. Charles Mfg. Company
1126 Blue Lake Square
zip 94040

Orange
J. B. Galloway, CKD
Carefree Kitchens, Inc.
453 North Anaheim Blvd.
zip 92668

R. L. Pizzuit, CKD
Diamond Industries/
Div. Medford Corp.
210 West Taft
zip 92665

Palo Alto
P. D. Provost, CKD
Butterfield, Kitchens & Baths
3626 El Camino Real
zip 94306

Sacramento
J. W. Aievoli, CKD
Kitchens, Inc.
2015 Q Street
zip 95814

Ellen M. Cheever-Aievoli, CKD
Kitchens, Inc.
2015 Q Street
zip 95814

M. Cohn, CKD
Kustom Kitchens
1220 "X" Street
zip 95818

J. M. Liston, CKD
Horrell & Son, Inc.
3130 L Street
zip 95816

L. C. Lundell, CKD
Home & Kitchen Interiors
4601 H Street
zip 95819

D. J. Schickling, CKD
Home & Kitchen Interiors
4601 H Street
zip 95819

San Carlos
S. M. Macey, CKD
Galli Homes, Inc.
778 El Camino Real
zip 94070

San Francisco
G. A. Taylor, CKD
Continental Home Improvement
340 West Portal
zip 94127

San Leandro
B. Peck, CKD
Somerset Remodeling, Inc.
15225 Hesperian Blvd.
zip 94578

San Mateo
D. W. Quest, CKD
Quesco Cabinets, Inc.
1011 South Claremont Street
zip 94402

San Pedro
Mary Grace Satterfield, CKD
Cook's Kitchen Center
402 W. 7th St.
zip 90731

Walnut Creek
J. Palazzolo, CKD
East Bay Kitchens
2659 North Main Street
zip 94596

West Hollywood
Jeannette N. Coppes, CKD-ASID
Distinctive Kitchens & Baths
720 Ramage Street
zip 90069

CANADA

ALBERTA

Edmonton
G. A. Dreger, CKD
Dreger's Kitchen Corner Ltd.
10442 — 82nd Avenue
zip T6E 2A2

Lily D. Dreger, CKD
8331 120th St.
zip T6E 2A2

ONTARIO

Dorchester
R. L. Bannerman, CKD
Kitchen Salon, Inc.
Village Center Plaza
61 Dorchester Road
zip N0L 1G0

London
K. H. Cassin, CKD
Cassin Remco Limited
#135 Highway
zip N6A 4B8

Toronto
G. N. Riepert, CKD
Kitchen Planning & Design, Inc.
Suite 504 — 207 Queen's Quay, West
zip M5J 1A7

COLORADO

Colorado Springs
R. D. Bailey, CKD
Bailley's Kitchens, Inc.
530 N. Tejon
zip 80903

W. B. Jordan, CKD
Jordan's, Inc.
121 E. Bijou
zip 80902

N. L. Van Nattan, CKD
Elm Distributors
120 West Rio Grande
zip 80903

Denver
E. Hanley, CKD
Edward Hanley & Company
1448 Oneida Street
zip 80220

Esther M. Hartman, CKD
Kitchen Distributors, Inc.
1235 South Broadway
zip 80210

C. W. Kline, CKD
Kitchens by Kline
2640 E. 3rd Avenue
zip 80206

Betsy H. Smith, CKD
Carriage Cabinet Concepts, Inc.
1030 W. Ellsworth Ave.
zip 80223

E. Winger, CKD
Kitchen Distributors, Inc.
1235 South Broadway
zip 80210

CONNECTICUT

Ansonia
G. H. Mann, CKD
Ralph Mann & Sons
505 Main Street
zip 06401

Bridgeport
I. Effron, CKD
City Lumber Company of Bridgeport
75 Third St.
zip 06601

Bristol
A. S. Audibert, CKD
Audibert's
781 King Street
zip 06010

Darien
L. F. Maceli, CKD
2 Clock Avenue
zip 06820

East Haven
J. A. Kmetzo, CKD
Metzo Kitchens — Baths
334 Main Street
zip 06512

Essex
G. D. Crane, CKD
Paul Dolan Company, Inc.
Route 9A
zip 06426

Greenwich
L. J. Kowalski, CKD
Kowalski's Kitchen Originals
202 Field Point Road
zip 06830

Litchfield
R. L. Gelormino, CKD
Kustom Kitchens of Litchfield, Inc.
Torrington Road
zip 06759

Norwalk
A. Kasper, CKD
Kitchens by Benson
691 Main Avenue
zip 06851

Plantsville
K. L. Bell, CKD
Bell Kitchens, Inc.
363 Mulberry St.
zip 06479

Southington
E. C. Brady, CKD
Kitchens of Distinction by Brady
90 Center Street
zip 06489

Gertrude I. Greaves, CKD
4 Stoughton Road
zip 06489

Stamford
Eleanor L. Chadwick, CKD
Mohawk Service, Inc.
Kitchen & Appliance Div.
21 Myrtle Ave.
zip 06902

West Hartford
R. C. Aldridge, CKD
M. A. Peterson, Inc.
607 New Park Avenue
zip 06110

D. L. Davis, CKD
Bradley Kitchens, Inc.
214 Park Road
zip 06119

J. S. Dowling, CKD
M. A. Peterson, Inc.
607 New Park Avenue
zip 06110

R. O. Geddes, CKD
M. A. Peterson, Inc.
607 New Park Ave.
zip 06110

Brita O. Peterson, CKD
M. A. Peterson, Inc.
607 New Park Ave.
zip 06110

M. A. Peterson, CKD
M. A. Peterson, Inc.
607 New Park Avenue
zip 06110

Westport
S. M. Lefler, CKD
Kitchens by Lefler
431 Post Road East
zip 06880

DELAWARE

Wilmington
W. G. Magan, CKD
Craft-Way Kitchens, Inc.
Evelyn Drive at Kirkwood Highway
zip 19808

DISTRICT OF COLUMBIA

Washington
R. W. Baur, CKD
The Kitchen Guild
Day-Schafer, Inc.
5002 Connecticut Avenue N.W.
zip 20008

A. R. Dresner, CKD
Douglas Distributing Corporation
3521 "V" Street N.E.
zip 20018

R. D. Schafer, CKD
The Kitchen Guild
Day-Schafer, Inc.
5002 Connecticut Avenue N.W.
zip 20008

L. E. Schucker, III, CKD
Kitchens, Inc.
5027 Connecticut Avenue N.W.
zip 20008

Betta J. Scoby, CKD
Kitchens, Inc.
5027 Connecticut Ave. N.W.
zip 20008

FLORIDA

Ft. Lauderdale
P. B. Gunter, CKd
Bath & Kitchen Designers, Inc.
5060 North Dixie Hwy.
zip 33331

R. L. Welky, CKD
Mutschler Kitchens of Ft. Lauderdale
1881 N.E. 26th Street, Suite 102
zip 33334

Hollywood
R. Horowitz, CKD
2230 Polk Street
zip 33020

Jacksonville
C. W. Bailey, CKD
Bailey Brothers, Inc.
4547 Wesconnett Blvd.
zip 32210

W. F. Voyles, CKD
Murray Hill Corporation
416 Ryan Street
zip 32205

Jacksonville Beach
W. T. Langohr, CKD
Townsend Kitchens
1315 North Third Street
zip 32250

Miami
R. F. Braithwaite, CKD
Benchmark Cabinetry Inc.
4308 N.E. 2nd Avenue
zip 33137

R. V. Kucera, CKD
Kitchen Center, Inc.
5124 Biscayne Boulevard
zip 33137

G. Ann Nunnally, CKD
Benchmark Cabinetry, Inc.
4308 N.E. 2nd Avenue
zip 33137

North Palm Beach
F. B. Shone, CKD
Kitchen Specialist
833 Cinnamon Road
zip 33408

Pensacola
F. D. Kay, CKD
Kay's Kitchen & Bath Designs
2901 North "E" Street
zip 32501

Sarasota
E. O. Feagans, CKD
Sarasota Kitchens, Inc.
5945 North Washington Blvd.
zip 33580

Tampa
R. D. Arnold, CKD
Scruggs House of Cabinets
5214 Nebraska Avenue
zip 33603

GEORGIA

Albany
A. H. Snelling, Jr., CKD
Custom Kitchens Company
808 West Oglethorpe Avenue
zip 31705

Nashville
D. H. Powell, CKD
Berrien Cabinet Works
519 South Bartow Street
P.O. Box 766
zip 31639

Savannah
D. B. McCullough, CKD
Kitchens by McCullough
1311 East 59th Street
zip 31404

Waycross
W. L. Oxley, Jr., CKD
HOM Kitchens, Inc.
331 Albany Avenue
zip 31501

HAWAII

Honolulu
M. L. Smith, CKD
The Kitchen Center of Hawaii
250 Ward Street, Oahu
zip 96814

ILLINOIS

Addison
H. H. Sersen, CKD
Woodland Sales Company
823 South Route 53
zip 60101

Arlington Heights
E. J. Keegan, CKD
Key Kitchens
1628 W. Northwest Highway
zip 60004

Belleville
R. W. Lautz, CKD
Schifferdecker Kitchens & Baths
747 East Main
zip 62221

V. P. Schifferdecker, CKD
Schifferdecker Kitchens & Baths
747 East Main
zip 62221

Champaign
Marilyn R. Stalter, CKD
Colbert's
1602 South Neil St.
zip 61820

Chicago
C. L. Anderson, CKD
Lectroglaz Corporation
4014 West Armitage
zip 60639

Bernice G. Greenwald, CKD
Suburban Designers, Inc.
2412 W. 111th St.
zip 60655

G. A. Reilly, CKD
Peoples Gas Company
122 South Michigan Avenue
Room 1701
zip 60603

J. C. Turkstra, CKD
Turkstra's Modernizing Center
10958 South Halsted Street
zip 60628

Decatur
G. E. Coutant, CKD
Kitchen Distributors
1449 East Eldorado
zip 62525

L. C. Rice, CKD
J. J. Swartz Company
2120 North Oakland Avenue
zip 62526

Des Plaines
E. L. Johnson, CKD
Mutschler Kitchens of Chicago, Inc.
2434 Dempster Street
zip 60016

Edwardsville
R. V. Mueller, CKD
Edwardsville Lumber Co.
201 West High
zip 62025

El Paso
D. A. Rohrberg, CKD
Beemer Enterprises
657 East 2nd Street
zip 61738

Evanston
B. E. Karlson, CKD
Karlson Home Center, Inc.
1815 Central Street
zip 60201

Fairview Heights
Verla M. Stratton, CKD
American Kitchen Designs
10606 Lincoln Trail
zip 62208

Flossmoor
D. C. Johnson, CKD
Kitchens by Don Johnson Enterprises
2044 Cummings Lane
zip 60422

Freeport
C. S. Schroeder, CKD
Mutschler
404 West American Street
zip 61032

Galatia
B. G. Stidman, CKD
Galatia Building Center
Hickory and Mill Streets, Box 127
zip 62935

Galena
S. C. Gilfoyle, CKD
Galena Lumber Company
233 N. Commerce St.
zip 61036

Harrisburg
H. L. Wilson, CKD
Wilson Custom Kitchens
South Feazel Street
zip 62946

Jacksonville
F. R. Taylor, CKD
Andrews Lumber Company, Limited
320 North Main Street
zip 62650

Kildeer
L. R. Svendson, CKD
Les Svendson, & Assoc.
21341 N. Grove
zip 60047

Monmouth
D. M. Warfield, CKD
Warfield McCullough
111 East 4th Avenue
zip 61462

Niles
E. L. Zielinski, CKD
Better Kitchens Inc.
7640 Milwaukee Avenue
zip 60648

Normal
K. L. Devlin, CKD
Devlin Kitchen & Home
Improvement Center
507 East Pine Street
zip 61761

Oak Brook
J. G. Licher, CKD
St. Charles Manufacturing Company
610 Enterprise Drive
zip 60521

Paris
R. P. Junghans, CKD
The Building Specialties Co.
Tucker Beach Road
zip 61944

Pinckneyville
Shirley M. Woosley, CKD
The Cupboard Shop
111 South Walnut
zip 62274

Plainfield
A. G. Ackerberg, Jr., CKD
Ideal Millwork Company
Route 1
zip 60544

River Grove
G. Cernauske, CKD
Reynolds Enterprises
2936 River Road
zip 60171
W. A. Reynolds, Jr., CKD
Reynolds Enterprises, Inc.
2936 River Road
zip 60171

Rochelle
F. W. Eber, CKD
Eber Remodelers &
   Kitchen Specialists
426 N. 11th
zip 61068

Rockford
D. C. Johnson, CKD
Dahlgren-Johnson Custom Cabinets
1000 - 9th Street
zip 61108

Springfield
H. R. Buckhold, CKD
McDermand Kitchens
1831 So. 11th Street
zip 62703
R. J. Kansy, CKD
Kitchens by Kansy
1516 South Sixth Street
zip 62703

St. Charles
O. R. Beardsley, CKD
St. Charles Manufacturing Co.
1611 East Main Street
zip 60174
R. J. Rodgers, CKD
St. Charles Manufacturing Company
1611 East Main St.
zip 60174
L. P. Thompson, CKD
St. Charles Manufacturing Co.
1611 East Main Street
zip 60174

Taylorville
C. D. Brown, CKD
Brown & Sons Cabinetry
405 Springfield Road
zip 62568

Waukegan
J. P. Descour, CKD
Joe Kohn — Kitchens & Baths
141 South Genesee Street
zip 60085
J. Kohn, CKD
Joe Kohn — Kitchens & Baths
141 South Genesee Street
zip 60085

Wilmette
K. G. Knobel, CKD
Karl G. Knobel, Inc.
1218 Washington Avenue
zip 60091
K. P. Knobel, CKD
Karl G. Knobel, Inc.
1218 Washington Avenue
zip 60091

INDIANA

Bargersville
R. E. Nichols, CKD
Cabinets by Nichols, Inc.
P.O. Box 311, State Road 144
zip 46101

Bloomington
R. S. Penrod, CKD
Penn Kitchens
2600 South Walnut
zip 47401
L. G. Routen, CKD
The Kitchen Center, Inc.
702 North Rogers St.
zip 47401

Clarksville
E. J. McLaughlin, CKD
Wholesale Kitchen Distributors
1518 Altawood Drive
zip 47130

Columbus
L. W. Alexander, CKD
Alexander's Cabinets & Appliances
1817 24th Street
zip 47201

Evansville
Anna L. Skomp, CKD
Cliff's Kitchens, Inc.
1415 E. Division St.
zip 47714
C. E. Skomp, CKD
Cliff's Kitchens, Inc.
1415 E. Division St.
zip 47714

Gary
S. Kaplan, CKD
American Supply Company
of Gary, Inc.
1030 East 10th Place
zip 46402

Indianapolis
J. M. Boarman, CKD
1814 West Wyoming Street
zip 46221
J. D. Foley, CKD
Wonderlife, Div. of ADI
8399 Zionsville Road
zip 46268
C. L. Gray Jr., CKD
Gray-Breese Co. Inc.
3750 W. 16th Street
zip 46222
J. S. Jordan, CKD
Jordan Showplace Kitchens
2206 Lafayette Road
zip 46222
A. C. Raup, CKD
Raup Tile & Cabinet Company
5349 Keystone Avenue
zip 46220

Mishawaka
D. P. Guckenberger, CKD
Valley Kitchens & Baths, Inc.
1020 West Jefferson Blvd.
zip 46544

Muncie
C. P. Pippen, CKD
Pippens Kitchens, Inc.
428 W. Washington St.
zip 47305
J. P. West, CKD
United Home Supply Inc.
300 Hoyt Avenue
zip 47302

Nappanee
R. S. Ringenberg, CKD
Mutschler
302 South Madison Street
zip 46550

New Castle
R. John CKD
Foust Lumber &
   Building Supplies, Inc.
402 North 14th Street
zip 47362

Newburgh
J. D. Mitchell, CKD
Kitchen Interiors
R.R. 3 Box 6
zip 47630

Schererville
V. A. Wietbrock, CKD
Koremen Company, Inc.
2142 U.S. #41
zip 46375

Shelbyville
J. L. Risley, CKD
Risley's Kitchen Specialists
212 East Broadway
zip 46176

South Bend
D. E. Carpenter, CKD
Beemer Enterprises
1563 Turtle Creek Drive
zip 46637
L. M. Seago, CKD
Louie Seago's
   Remodeling Service, Inc.
1413 West Western Avenue
zip 46619

Syracuse
W. M. Beemer, CKD
Beemer Enterprises, Inc.
R.R. 1
zip 46567

Terre Haute
W. F. Frazier, CKD
Frazier Distr. Co., Inc.
Kitchens & Interior Designs
1318 Ohio Street
zip 47807

Valparaiso
C. A. Berg, CKD
M & B Lumber Company, Inc.
1002 Locust Street
zip 46383

IOWA

Burlington
W. C. Fox, CKD
Fox Appliance & Kitchen Center, Inc.
705-11 Jefferson Street
zip 52601

W. M. Hoffman, CKD
Keystone Products Company, Inc.
2880 Mount Pleasant Street
zip 52601

Carroll
R. E. Watters, CKD
Watters Distributing Company
527 North Adams Street
zip 51401

Cedar Rapids
H. R. Ek, CKD
St. Charles Kitchens by Friedl, Inc.
1013 Mt. Vernon Road, S.E.
zip 52403
F. B. Friedl, CKD
St. Charles Kitchens by Friedl, Inc.
1013 Mt. Vernon Road, S.E.
zip 52403
D. Novak, CKD
Custom Cabinets & Wood Products
Rural Route 2
zip 52401

Davenport
O. F. Maxwell, CKD
Brammer Mfg. Company
1701 Rockingham Road
zip 52808
G. E. Nordeen, CKD
Home Supply Company
314 East 2nd Street
zip 52801

Des Moines
A. A. Johnson, CKD
Kitchen Center, Inc.
5055 Second Avenue, Box 4000 H.P.
zip 50333
P. M. Negley, CKD
N D S Company
3839 Merle Hay Road
Suite 100
zip 50310

Marshalltown
R. B. Springer, CKD
Custom Designs, Inc.
1211 Glenwood Terrace
zip 50158
C. Swanson, CKD
Swanco Enterprises, Inc.
815 North 3rd Avenue
zip 50158

KANSAS

Wichita
S. Culbertson, Jr., CKD
The Kitchen Place
1634 East Central
zip 67214

Winfield
J. G. Gordon, CKD
Gordon's House of Cabinetry
109 West 9th St., Box 825
zip 67156

KENTUCKY

Lexington
D. M. Butcher, CKD
Creative Kitchens, Inc.
1269 Eastland Drive
zip 40505
R. B. Cornett, CKD
Kitchen Planning Center, Inc.
101 W. Loudon
zip 40508
B. L. Cowgill, CKD
Southern Supply Co., Inc.
768 East Third Street
zip 40502
F. R. Smith, CKD
Kitchen Planning Center, Inc.
101 W. Loudon
zip 40508

Louisville
Lorraine Allen, CKD
General Electric/Hotpoint
AP4-214, Appliance Park
zip 40225
J. U. Forst, CKD
General Electric/Hotpoint
AP4-214, Appliance Park
zip 40225
R. W. Harlan, CKD
General Electric/Hotpoint
AP4-214, Appliance Park
zip 40225
W. J. Ketcham, CKD
General Electric/Hotpoint
AP4-214, Appliance Park
zip 40225
C. Jean Mattingly
General Electric/Hotpoint
AP4-214, Appliance Park
zip 40225
P. M. Pittenger, CKD
The House of Kitchens, Inc.
106 Bauer Avenue
zip 40207
J. W. Riley, Jr., CKD
Jefferson Kitchens, Inc.
1034 Rogers Street
zip 40204

LOUISIANA

New Orleans
C. B. Gamble, CKD
Kitchens by Cameron, Inc.
8019 Palm Street
zip 70125

Shreveport
W. J. Patten, CKD
Richmond Floors & Kitchens, Inc.
3856 Southern Avenue
zip 71106

MAINE

Kittery
D. L. Callanan, CKD
Dion Lumber Company
State Road, Route 1
zip 03904

Lewiston
C. Bellegarde, Jr., CKD
Bellegarde Custom Kitchens
516 Sabattus Street
zip 04240
P. Clifford, CKD
Bellegarde Custom Kitchens
516 Sabattus Street
zip 04240
R. O. Dion, CKD
BCD Distributors
Pepperell Mill Bldg. 14
zip 04240

MARYLAND

Baltimore
D. R. Cahlander, CKD
Cox Kitchens & Baths, Inc.
5011 York Road
zip 21212
R. F. Cox, CKD
Cox Kitchens & Baths, Inc.
5011 York Road
zip 21212
C. N. Ellrich, CKD
Cox Kitchens & Baths, Inc.
5011 York Road
zip 21212
J. L. Feeley, Jr., CKD
Feeley Kitchens
6239 Fernway
zip 21212
R. L. Gibbs, CKD
Cox Kitchens & Baths Inc.
5011 York Road
zip 21212
B. Kirk, CKD
Kitchen Fair, Inc.
417 South Highland Avenue
zip 21224
A. V. Taylor, CKD
Taylor's Kitchens
2214 E. Monument Street
zip 21205

Beltsville
J. S. Bendheim, CKD
Builder Kitchens, Inc.
10710 Tucker Street
zip 20705
W. E. Pugh, CKD
Builder Kitchens, Inc.
10710 Tucker Street
zip 20705

Bethesda
J. F. Edwards, CKD
Wailes and Edwards Inc.
8013 Woodmont Avenue
zip 20014
B. R. Wailes, CKD
Wailes and Edwards Inc.
8013 Woodmont Avenue
zip 20014

Cambridge
W. E. Murphy, Jr., CKD
Cambridge Interiors
313 High Street
zip 21613

Chevy Chase
P. V. Chadik, CKD
2920 Greenvale Road
zip 20015
R. M. Tunis, CKD
Richard M. Tunis, Inc.
7032 Wisconsin Avenue
zip 20015

Gaithersburg
R. L. Alexander, CKD
Gaithersburg Lumber &
Supply Co., Inc.
11 S. Frederick Avenue
zip 20760
R. B. Cutler, CKD
Capitol Kitchens & Bldg. Supply, Inc.
9 North Frederick Avenue
zip 20760

Kensington
R. D. Rutter, Sr., CKD
Custom Crafters Inc.
4000 Howard Avenue
zip 20795

Silver Spring
J. Dobbs, CKD
Creative Kitchens, Inc.
8480 Fenton Place
zip 20910
N. Granat, CKD
Creative Kitchens, Inc.
8480 Fenton Place
zip 20910

Waldorf
H. E. Fowler, CKD
Waldorf Supply, Inc.
Fowler Building - P.O. Box 578
zip 20601

MASSACHUSETTS

Adams
R. T. Arnold Jr., CKD
Arnold's 1788 Yards Inc.
44 Spring Street
zip 01220

Agawam
J. Herzenberg, CKD
Kitchens by Herzenberg, Inc.
South End Bridge Circle
zip 01001

Boston
L. K. Johnson, CKD
Lee Kimball Kitchens
119 Canal Street
zip 02114

Charlestown
P. T. Lowell, III, CKD
Wholesale Cabinets, Inc.
295 Medford Street
zip 02129

Chicopee
J. F. Burns, CKD
Doane & Williams Inc.
955 Chicopee Street
zip 01013

Danvers
S. F. Brown, CKD
Brown's Kitchen & Bath Center
56 N. Putnam Street
zip 01923

Dedham
T. J. Pitkanen, CKD
Boyd Craft, Inc.
62 Walnut Street
zip 02026

Fitchburg
R. J. Egan, CKD
Engineered Kitchens, Inc.
360 Summer Street
zip 01420
N. J. Thibault, CKD
Engineered Kitchens Inc.
360 Summer Street
zip 01420

Framingham
R. W. Burke, CKD
Kitchen Center of Framingham, Inc.
597 Waverly Street
zip 01701
K. W. Doody, CKD
Kitchen Center of Framingham, Inc.
697 Waverly Street
zip 01701

Lawrence
D. Lemkin, CKD
Jalco Kitchen Center
Div. of Jackson Lumber Co., Inc.
239 Market Street
zip 01843

Leominster
R. E. Sponenberg, CKD
Kitchen Associates, Inc.
112 Whitney Street
zip 01453

Mattapoisett
W. Walega, CKD
New Design, Inc.
92 North Street
zip 02739

New Bedford
R. G. Peckham, CKD
Peckham's Custom Kitchens
896 Hathaway Rd.
zip 02740
N. E. Robitaille, CKD
Tailored Kitchens Supply Co.
100 Tarkiln Hill Road
zip 02745

North Adams
L. S. Gagliardi, CKD
Gagliardi's, Inc.
9-13 Union Street
zip 01247

North Attleboro
B. A. Cavallaro, CKD
Inel Kitchens
560 Kelley Blvd.
zip 02760

Orleans
J. S. P. Loffstadt, CKD
Nickerson Furniture & Interiors
47 Main Street
zip 02653

Readville
R. P. Gerth, CKD
Gerrity Company, Inc.
Whiting Avenue Ext.
zip 02137

Roslindale
R. L. Norberg, CKD
Charl Marc Kitchens
4174 Washington St.
zip 02131

Shrewsbury
F. R. Angel, CKD
Modular Interiors, Inc.
33 Boston Tpke., Route 9
zip 01545

R. A. Cuccaro, CKD
R. A. Cuccaro Associates
33 Boston Turnpike Rt. 9
zip 01545

H. R. Howard, CKD
Modular Interiors, Inc.
33 Boston Turnpike, Route 9
zip 01545

Waltham
P. R. Lipkin, CKD
St. Charles of Boston
473 Winter St.
zip 02154

C. H. Sandford, CKD
St. Charles of Boston
473 Winter Street
zip 02154

Wilmington
B. F. Rice, CKD
Kitchens by Rice Bros., Inc.
3-Rear-Church Street
zip 01887

W. E. Rice, CKD
Kitchens by Rice Bors., Inc.
3-Rear-Church Street
zip 01887

MICHIGAN

Ann Arbor
D. J. Thibodeau, CKD
Michigan Kitchens & Bathrooms
3162 Packard Road
zip 48104

Birmingham
Charlotte E. Clark, CKD
Charlotte Clark Kitchens
4068 West Maple
zip 48010

Blissfield
W. M. Weinlander Jr., CKD
Weinlander Wood Products &
    Home Supply, Inc.
8593 E. U.S. 223
zip 49228

Bloomfield Hills
R. E. Martens, CKD
St. Charles of Detroit
2713 Woodward
zip 48013

Bridgeport
B. J. Maday, CKD
Maday Kitchens, Inc.
7483 Dixie Highway
zip 48722

Coldwater
D. N. Streets, CKD
H & S Supply, Inc.
317 North Fiske Road
zip 49036

Detroit
J. R. Allcom, CKD
Artisan Plastic, Inc.
12001 Greenfield
zip 48227

Farmington Hills
Frances B. Terpstra, CKD
32149 West Twelve Mile Road
zip 48024

Flint
D. B. Gavulic, CKD
Peoples Kitchen Center
G-3490 Miller Road
zip 48507

Grand Rapids
J. M. Damstra, CKD
Gallery of Kitchens
5243 Plainfield NE
zip 49505

Grosse Pointe Woods
Christine A. Kosmalski, CKD
Mutschler Kitchens, Inc.
20227 Mack Avenue
zip 48236

Jackson
D. C. Nicholson, CKD
The Kitchen Shop, Inc.
407 Ist Street
zip 49201

Lansing
M. E. Blake, CKD
The Kitchen Shop, Inc.
5320 S. Pennsylvania Avenue
zip 48910

R. A. Ferle, CKD
Custom Kitchens, Inc.
724 E. Shiawassee
zip 48912

R. E. Paspas, CKD
Beemer Enterprises, Inc.
1728 Holly Way
zip 48910

T. A. Richards, CKD
Kitchens by Richards
2501 South Cedar Street
zip 48910

R. B. Vandervoort, CKD
Hager-Fox Distributing Company
1115 S. Pennsylvania Avenue
zip 48901

Muskegon
R. E. Hill, CKD
Style Trend Kitchens
2390 Henry Street
zip 49441

Royal Oak
R. E. Holton, CKD
Royal Oak Kitchens, Inc.
4518 North Woodward
zip 48072

St. Clair
R. H. Nauman, Sr., CKD
Tri-Star Kitchens
1880 South Range Road
zip 48079

Tecumseh
L. G. Fogelsong, CKD
Tecumseh Building Supply Co.
214 E. Chicago Blvd.
zip 49286

Roma L. Fogelsong, CKD
Tecumseh Building Supply Co.
214 E. Chicago Blvd.
zip 49286

Troy
L. E. Trevarrow, Jr., CKD
Trevarrow, Inc.
2800 Industrial Row
zip 48084

MINNESOTA

St. Paul
R. J. Gorman, CKD
Kitchens by Krengel, Inc.
1688 Grand Avenue
zip 55105

J. W. Krengel, CKD
Kitchens by Krengel, Inc.
1688 Grand Avenue
zip 55105

Virginia
R. K. Lahti, CKD
Iver Johnson Lumber Company
Northgate Plaza
zip 55792

MISSISSIPPI

Gulfport
J. P. Campbell, CKD
Campbell Company, Inc.
1742 East Railroad
zip 39501

MISSOURI

Crestwood
R. R. Brumley, CKD
M-W Home Center
9280 Watson Road
zip 63126

Hannibal
S. C. Keck, CKD
Broadway Kitchens
520 Broadway
zip 63401

Kansas City
M. P. Daily, CKD
Quaker Maid Kitchens
4734 Harrison
zip 64110

St. Charles
J. E. Weaver, CKD
Hackmann Lumber Company
3030 Highway 94, South
zip 63301

St. Louis
A. Baum, CKD
The Kitchen Shop
1063 S. Brentwood Blvd.
zip 63117

Jean Baum, CKD
The Kitchen Shop
1063 S. Brentwood Blvd.
zip 63117

W. C. Karr, CKD
Kitchens by Karr, Inc.
8456 Watson Road
zip 63119

C. J. Polley, CKD
Morgan Wightman Supply Company
9910 Page
zip 63114

St. Louis County
R. E. Duenke, CKD
Roy E. Dunke Cabinet Company
510 Manchester Road
zip 63011

MONTANA

Billings
J. W. Bergeson, CKD
Modern Kitchens, Inc.
2710 Montana Avenue
zip 59102

W. A. Shaffer, CKD
Modern Kitchens, Inc.
P.O. Box 1881
2710 Montana Avenue
zip 59103

NEBRASKA

Lincoln
R. E. Crowl, CKD
Crowl's Kitchens
137 South 9th
zip 68508

Las Vegas
H. H. Schmidt, CKD
St. Charles of Nevada
5006 Maryland Pkwy.
zip 89119

NEW HAMPSHIRE

Laconia
H. A. Lovell, CKD
R. H. Smith Company
1150 Union Avenue
zip 03246

R. C. Elliott, CKD
Home Improvement Co., Inc.
Meriden Road
zip 03766

Manchester
J. R. Higgins, CKD
J. R. Higgins, Inc.
449 Hayward Street
zip 03103

Portsmouth
J. Mitrook, CKD
Mitrook's Custom Kitchen Center
100 Albany Street P.O. Box 1152
zip 03801

NEW JERSEY

Barrington
S. L. Rabinowitz, CKD
AV Custom Kitchens
222 White Horse Pike
zip 08007

Bayonne
D. P. Pietruska, CKD
Woodward Lumber & Supply Co.
37 Linnett St.
zip 07002

J. F. Pietruszka, CKD
Woodward Lumber &
    Supply Company
37 Linnet Street
zip 07002

Bridgeton
C. J. Curtis, CKD
Kitchen Creations by Kelly
South Laurel Street
zip 08302

W. J. Kelly, CKD
Kitchen Creations by Kelly
Div. of Smith & Richards
    Lumber Co., Inc.
110 South Laurel Street
zip 08302

Caldwell
A. S. Franzblau, CKD
Kitchen Cottage Corporation
375 Bloomfield Avenue
zip 07006

J. R. Taylor, CKD
Kitchen Cottage Corporation
375 Bloomfield Avenue
zip 07006

Cherry Hill
A. E. Rosner, CKD
Rosner's Custom Kitchens
1700 State Highway 70
zip 08002

M. Rosner, CKD
Rosner's Custom Kitchens
1700 State Hghway 70
zip 08002

Clifton
A. J. Giannaula, CKD
Allied Woodcraft
421 Allwood Road
zip 07012

C. A. Schneider, CKD
C. Schneider & Co., Inc.
158-166 Highland Avenue
zip 07011

Dumont
J. V. D'Aloisio, CKD
Nick's Kitchen Center
71 New Milford Road
zip 07628

Virginia R. Loretto, CKD
Allied Craftsmen, Inc.
409 E. Madison Ave.
zip 07628

East Newark
J. P. Castronova, CKD
Paramount Kitchens
211 Central Avenue
zip 07029

Garwood
M. E. Dudick, CKD
Dudick & Son
40 North Avenue, P.O. Box 204
zip 07027

Hackettstown
R. W. Afflerbach, CKD
A.I.K.D.
114 Main Street
zip 07840

R. R. Oxley, CKD
A.I.K.D.
114 Main Street
zip 07840

Hawthorne
T. J. Bogusta, CKD
Van Beuzekom Kitchens Inc.
301 Lafayette Avenue
zip 07506

J. Van Beuzekom, CKD
Van Beuzekom Kitchens, Inc.
301 Lafayette Avenue
zip 07507

Kinnelon
H. H. Fichtler, CKD
16 Birch Road
zip 07405

Oradell
H. B. Sobel, CKD
Home Fiar Contractors
119 Gordon Court
zip 17649

Parsippany
M. A. Waimon, CKD
Richmain Kitchens
7 Quimby Court
zip 07054

Paterson
A. M. Kessler, CKD
Paterson Stove & Kitchen Center
88 Broadway
zip 07505

Pompton Plains
T. E. Lutjen, CKD
Jeffreys and Lutjen, Inc.
29 Evans Place
zip 07444

Princeton
Ethel M. Peresett, CKD
Kitchens of Distinction by Peresett
249 Moore St.
zip 08540

Rahway
H. J. Aulert, Jr., CKD
Beautiful Homes Center, Inc.
29 E. Milton Avenue
zip 07065

G. E. Fross, CKD
Beautiful Homes Center, Inc.
29 East Milton Avenue
zip 07065

Ridgewood
P. W. Fluhr, CKD
Ulrich, Inc.
100 Chestnut Street
zip 07450

J. D. Ulrich, CKD
Ulrich, Inc.
100 Chestnut Street
zip 07450

Roselle Park
G. C. Horvath, CKD
Proven Design, Inc.
111 E. Westfield Ave.
zip 07204

P. E. Horvath, CKD
Proven Design, Inc.
111 E. Westfield Avenue
zip 07204

Saddlebrook
J. A. Yesbek, CKD
Kinzee Industries
259 - 2nd Street
zip 07662

Somerville
C. A. Bothers, CKD
A. R. Bothers Woodworking Inc.
236 Dukes Pky., P.O. Box 127
zip 08876

Springfield
L. Shur, CKD
Home Fair Contractors, Inc.
22 Route 22, Westbound
zip 07081

Summit
Maria Brisco, CKD
Cabri, Inc.
323 Springfield Avenue
zip 07901

E. J. Rawnsley, CKD
St. Charles Designer Kitchens, Inc.
66 River Road
zip 07901

Upper Montclair
G. C. Murphy, CKD
Designers Plus+
590 Valley Road
zip 07043

West Belmar
Michelle F. Salinard CKD
Du-Craft, Inc.
1919 Rt. 71
zip 07719

B. R. Tunbridge, CKD
Du-Craft, Inc.
1919 Route 71
zip 07719

West Collingswood
A. J. Terragrossa, CKD
810 Collings Avenue
zip 08107

West Orange
L. Lemchen, CKD
Barmark Design
200 Mt. Pleasant Avenue
zip 07052

Westmont
G. G. Hurwitz, CKD
Haddon-Towne Design Center, Inc.
112 Haddon Avenue
zip 08108

Westwood
J. L. Whittaker, CKD
Jay L. Whittaker Co., Inc.
15 Bergenline Avenue
zip 07675

NEW MEXICO

Albuquerque
H. L. Chapman, CKD
Creative Kitchens, Inc.
503 Slate Avenue, NW
zip 87102

NEW YORK

Albany
P. R. Cloutier, CKD
Kitchen Distributors, Inc.
5 Interstate Avenue
zip 12205

J. Mendelsohn, CKD
Mayfair Kitchen Center, Inc.
87 Homestead Avenue
zip 12203

Amsterdam
J. J. Miller, CKD
Kreative Kitchens by Miller, Inc.
309 Forest Avenue
zip 12010

Auburn
R. W. Quigley, CKD
Quig Enterprises
203 State Street
zip 13021

Baldwin
H. Gainsburg, CKD
Baldwin Sales Corporation
795 Merrick Road
zip 11510

B. C. Max, CKD
Baldwin Sales Corporation
795 Merrick Road
zip 11510

Boonville
H. R. Myers, CKD
H. R. Myers Lumber Co., Inc.
Box 147 Route 12
zip 13309

Brooklyn
J. L. Langan, CKD
Kitchen Fashions, Inc.
1899 Coney Island Avenue
zip 11230

Buffalo
J. A. Barth, CKD
Kitchens by Barth
306 Ayer Road
zip 14221

S. V. DiLeo, CKD
Di-Tell Mastercraft Cabinet Co., Inc.
1670 Kenmore Avenue
zip 14216

F. Thayer, Jr., CKD
St. Charles of Western New York
9266 West Lane, Angola
zip 14006

Corning
R. F. Kennedy, CKD
Adamy's, Inc.
Route 17
zip 14830

Cornwall
J. L. Clouser, CKD
Clouser Sales, Inc.
Rt. 32
zip 12518

Elmira
L. J. Ryder, CKD
Ryder's Kitchens, Inc.
2026 Lake St.
zip 14903

Farmingdale
D. W. Fioretti, CKD
Roseline Formica Kitchens
120 Schmitt Blvd.
zip 11735

Florida
N. Papaceno, CKD
124A Trading Corporation
Route 17A
zip 10921

Garden City Park
F. M. Frank, CKD
Alamode Kitchen Center, Inc.
2272 Jericho Tpke.
zip 11040

T. L. Frank, CKD
Alamode Kitchen Center, Inc.
2272 Jericho Tpke.
zip 11040

Garden City South
M. Berkoff, CKD
Herbert P. Bisulk, Inc.
295 Nassau Blvd.
zip 11530

J. F. Werner, CKD
Herbert P. Bisulk, Inc.
295 Nassau Blvd.
zip 11530

Glendale
F. P. Frederick, CKD
Frederick Construction Co.
79-49 Myrtle Avenue
zip 11227

H. Jacoby, CKD
Frederick Construction Co.
79-49 Myrtle Avenue
zip 11227

Glens Falls
R. J. Dorey, CKD
Warner Pruyn
P.O. Box 900, Quaker Road
zip 12801

Grand Gorge
D. C. Tait, CKD
Dan Tait, Inc.
zip 12434

Great Neck
C. Mustello Jr., CKD
D & M Kitchens, Inc.
400 Great Neck Road
zip 11021

Hawthorne
E. E. Berger, CKD
Berger Appliances, Inc.
441 Commerce St.
zip 10532

Hewlett
C. T. Passaro, CKD
Whitehall Kitchen & Bath Center
Div. of Whitehall Home
   Improvement Centers, Inc.
1598 Broadway
zip 11557

Horseheads
J. M. Kennedy Jr., CKD
Kennedy Kitchens, Inc.
727 Fox Street
zip 14845

Ithaca
R. M. Baker Jr., CKD
Bob Baker's Kitchens
401 E. State Street
zip 14850

Jill M. Stoughton, CKD
Bob Baker's Kitchens
401 East State Street
zip 14850

Johnson City
Susan Y. Adams, CKD
Valley Crafts, Inc.
Valley Plaza, Oakdale
zip 13790

R. F. Carbrey, CKD
Valley Crafts, Inc.
Valley Plaza, Oakdale
zip 13790

Massapequa
J. B. Ciccarello, CKD
Aladdin Remodelers, Inc.
7 Broadway
zip 11758

Mineola
F. J. Schneider, CKD
Frederick J. Schneider, Inc.
550 Jericho Tpke.
zip 11501

Nassau
R. W. Baum, CKD
Millbrook Kitchens, Inc.
Route 20
zip 12123

New Hartford
C. R. Spetts, CKD
Charm Kitchens by Spetts
Commercial Drive, Route 5A
zip 13413

New York City
F. Berg CKD
Berg & Brown, Inc.
1424 Lexington Avenue
zip 10028

M. Bomstein, CKD
St. Charles of New York City
964 - 3rd Avenue
zip 10022

R. J. Brady, CKD
General Electric Company
205 E. 42nd Street, Room 420
zip 10017

F. S. Feinstein, CKD
Atlas Kitchens, Inc.
205 Lexington Avenue
zip 10016

J. F. Hammill, CKD
Kitchen Associates, Inc.
220 East 78 Street
zip 10021

L. N. Newman, CKD
Kitchen Associates Inc.
220 East 78 Street
zip 10021

Florence Perchuk, CKD
SVP Kitchen & Bath Designs
54 Riverside Drive
zip 10024

I. Schwartz, CKD
Bakit Industries, Inc.
32 E. 30th St.
zip 10016

Plattsburgh
E. M. Scardaccione, CKD
Lee Appliance Company, Inc.
Morrisonville Road, RD 16
zip 12901

Potsdam
D. L. Thomas, CKD
D. L. Thomas Kitchens & Baths
Outer Market St. - P.O. Box 636
zip 13676

Richmond Hill
J. C. Ferrara, CKD
Joseph O. Ferrara & Sons, Inc.
125-01 Liberty Avenue
zip 11419

Riverhead
F. A. Tommasini, CKD-ASID
Kitchen & Bath, Inc.
1179 Route 58
zip 11901

Rochester
S. L. Ayres, III, CKD
Dell's House of Kitchens
1658 Portland Avenue
zip 14608

L. A. Raggi, CKD
Windsor Kitchens Inc.
1461 Hudson Avenue
zip 14621

Rockville Centre
I. Taras, CKD
Art-Carft Kitchens, Inc.
144 Sunrise Highway
zip 11570

Rome
J. D. Opper, CKD
Opper's, Inc.
303 Erie Blvd., West
zip 13440

Saranac Lake
M. V. Watson, CKD
Casier Appliances, Inc.
12 Bloomingdale Avenue
zip 12983

Scarsdale
C. J. Arzonetti, CKD
Garth Custom Kitchens, Inc.
24 Garth Road
zip 10583

Schenectady
H. Horowitz, CKD
Sheridan Village, Apt. 11A-1
Gerling Street
zip 12308

B. M. Kolner, CKD
Kolner Kitchens
1468 State St.
zip 12304

R. L. McCoy, CKD
Kolner Kitchens
1468 State St.
zip 12304

Sidney
D. J. Zieno, CKD
Sidney Appliance &
   Modern Kitchens, Inc.
89 Main Street
zip 13838

Staten Island
D. P. Pietruska, CKD
Anderson Kitchens
77 Lincoln Avenue
zip 10306

J. F. Pietruszka, CKD
Anderson Kitchens
77 Lincoln Avenue
zip 10306

C. L. Van Name, CKD
Statwood Kitchens
1475 Hylan Blvd.
zip 10305

Syracuse
R. F. Martino Jr., CKD
Modern Kitchens of Syracuse, Inc.
2380 Erie Blvd. East
zip 13224

E. J. McLaughlin, CKD
160 Farm Acre Road
zip 13210

Troy
F. R. Casey, CKD
Casey Remodelers
108 Main Avenue
zip 12198

A. Miller, CKD
Mid State Kitchens Inc.
351 Fifth Avenue
zip 12182

Tuckahoe
A. Gulbis, CKD
Lifetime Kitchens, Inc.
269 Columbus Avenue
zip 10707

Erna Gulbis, CKD
Lifetime Kitchens, Inc.
269 Columbus Ave.
zip 10707

Valley Stream
D. D'Anna, CKD
Danark Associates, Inc.
78 Rockaway Avenue
zip 11580

Wappingers Falls
W. H. Algier, CKD
Empire Kitchen & Woodworking Inc.
862 South Road
zip 12590

Warnerville
R. A. Coons, CKD
R. C. Supply
Warnerville & Mineral Springs Road
Box 155
zip 12187

Waverly
T. G. Burns, CKD
Burns Kitchen Center Ltd.
220 Broad Street
zip 14892

White Plains
R. J. Beech, Jr., CKD
Westchester Custom Kitchens, Inc.
145 East Post Road
zip 10601

Williston Park
J. P. Rupolo, CKD
Tommasini Building Corporation
485 Willis Avenue
zip 11596

S. B. Wechter, CKD
Sidney B. Wechter Corp.
30 Hillside Avenue
zip 11596

Yorktown Heights
R. N. Smith, CKD
Yorktown Interior Woodworking Co.
1776 Front Street
zip 10598

NORTH CAROLINA

Charlotte
R. D. Finlayson, CKD
Kitchen Creations of Charlotte
130 West Boulevard
zip 28203

Elizabeth City
F. C. Stahl, CKD
IXL Westinghouse
Route 1
zip 27909

Fayetteville
S. E. Holt, CKD
Kitchen Kreations
165 Westwood Shopping Center
zip 28303

Greensboro
K. R. Key, Sr., CKD
K & W Custom Kitchens
725 Winston Street
zip 27405

J. P. Mitchell, Jr., CKD
Old Master Cabinet Co.
Burlington Dist. Co., Inc.
2232 Westbrook Street.,
P.O. Drawer 5486
zip 27402

Raleigh
J. H. G. Raiser, CKD
Triangle Design Center
5216 Hollyridge Drive
zip 27612

Southern Pines
R. F. Carbrey, CKD
Kitchens by Carder, Inc.
236 S.W. Broad St., Box 23
zip 28387

L. J. Ryder, CKD
Kitchens by Carder, Inc.
236 S.W. Broad St., Box 23
zip 28387

NORTH DAKOTA

Fargo
D. W. Smith, CKD
Cabinets, Inc.
2600 Main Avenue
P.O. Box 626
zip 58102

OHIO

Akron
H. S. Hembury, CKD
Tailormade Kitchen Co.
1063 S. Arlington Street
zip 44306

Canton
F. A. Valentine, CKD
Ed Williams Home Center
5570 Fulton Drive, NW
zip 44718

Cincinnati
R. E. Bolte, CKD
Agean Kitchens & Baths
9526 Winton Road
zip 45231

R. P. Halpin, CKD
Nickoson Sink Top Co.
3511 Harrison Ave.
zip 45211

R. E. Klein, CKD
Roland "Lou" Klein, Inc.
6900 Gracely Drive
zip 45233

J. F. Rugh, CKD
Valley Floor Covering &
   Kitchen Specialist
417 Wyoming Avenue
zip 45215

Cleveland
G. J. Baird, CKD
Schwede Kitchens
22080 Center Ridge Road
zip 44116

R. O. Click, CKD
Cleveland Tile & Cabinet Co.
131 Terminal Tower Arcade
zip 44113

A. G. Luzius, CKD
Mutschler Kitchens of Cleveland, Inc.
10523 Camegie Avenue
zip 44106

D. Wallace, CKD
Cleveland Tile & Cabinet Co.
131 Terminal Tower Arcade
zip 44113

Cleveland Heights
P. J. Orobello, CKD
National Heating & Plumbing Co.
3962 Mayfield Road
zip 44121

A. C. Zigerelli, CKD
National Heating & Plumbing Co.
3962 Mayfield Road
zip 44121

Columbus
J. F. Fehn, CKD
Scioto Kitchen Sales, Inc.
3232 Alleghany Avenue
zip 43209

W. A. Hagedom, CKD
H & C Kitchens & Bathrooms, Inc.
1290 West Broad Street
zip 43222

J. A. Jacobs, CKD
JAE Company Kitchens
955 W. Fifth Avenue
zip 43212

R. L. Jacobs, CKD
266 South Virginia Lee Road
zip 43212

T. W. Salt, CKD
Lucas Appliances & TV –
   Lucas Kitchens
4369 East Broad Street
zip 43213

Dayton
A. J. Boczonadi, CKD
Better Kitchens & Baths
3333 Dayton Xenia Road
zip 45432

S. F. Lamberth, CKD
Dayton Showcase Company
2601 West Dorothy Lane
zip 45439

Eastlake
F. A. Lasorella, CKD
Lakeland Building & Construction Co.
1450 East 357th Street
zip 44094

Hamilton
R. P. Campbell, CKD
Roth U. Bertsch & Co. Inc.
118 Main Street
zip 45013

A. R. Lingler, CKD
Roth U. Bertsch & Co. Inc.
118 Main Street
zip 45013

Mansfield
A. R. Driskell, CKD
Tappan Co.
Tappan Park
zip 44901

Mentor
W. C. Pike, CKD
Fashion Trend Kitchens & Baths
7515 Tyler Blvd.
zip 44060

New Knoxville
O.H. Hoge, CKD
Hoge Lumber Co.
South Main Street
zip 45871

Stow
H. J. Harris, CKD
Bauer Enterprises, Inc.
4575 Hudson Dr.
zip 44224

Sylvania
R. E. Chapman, CKD
Coppes, Inc.
4902 Burkewood Ct. 102A
zip 43560

Tallmadge
C. G. Schweikert, CKD
White Hall Apts.,
370 Caruthers Avenue
zip 44278

Toledo
J. B. Waxman, CKD
Custom Kitchens by Jerome
2138 North Reynolds Road
zip 43615

Warren
J. B. Knowlton, CKD
The Morgan Company
5400 Oakhill Drive N.W.
zip 44481

OREGON

Portland
V. R. Greb, CKD
J. Greb & Son, Inc.
5027 N.E. 42nd Avenue
zip 97218

N. B. Kelly, CKD
Neil Kelly Co., Inc.
735 North Alberta
zip 97217

Martha Kerr, CKD
Neil Kelly Co., Inc.
735 North Alberta
zip 97217

K. P. Stanley, CKD
Neil Kelly Co., Inc.
735 North Alberta
zip 97217

PENNSYLVANIA

Aliquippa
G. D. Lucci, Jr., CKD
Lucci Kitchen Centers, Inc.
1828 N. Brodhead Rd.
zip 15001

M. A. Lucci, CKD
Lucci Kitchen Centers, Inc.
1828 N. Brodhead Rd.
zip 15001

R. J. Lucci, CKD
Lucci Kitchen Centers, Inc.
1828 N. Brodhead Rd.
zip 15001

Allentown
R. L. Wieland, CKD
Kitchens by Wieland, Inc.
4210 Tilghman Street
zip 18104

Bally
H. F. Measler, CKD
Longacre Electrical Service
602 Main Street
zip 19503

Bristol
J. D'Emidio, CKD
Cameo Kitchens, Inc.
Route 13 and 2nd Avenue
zip 19007

F. Licause, CKD
Cameo Kitchens
2nd Avenue & Route 13
zip 19007

Brodheadsville
M. F. Weiss Jr., CKD
M. F. Weiss, Inc.
P.O. Box 97
zip 18322

Carlisle
H. B. Gibb, Jr., CKD
Carlisle Kitchen Center
1034 Harrisburg Pike
zip 17013

Chester
J. H. Stefanide, CKD
Chester Woodworking, Inc.
503 E. 7th Street
zip 19013

Clarks Summit
A. W. Trivelpiece, CKD
Abington Cabinetry
Routes 6 & 11 Glenburn
zip 18411

Corry
R. A. Anderson, CKD
The Kitchen Village
Corner Route 6 and 89
zip 16407

Cresson
J. F. Glunt, CKD
Aaron Kitchen Design Center
508 Ninth Street
zip 16630

Erie
R. V. Robertson, CKD
Robertson's Kitchen & Remodeling
 Services of Erie, Inc.
2608 West 8th Street
zip 16505

Frazer
Josephine D. Cox, CKD
Coventry Kitchens, Inc.
446 West Lancaster Avenue
zip 19355

Glen Mills
J. C. Stefanide, CKD
Chester Woodworking, Inc.
15 Gov. Narkham Drive
zip 19342

Gettysburg
J. J. Dagenhardt, CKD
Gettysburg Building Supply Co.
225 South Franklin Street
zip 17325

Greensburg
W. Z. Peterson, CKD
Peterson Cabinet & Supply
503 New Alexandria Road
zip 15601

Harrisburg
C. H. Dissinger, CKD
Disco Sales & Service, Inc.
7 North Progress Avenue
zip 17109

R. M. Fromme, CKD
D & H Distributing Co.
2525 N. 7th Street
zip 17105

Huntingdon
R. J. Endres, CKD
E. B. Endres Lumber Co.
11th Susquehanna Avenue
zip 16652

Johnstown
P. J. Formica, CKD
Patsy Formica's Kitchen
 Design Center
734 Railroad Street
zip 15902

A. S. Trigona, CKD
A. S. Trigona & Sons, Inc.
110 Lundy Lane
zip 15904

Kittanning
H. A. Montgomery, CKD
202 Rear North McKean Street
zip 16201

Kreamer
C. K. Battram, Jr., CKD
Charles Associates, Inc.
Route 522
zip 17833

G. R. Callender, CKD
Wood-Mode Cabinetry
Snyder Country
zip 17833

C. H. Lemmerman, CKD
Wood-Moode Cabinetry
Snyder County
zip 17833

Lansdale
D. R. Oberholtzer, CKD
Oberholtzer Kitchens, Inc.
1801 North Broad Street
zip 19446

R. R. Oberholtzer, CKD
Oberholtzer Kitchens, Inc.
1801 North Broad Street
zip 19446

Leola
M. R. Bowers, CKD
Krown Kitchens, Inc.
522 Hess Rd.
zip 17540

Macungie
D. J. Bubba, CKD
Dries Building Supply Company
RD #2, Brookside Road
zip 18062

H. B. Dries, CKD
Dries Building Supply Company
RD #2, Brookside Road
zip 18062

P. A. Hoffman, Jr., CKD
Dries Building Supply Company
RD #2, Brookside Road
zip 18062

Milesburg
R. A. Knarr, CKD
Knarr's Kitchen Design Center
Turnpike Street, (Centre County)
zip 16853

Northumberland
D. C. Broscious, CKD
Broscious Building Center
4th & Duke Streets
zip 17857

Parkesburg
B. W. Fenninger, CKD
Fenninger Custom Kitchens
RD #2
zip 19365

Philadelphia
L. G. Ciliberti, CKD
Donze Kitchens & Bathrooms
1834 E. Passyunk Avenue
zip 19148

B. Fleet, CKD
Mayfair Kitchen
 Remodeling Center, Inc.
7400 Frankford Avenue
zip 19136

S. Kulla, CKD
Kulla Kitchens
7800 Rockwell Avenue
zip 19111

R. E. Mayer, CKD
A. A. Perry & Sons
4709 Frankford Avenue
zip 19124

T. R. Moser, CKD
Moser Corporation
5702 N. 5th Street
zip 19120

A. A. Perry, Jr., CKD
A. A. Perry & Sons, Inc.
4709 Frankford Avenue
zip 19124

L. Raider, CKD
Raider Associates, Inc.
843 Disston Street
zip 19111

N. L. Rossi, CKD
Rossi Kitchens
1227 Jackson Street
zip 19148

L. P. Scarani, CKD
S. S. Fretz, Jr., Inc.
2001 Woodhaven Blvd.
zip 19116

L. A. Scarf, CKD
Rich Maid Kitchens
2255 Faunce Street
zip 19152

J. B. Wagner, CKD
Mayfair Kitchen
 Remodeling Center, Inc.
7400 Frankford Avenue
zip 19136

Pittsburgh
F. R. Boyd, CKD
Style-Rite Kitchens
1401 Frey Road
zip 15235

L. J. Frey, CKD
701 Greenlee Road
zip 15227

W. J. Glivic, CKD
Bill Glivic Kitchens
3845 Willow Avenue
zip 15234

J. J. Molek, CKD
Morr-Craft Products, Inc.
1414 Spring Garden Avenue
zip 15212

R. Morra, CKD
Morr-Craft Products, Inc.
1414 Spring Garden Avenue
zip 15212

C. P. Morrison, CKD
Morrison Kitchens
5121 Clairton Blvd.
zip 15236

J. H. Safyan, CKD
Marcus Kitchens, Inc.
5954 Baum Blvd.
zip 15206

A. Sambol, CKD
Stein's Custom Interiors
3559 Bigelow Blvd.
zip 15213

G. R. Scull, CKD
Morrison Kitchens
5121 Clairton Blvd.
zip 15236

S. Z. Stein, CKD
Steins Custom Interiors
3559 Bigelow Blvd.
zip 15213

A. C. Winterhalter, CKD
Kitchen Center, Inc.
968 Route 8, (Glenshaw)
zip 15116

Quakertown
W. L. Rotenberger, CKD
Rotenberger Kitchens
527 West Broad Street
zip 18951

R. G. Snyder, CKD
Willow Grove Plumbing & Heating
 Supply Company
461 N. West End Blvd.
zip 18951

Reading
J. G. Heffleger, CKD
J & J Heffleger Custom Kitchens, Inc.
RD #2, Cross Keys Road
zip 19605

Sharon
C. H. Miller, CKD
Miller-Renz Kitchen Center of Sharon
3005 East State Street
zip 16146

J. Parry, CKD
Miller-Renz Kitchen Center of Sharon
3005 East State Street
zip 16146

E. C. Renz, CKD
Miller-Renz Kitchen Center of Sharon
3005 E. State Street
zip 16146

Southampton
A. J. Moeser, CKD
Suburban Kitchen Company, Inc.
650 Street Road
zip 18966

Springfield
A. L. Donze, CKD
Donze Kitchens & Bathrooms
512 Baltimore Pike
zip 19064

S. J. Donze, CKD
Donze Kitchens & Bathrooms
512 Baltimore Pike
zip 19064

U. L. Tomassone, CKD
Bertoma, Inc.
428 Baltimore Pike
zip 19064

Upper Darby
C. J. Walsh, CKD
Wall & Walsh, Inc.
8320 West Chester Pike
zip 19082

West Chester
H. R. Hurlbrink, CKD
Hurlbrink House of Kitchens
701 Westtown Road
zip 19380

C. E. Muhly, III, CKD
Conrad E. Muhly Co.
5 Westtown Road
zip 19380

Wynnewood
P. L. Heath, CKD
1209 W. Wynnewood Rd.
Apt. 202
zip 19096

Wyoming
L. Platsky, CKD
Betterhouse, Inc.
1140 Wyoming Avenue
zip 18644

M. L. Weisberger, CKD
Betterhouse, Inc.
1140 Wyoming Avenue
zip 18644

York
R. C. Harry, CKD
Bob Harry's Kitchen Center Inc.
3602 East Market Street
zip 17402

H. B. Murray, CKD
Murray Equipment Co., Inc.
1228 E. Philadelphia Street
zip 17405

G. M. Nicolaisen, CKD
Robert's Kitchens by George
829 West Market Street
zip 17404

RHODE ISLAND

Cranston
D. H. Ingalls, CKD
Ingalls Kitchens, Inc.
25 Carlsbad Street
zip 02920

Providence
J. A. McClure, CKD
American Custom Kitchens Inc.
145 Chad Brown Street
zip 02908

SOUTH CAROLINA

Columbia
J. A. Clarkson, CKD
Kitchen Distributing Company
946 Harden Street
zip 29205

Goose Creek
R. J. Millard, Sr. CKD
333 Holly Avenue
zip 29445

TENNESSEE

Knoxville
J. H. Lady, CKD
John Beretta Tile Co., Inc.
2706 Sutherland Ave.
zip 37919

M. L. Robinson, CKD
Modern Supply Company
Western Avenue at Dale
zip 37921

Memphis
W. M. Carruthers, CKD
Kitchens, Inc.
2665 Broad Ave.
zip 38112

J. E. Mason, CKD
Kitchens, Inc.
2665 Broad Avenue
zip 38112

Nashville
H. P. Dean, CKD
Dean's Kitchen Center, Inc.
1023 — 16th Avenue, South
zip 37212

G. Fleischer, CKD
Hermitage Kitchen Gallery
531 Lafayette Street
zip 37210

J. R. Henry, CKD
Henry Kitchens, Inc.
1808 Broadway
zip 37203

H. S. Moulder, Jr., CKD
Hermitage Kitchen Gallery
531 Lafayette Street
zip 37210

W. B. Pybas, CKD
Hermitage Kitchen Gallery
531 Lafayette Street
zip 37210

TEXAS

Dallas
W. R. Gedney, CKD
William R. Gedney & Company
Suite 254, 5952 Royal Lane
zip 75230

Houston
G. H. Gerdes, Jr., CKD
Wood-Mode Cabinetry
3637 West Alabama, Suite 370
zip 77027

C. B. Omo, CKD
Wood-Mode Cabinetry
3637 West Alabama, Suite 370
zip 77027

D. B. Steffan, CKD
Cabinet Systems
3637 West Alabama, Suite 370
zip 77027

D. W. Yeager, CKD
Kitchen Designers of Houston, Inc.
6131 Kirby Drive, P.O. Box 6723
zip 77005

Midland
J. T. Darsey, CKD
West Texas Kitchen Mart
2313 West Storey Ave.
zip 79701

UTAH

Heber City
L. D. Sheffield, CKD
Heber Cabinets
20 North 600 West
zip 84032

Salt Lake City
K. L. Cowan, CKD
Craftsman Cabinets, Inc.
2200 South Main Street
zip 84115

J. B. Curtis, CKD
Craftsman Cabinets
2200 South Main
zip 84115

V. Daniels, CKD
Olympia Kitchen Center Inc.
965 East 33rd South
zip 84106

D. Denning, CKD
Craftsman Cabinets, Inc.
2200 South Main Street
zip 84115

C. D. Lindquist, CKD
Craftsman Cabinets, Inc.
2200 South Main Street
zip 84115

C. W. Millet, CKD
Millet's Kitchens
1344 South 2100 East
zip 84108

G. N. Sheffield, CKD
Craftsman Cabinets, Inc.
2200 S. Main Street
zip 84115

West Jordan
L. A. Carolson, CKD
Carlson Kitchens, Inc.
3412 West 8600 South
zip 84084

VERMONT

Montpelier
R. A. Copping, CKD
Martin's Home Center, Inc.
114 River St. Box 39
zip 05602

Rutland
P. L. Hackel, CKD
Vermont Electric Supply Co. Inc.
299 N. Main Street
zip 05701

VIRGINIA

Arlington
W. A. Dembo Sr., CKD
Kitchen Classics, Inc.
6023 Wilson Blvd.
zip 2205

W. T. Lowe, CKD
William Lowe & Sons, Inc.
Kitchen Komer
1611 South Walter Reed Drive
zip 22204

Bluemont
D. R. Manire, CKD
Shenandoah Kitchens, Inc.
RR #2, Box 213, B-1
zip 22012

Fairfax
R. F. Bartholomew, Sr., CKD
Rich Craft Kitchens, Inc.
9411 Lee Hwy., Apt. 404
zip 22030

Glen Allen
R. A. Cecchini, CKD
The Kitchen Center
Route 2, Box 343
Mountain Road & No. 1 Highway
zip 23060

Norfolk
Ann R. Hux, CKD
Kitchen Towne
2600 Hampton Blvd.
zip 23508

Meredith M. Johnson, CKD
Kitchen Towne
2600 Hampton Blvd.
zip 23508

Richmond
G. A. Bernat, CKD
Custom Kitchens, Inc.
6412 Horsepen Road
zip 23226

R. E. Hammack, CKD
Custom Kitchens, Inc.
6412 Horsepen Road
zip 23226

A. C. Hendrick, Jr., CKD
Custom Kitchens, Inc.
6412 Horsepen Road
zip 23226

WASHINGTON

Snohomish
O. W. Strobel, CKD
Creative Kitchens & Baths
14430 Connelly Road
zip 98290

WEST VIRGINIA

Charleston
C. H. Coles, CKD
Save Supply Company, Inc.
P.O. Box 71, 711 Park Avenue
zip 25321

Huntington
R. E. Stepp, CKD
Creative Kitchens, Inc.
1242 Fifth Ave.
zip 25701

WISCONSIN

Appleton
J. A. Klinkert, CKD
Kitchens by Klinkert, Inc.
337 West Wisconsin Avenue
zip 54911

Delevan
V. L. Matousek, CKD
Kitchens, Bathrooms, Remodeling
Box 429A, RR5
zip 53115

Elm Grove
H. M. Eberhart, CKD
Coppes, Inc.
805 Park Lane
zip 53122

Green Bay

G. F. Soik, CKD
Green Bay Kitchen Mart
3110 Market Street
zip 54303

W. N. Thomas, CKD
Green Bay Kitchen Mart
3110 Market Street
zip 54303

Hartland

P.K. Johnson, CKD
Old World Craftsmen
643 Industrial Drive
zip 53029

Kenosha

T. W. Nelson, CKD
Nelson Millwork & Supplies
6935 - 14th Avenue
zip 53140

Madison

J. E. Abrahamson, CKD
Wisconsin Supply Corporation
630 West Mifflin Street
zip 53701

M. J. Ebben, CKD
Herman & Ebben Kitchen Mart
4613 West Beltline Highway
zip 53711

S. P. Emerson, C KD
Herman & Ebben Kitchen Mart
4613 West Beltline Highway
zip 53711

B. J. Herman, CKD
Herman & Ebben Kitchen Mart
4613 West Beltline Highway
zip 53711

R. F. Jones, CKD
Kitchens of Distinction
6719 Seybold Road
zip 53719

J. R. Luck, CKD
Modern Kitchen Supply, Inc.
3003 Kapec Road, Box 4133
zip 53711

J. D. Strand, CKD
Herman & Ebben Kitchen Mart
4613 West Beltline Highway
zip 53711

L. C. Thomas, CKD
Kitchens by Findorff
Div. of J. H. Findorff & Son, Inc.
601 West Wilson Street
zip 53703

Manitowoc

J. J. Sleger, CKD
Town & Country Kitchens
Div. of J. J. Schmitt
1117 Franklin Street
zip 54220

Milwaukee

E. L. Delfosse, CKD
Wisconsin Kitchen Mart
5226 West Hampton Avenue
zip 53218

W. M. Feradi, CKD
Built-In Kitchens, Inc.
7289 North Teutonia Avenue
zip 53209

F. J. Jones, Jr., CKD
Francis J. Jones Corp.
3803 North Oakland Avenue
zip 53211

E. J. Petry, CKD
Wisconsin Kitchen Mart
5226 West Hampton Avenue
zip 53218

R. K. Rossman, CKD
Wisconsin Kitchen Mart
5226 West Hampton Avenue
zip 53218

R. L. Wainwright, CKD
Wisconsin Kitchen Mart
5226 West Hampton Avenue
zip 53218

E. A. Wittig, CKD
Wisconsin Kitchen Mart
5226 West Hampton Avenue
zip 53218

Oconomowoc

R. W. Kotowski, CKD
Kotowski Kitchens
1383 West Wisconsin Avenue
zip 53066

Sheboygan

A. B. Mather, CKD
A. Mather Company
1002 Indiana Avenue
zip 53081

Schofield

T. E. De Lisle, CKD
De Lisle Company, Inc.
624 Moreland Avenue
zip 54476

Stratford

D. A. Burger, CKD
Stratford Building Supply, Inc.
215 East Railroad
zip 54484

Sun Prairie

B. J. Lessner, CKD
Lessner Cabinet, Inc.
35 North Walker Way
zip 53590

Wisconsin Rapids

M. D. Petta, CKD
Rapids Lumber Company
750 West Grand Avenue
zip 54494

Appendix 5

Addresses of Firms Mentioned in This Book

Ajax Hardware Corp., 825 S. Ajax Av., City of Industry, Cal. 91747

Allmilmo Corp., 122 Clinton Rd., Fairfield, NJ 07006

Amana Refrigeration, Sub. Raytheon, Amana, Iowa 52203

American Institute of Kitchen Dealers, 114 Main St., Hackettstown, N.J. 07840

American Olean Tile Co., Lansdale, Pa. 19446

Armstrong Cork Co., Liberty & Charlotte, Lancaster, Pa. 17604

Amtico Flooring, Div. American Biltrite Rubber, 3 Assumpink Blvd., Trenton, N.J. 08607

Bailey's Kitchens, 530 N. Tejon St., Colorado Springs, Colo., 80902

Barmark, 198 Central Av., East Orange, N.J. 07018

Betterhouse, 1150 Wyoming Av., Wyoming, Pa. 18644

Bisulk Kitchens, 295 Nassau Blvd., Garden City South, N.Y. 11530

Boise Cascade Cabinet Div., Box 514, Berryville, VA 22611

Broan Mfg. Co., 926 W. State St., Hartford, Wis. 53027

Caloric Corp., Sub. Raytheon, Topton, Pa. 19562

Charlotte Clark Kitchens, 18932 W. McNichols Rd., Detroit, Mich. 48219

City Lumber Co., 75 Third St., Bridgeport, Conn.

Champion Building Products, 1 Landmark Sq., Stamford, CT 06921

Congoleum Industries, Kearny, N.J. 07032

Connor Forest Industries, Box 847, Wausau, Wis. 54401

Coppes, Inc., Nappanee, Ind. 46550

Dacor Mfg. Co., Armory St., Worcester, Mass. 01601

DuPont Co., Room 25419, Wilmington, De. 19898

Durabeauty, Consolwed Corp., 700 Hooker St., Wisconsin Rapids, Wis. 54494

Duro-Test Corp., 17-10 Willow St., Fair Lawn, N.J. 07047

Dutch Built Kitchens, 1494 N. Charlotte St., Pottstown, Pa. 19464

Elkay Mfg. Co., 2700 S. 17 Av., Broadview, Ill. 60153

Enjay Fibers & Laminates, Enjay Chemical Co., Odenton, Md. 21113

Fasar Systems, 2801 Burton Av., Burbank, Ca. 91504

Formica Corp., 120 E. Fourth St., Cincinnati, Ohio 45202

Frigidaire, 300 Taylor St., Dayton, Oh. 45401

Funder America, Box 907, Mocksville, N.C. 27028

General Electric, Appliance Park, Louisville, Ky. 40225

General Electric, Large Lamp Div., Nela Park, Cleveland, Ohio 44112

Grabill Cabinet Co., Box 146, Grabill, Ind.

Gulf Corp., 615 Tchoupitoulas St., New Orleans, La. 70130

Halbeisen, Hen, Inc., 935 Penn St., Reading, Pa. 19601

Home Ventilating Institute, 360 N. Michigan Av., Chicago, Ill. 60601

Honeywell, 2701 Fourth Av. S., Minneapolis, Minn. 55408

Hotpoint, General Electric Co., Appliance Park, Louisville, Ky. 40225

Housing & Urban Development Dept., Washington, D.C. 20410

Imperial Cabinet Co., Box 427, Gaston, Ind. 47342

In-Sink-Erator, Div. Emerson Electric, 4700 21st St., Racine, Wis. 53406

IXL Furniture Co., Elizabeth City, N.C. 27909

Jenn-Air Corp., 3035 Shadeland, Indianapolis, Ind. 46226

Johnson, H. & R., Hwy. 35, Keyport, N.J. 07735

Karpy Kitchens, Rte. 17A, Florida, N.Y.

Kemper Div., The Tappan Co., 901 S. N St., Richmond, Ind.

Kennedy Kitchens, 727 Fox St., Horseheads, N.Y. 14845

Kich-n-vent, Div. Home-Metal Products, 750 Central Xway, Plano, Texas 75074

KinZee Industries, 259 Second St., Saddle Brook, N.J. 07662

KitchenAid Dishwasher Div., Hobart Mfg., Troy, Ohio 45373

Kitchen Concepts, 750 N.W. McNab Rd., Ft. Lauderdale, Fla. 33309

Kitchen Kompact, KK Plaza, Jeffersonville, Ind. 47130

Kitchen Originals, 5300 Merrick Rd., Massapequa, N.Y.

Kitchens by Krengel, 1688 Grand Av., St. Paul, Minn. 55105

Kitchens by Wieland, 4210 Tilghman St., Allentown, Pa.

Kitchens Inc., Narrowsburg, N.Y. 12764

Kitchens Unlimited, 320 S. Robertson Blvd., W. Los Angeles, Cal.

Kohler Co., Kohler, Wis. 53044

Koss Corp., 4129 N. Port Washington Av., Milwaukee, Wis. 53212

Lightolier, 346 Claremont Av., Jersey City, N.J. 07305

Long-Bell, Div. International Paper, Box 579, Longview, Wash. 98632

MarVell Kitchens, 1150 Wyoming Av., Wyoming, Pa. 18644

Merillat Industries, 2895 W. Beecher Rd., Adrian, Mich. 49221

Micarta, Div. Westinghouse Electric, Hampton, S.C.

Miami-Carey, Div. Panacon Corp., 203 Garver Rd., Monroe, Ohio

Modern Kitchens of Syracuse, 2380 Erie Blvd. East, Syracuse, N.Y.

Modern Maid, E. 14 St., Chattanooga, Tenn. 37401

Monarch Tile, Box 2041, San Angelo, Tx. 76901

Mutschler Kitchens, Madison at Randolph, Nappanee, Ind. 46550

National Assn. of Plastic Fabricators, 4720 Montgomery Lane, Washington, D.C. 20014

National Industries, Div. AVM Corp., Odenton, Md. 21113

Noblecraft Industries, Box 88, Hillsboro, Ore. 97123

NuTone, Div. Scovill Mfg. Co., Madison & Red Bank Rds., Cincinnati, Ohio 45227

Overton Co., Box 848, Kenly, N.C. 27542

Owens-Corning Fiberglas, Fiberglas Tower, Toledo, Ohio 43659

Panelyte (See Reliance Panelyte)

Paris Kitchens, Box 8, Paris, Ontario, Can. N3L 2Z6

Pioneer Craftsman, 330 Rose St., Reading, Pa. 19601

Pioneer Plastics Corp., Pionite Rd., Auburn, Me. 04210

Poggenpohl, 222 Cedar Lane, Teaneck, N.J. 07666

Progress Lighting, Erie Av. & G St., Philadelphia, Pa. 19134

Quaker Maid Kitchens, Div. The Tappan Co., Leesport, Pa. 19533

Rangaire Corp., Roberts Cobell Div., Box 177, Cleburne, Texas 76031

Reliance Panelyte, Box 1667, Tupelo, Miss. 38801

Reneer Films, Box 40, Auburn, Pa. 17922

Reynolds Enterprises, 2936 River Rd., River Grove, Ill. 60171

Riviera Products, 1960 Seneca Rd., St. Paul, Mn. 55122

Ronson Corp., 1 Ronson Rd., Woodbridge, N.J. 07095

Rutt-Williams, 1536 Grant St., Elkhart, Ind. 46514

Saint Charles Mfg. Co., 1611 E. Main St., St. Charles, Ill.

Scheirich, H. J. Co., Box 21037, Louisville, Ky. 40221

Southern Cal. Assn. Wood Cabinet Mfrs., 9126 S. Western Av., Los Angeles, Cal.

Springfield Cabinet, 932 Dayton Av., Springfield, Ohio 45506

Sub-Zero, Box 4130, Madison, Wis. 53711

Swearingen, Ray Co., 4625 41st St. NW, Washington, D.C.

Tappan Div., The Tappan Co., 250 Wayne St., Mansfield, Ohio 44902

Textolite Div., Laminated Products Dept., General Electric, Coshocton, Ohio 43182

Thermador Div., Norris Industries, 5119 S. District Blvd., Los Angeles, Cal. 90022

Union-Carbide, 270 Park Av., New York, N.Y. 10017

Ultraflo Corp., Box 2294, Sandusky, Oh. 44870

Vaughan, Geo. & Son., 223 S. Frio St., San Antonio Texas 78207

Waste King Universal, Sub. Norris Ind., 3300 E. 50 St., Los Angeles, Cal. 90058

Wehco Plastics, Box 26, Bloomsbury, N.J. 08804

Westinghouse Electric, 1 Allegheny Sq., Pittsburgh, Pa. 15212

Whirlpool Corp., Benton Harbor, Mich.

Whitehall Cabinets, Whitehall Bldg., E. Rockaway, N.Y. 11518

White-Meyer Industries, 141 & Rte. 45, Orland Park, Ill. 60462

Wilson-Art, Ralph Wilson Plastics, Div. Dart Industries, 600 Gn. Bruce Dr., Temple, Texas

Wilson Cabinet Co., Box 489, Port Clinton, Ohio 43452

Wood-Mode Cabinetry, Kreamer, Pa. 17833

Yatron Bros., 3000 Penn Av., West Lawn, Pa.

Yorktowne Cabinets, Box 231, Red Lion, Pa. 17356

Appendix 6

Members, National Kitchen Cabinet Assn.

There are about 6,000 manufacturers of kitchen cabinets in the United States, not counting the "garage operators" that could add many thousands to the total.

However, less than 150 cabinet manufacturers account for $500 million in cabinet shipments, or one-third of all U.S. production.

Purpose of this appendix is to provide a representative nationwide list of manufacturers, and the membership of the National Kitchen Cabinet Assn. includes most major manufacturers and provides such a list. A few non-members have been added at the end of the list because they are of such stature that it would be a disservice to exclude them.

Members

AAA-Lapco, Inc., 11223 Plano Rd., P.O. Box 38269, Dallas, Texas 75238

Acme Cabinet Corp., 909 Hwy. 37, Toms River, N.J. 08753

Adler Kay Co., Inc., 3737 Venoy Road, Wayne, Mich. 48184

Alderman Interior Systems, Inc., 4511 W. Buffalo Ave., P.O. Box 15557, Tampa, Fla. 33614

American Cabinet Corp., 301 N. Seventh Ave., Scranton, Pa. 18503

American Evans, Inc., W. Main St., Evans City, Pa. 16027

Arnold Mfg. Co., 4180 E. Raines Rd., Memphis, Tenn. 38118

Artcraft Cabinets, Inc., 1861 E. Bergman, Springfield, Mo. 65802

Belwood Industries, Inc., P.O. Box A, Ackerman, Miss. 39735

Bilt-In Wood Products Co., 808 Low St., Baltimore, Md. 21202

Boise Cascade/Raygold Div., P.O. Box 1028, Winchester, Va. 22601

Boro Industries, 2901 Stanley, P.O. Box 11558, Ft. Worth, Texas 76110

Boro Wood Products Co., Inc., Box 636, Bennettsville, S.C. 29512

Brammer Mfg. Co., 1441 Rockingham Rd., Box 3547, Davenport, Iowa 52808

Brandom Mfg. Corp. of Texas, P.O. Box 437, Keene, Texas 76059

Brennan Western, Inc., 11803 N.W. 116 St., Kirkland, Wash. 98033

Cabinet Group, The Tappan Co., Kemper/Tappan/Quaker Maid Cabinets, 701 South N St., Richmond, Ind. 47374

Cabinet N Counter, P.O. Box 304, Waldorf, Md. 20601

Carr, Henry M., Inc., 1150 Vermont St., Frankfort, Ind. 46041

Carroll Industries, Inc., Box 510, Conway, N.H. 03818

Colonial Products Co., Redco Ave., P.O. Box 231, Red Lion, Pa. 17356

Connor Forest Industries, Inc., 131 Thomas St., Wausau, Wis. 54401

Conwed Cabinetry, Ladysmith, Wis. 54848

Coppes, Inc., 401 E. Market St., Nappanee, Ind. 46550

Crestwood Kitchens Ltd., 225 No. 5 Rd., Richmond, B.C., Canada

Del Mar Div., U.S. Plywood-Champion Papers, 2865 Gordon Rd., N.W., Atlanta, Ga. 30311

Dixie Cabinet Co., Inc., 1007 Trade St., P.O. Box 457, Morristown, Tenn. 37814

Dura Supreme, Inc., 10710 County Rd. #15, Minneapolis, Minn. 55441

E. & E. Mfg. Co., 912 W. Cedar, Box 447 Cedar Hill, Texas 75104

Excel Wood Products Co., Inc., P.O. Box 819, Lakewood, N.J. 08701

Francisco Cabinet Corp., 1525 Illinois St., Des Moines, Iowa 50314

Gregg Cabinets, Ltd., 200 Bedard Ave., Chambly, Quebec, Canada

Haas Cabinet Co., 613 Utica St., Sellersburg, Ind. 47172

Hager Mfg. Co., 1512-32 N. Front St., Mankato, Minn. 56001

Hogan-Scarboro Corp., P.O. Box 60, Dudley, Ga. 31022

Home Crest Corp., Goshen Industrial Park, Eisenhower Dr. E., P.O. Box 595, Goshen, Ind. 46526

Imperial Cabinet Co., Inc., P.O. Box 427, Gaston, Ind. 47342

International Paper Co., Long-Bell Div., Box 579, Longview, Wash. 98632

IXL Furniture Co., Inc., R.R. #1, Elizabeth City, N.C. 27909

Kabinart Corp., 2515 Bransford Ave., Nashville, Tenn. 37210

Keller Kitchen Cabinets Southern, Inc., State Road #44 W., Box 1089, Leland, Fla. 32720

Kemper Bros., Div. of The Tappan Co., 701 So. N St., Richmond, Ind. 47374

Kinzzee Products, Inc., 259 2nd St., Saddle Brook, N.J. 07662

Kitchen Kompact, Inc., KK Plaza, Jeffersonville, Ind. 47130

Kitchen Mart, Inc., 7815 National Tpke., Space Center, Louisville, Ky. 40214

Lady Fair Kitchens, Inc., 3447 S. Main St., Salt Lake City, Utah 84115

L-Co Cabinet Corp., S. Fifth St., Shamokin, Pa. 17872

J. P. Long Cabinets, 2500 Citrus Rd., P.O. Box 97, Rancho Cordova, Cal. 95670

N. J. MacDonald & Sons, Inc., 45 Johnson Lane, Braintree, Mass. 02185

Major-Line Products Co., Inc., P.O. Box 478, Hoquiam, Wash. 98550

Mastercraft, Inc., 6175 E. 39 Ave., Denver, Col. 80207

Medallion Kitchens, Inc., 8609 Lyndale Ave., S., Minneapolis, Minn. 55420

Merillat Industries, 2075 West Beecher Rd., Adrian, Mich. 49221

Mutschler Brothers Co., Nappanee, Ind. 46550

National Homes Corp., 1657 Grant Line Rd., New Albany, Ind. 47150

Noblecraft Industries, Inc., P.O. Box 88, Hillsboro, Ore. 97123

Olympia Sales Co., 1537 S. Sixth West, Salt Lake City, Utah 84115

Oxford Mfg. Co., U.S. Rte. 1, So., P.O. Drawer L, Oxford, Pa. 19363

Prestige Wood Products, Inc., P.O. Box 2329 Metropolitan, Kansas City, Kan. 66106

Raywal, Ltd., 68 Green Ln., Thornhill, Ontario, Canada

Riviera Products, Inc., 1960 Seneca Rd., St. Paul, Minn. 55122

Rutt-Williams Div. of Leigh Products, Inc., P.O. Box 42, Goodville, Pa. 17528

The Sanderson Harold Co., 1 Railway St., Paris, Ontario, Canada

Sawyer Cabinet, Inc., 12744 San Fernando Rd., P.O. Box 4157, Sylmar, Cal. 91342

H. J. Scheirich Co., P.O. Box 21037, 250 Ottawa Ave., Louisville, Ky. 40221

Schrock Bros. Mfg. Co., P.O. Box 247, Arthur, Ill. 61911

Texas Cabinet Mfg. Co., Div. of Ben Griffin Enterprises, Inc., 3000 W. Pafford, Fort Worth, Texas 76110

Thiokol Texas, Inc., 3215 N. Pan Am Expressway, San Antonio, Texas

Triangle Pacific Cabinets, Inc., 9 Park Pl., Great Neck, N.Y. 11201

United Cabinet Corp., 14th & Aristocraft, P.O. Box 420, Jasper, Ind. 47546

Valley Cabinet Mfg. Inc., 4339 Jetway Ct., North Highlands, Cal. 95660

Valley Kitchens, Inc., State Rd. 42, Mason, Ohio 45040

Geo. C. Vaughan & Sons, Box 7367, San Antonio, Texas 78207

Villa Mfg., 1 Curlew St., Rochester, N.Y. 14606

Weather-Seal Div., Georgia-Pacific Corp., 324 Wooster Rd. N., Barberton, Ohio 44203

Welsh Kitchens, 1312 W. Washington St., Orlando, Fla.

Westwood Products, Inc., 560 21st S.E., P.O. Box 506, Salem, Ore. 97038

White-Meyer Wood Products, Inc., 141st & Rte. 45, Orland Park, Ill. 60462

Whitehall Cabinets, Inc., Whitehall Bldg., East Rockaway, N.Y. 11518

Wilson Cabinet Co., Inc., Box 489, Port Clinton, Ohio 43452

Major Non-Member Manufacturers

Jeffrey Steel Products, 1345 Halsey St., Brooklyn, N.Y. 11227.

St. Charles Mfg. Co., 1611 E. Main St., St. Charles, Ill.

Wood-Mode Kitchens, Kreamer, Snyder County, Pa. 17833.

Excel Wood Products, Lakewood, N.J. 08701.

Acrite Industries, 1120 Leggett Av., Bronx, N.Y.

Geneva Industries, Geneva, Ill.

Index